THE FUTURE OF
THE MIDDLE EAST

THE FUTURE OF
THE MIDDLE EAST

Faith, Force, and Finance

Monte Palmer

ROWMAN & LITTLEFIELD
Lanham • Boulder • New York • London

Published by Rowman & Littlefield
An imprint of The Rowman & Littlefield Publishing Group, Inc.
4501 Forbes Boulevard, Suite 200, Lanham, Maryland 20706
https://rowman.com

Unit A, Whitacre Mews, 26-34 Stannary Street, London SE11 4AB,
United Kingdom

British Library Cataloguing in Publication Information Available

Library of Congress Cataloging-in-Publication Data
Names: Palmer, Monte, author.
Title: The future of the Middle East : faith, force, and finance / Monte Palmer.
Description: Lanham, Maryland : Rowman & Littlefield, 2018. | Includes bib-
    liographical references and index.
Identifiers: LCCN 2018030015 (print) | LCCN 2018032260 (ebook) | ISBN
    9781538117897 (electronic) | ISBN 9781538117880 | ISBN
    9781538117880 (cloth : alk. paper)
Subjects: LCSH: Middle East—History—20th century. | Middle East—Histo-
    ry—21st century. | Middle East—Religion—20th century. | Middle East—
    Religion—21st century. | Religion and politics—Middle East—History—
    20th century. | Religion and politics—Middle East—History—21st century.
    | Islam and politics—Middle East—History—20th century. | Islam and pol-
    itics—Middle East—History—21st century.
Classification: LCC DS62.8 (ebook) | LCC DS62.8 .P348 2018 (print) | DDC
    956.04—dc23
LC record available at https://lccn.loc.gov/2018030015

Printed in the United States of America

Dedicated to Carlyle. May the tradition continue.

CONTENTS

PREFACE

Having studied the Middle East most of my academic and consulting careers, no fact has become more apparent to me than the roles of faith, force, and finance in shaping the fate of the region. I firmly believe that these weapons of power will continue to have a major impact on the reshaping of the Middle East as the United States and other major powers find themselves embedded in Middle Eastern conflicts that defy resolution.

With this thought in mind, the object of this book is to illustrate how faith, force, and finance have shaped and reshaped a modern Middle East that began with World War I and how they are likely to reshape the Middle East during the coming decade.

Thanks are due to several of my colleagues at Florida State University and the American University of Beirut. They are also due to Donald Crosby, theologian and philosopher, for long hours of debate on the complexities of faith as a formidable force for good and evil.

I

THE POWER OF FAITH, FORCE, AND FINANCE

The soaring violence in the Middle East has become a global scourge with no end in sight. If this trend continues on its present course, the Middle East will be radically transformed as new countries emerge while others cease to exist. Among the emerging countries are self-proclaimed Islamic caliphates that serve as a staging ground for the terrorism and violence sweeping the region. The countries targeted for destruction include Israel, Saudi Arabia, Iraq, Syria, Libya, and Yemen. Others may not be far behind, including most US allies in the region. The transformation of the region is well underway. As in all classic tragedies, the script is there for all to see, but the solution remains elusive.

It could be argued that the script of the tragedy began with Genesis and the biblical wars that followed. This argument is difficult to ignore, for Genesis is the foundation of Judaism, Christianity, and Islam, the three Abrahamic faiths at the core of the unfolding drama of the Middle East. This in and of itself is a tragedy, for all three faiths believe in the same God, the One God. They also revere the same biblical prophets and have remarkably similar views of the end of time.

Modern historians, however, argue that the script of the modern Middle East began with the end of World War I and the fragmentation of the Turkish Empire into a multitude of tribal kingdoms controlled by Britain and France. The surge of Islamic extremism during this era was a response to the clash between Islamic culture and the secular culture of the European colonialists. The masses, by and large, retained their traditional culture, while an educated elite rapidly embraced the European ideologies of nationalism, communism, and democracy. The clash between tradition and modernity was immediate, as the educated elite began to view Islam as an obstacle to their dreams of independence, modernity, and power.

Even more changes in the drama of the Middle East occurred following World War II, when most countries in the region shed their subservience to the colonial powers that had ruled them and demanded total sovereignty in the new global order. Some of the new nations were tribal monarchies that clung to Islam, while others looked to the Soviet Union for economic and military support. Soviet help was readily forthcoming, for the Cold War that followed World War II had turned the Middle East into a proxy battleground between the United States and the Soviet Union. It was this proxy war between the two superpowers that pushed tensions between Islam and modernity to the breaking point. Henceforth, the Middle East would develop its own cold war between reformist military regimes supported by the Soviet Union and tribal monarchies supported by the United States. The US plan was to use Islamic faith to block Soviet expansion in the region. The Soviet plan was to push the United States out of the region by supporting democracy, equality, and socialist development. American support for Islamic extremism served its purpose at the time but also prepared the ground for the 9/11 attacks on the United States and the unfolding crises of jihadist terror that followed. What had begun as a clash between Islamic culture and Western ideologies was transformed into a global battle between radical Islamic extremists, intent on turning the Middle East into a time warp of seventh-century Arabia, and the most powerful country on earth and its regional allies.

The Arab Spring revolutions of 2010 and 2011 ushered in yet another chapter in the drama of the Middle East. It was at that point that an earthquake of mass despair overthrew the old order of tyrannical dictators who had ruled for decades. Everything in the Middle East was now up for grabs, or so it seemed. There was going to be a new Middle East, but no one was quite sure what it would look like or who would be in charge. How could anyone predict the future when no one had expected the Arab Spring in the first place?

Egyptian security officials admitted that the Arab Spring revolution had caught them by surprise. Gadi Eizenkot, an Israeli chief of staff, admitted that Israel, too, was taken by surprise by the spontaneous events of the Arab Spring of 2010 and 2011. He referred to the Arab Spring as an "Arab Shake-Up" and suggested that the old order had collapsed. He also said to be prepared for "unexpected twists" (Eizenkot, 2015).

Because no one had expected the Arab Spring revolutions, no one was prepared for the endless chain of violent consequences that followed. This was certainly true of the United States and its allies, who had failed to anticipate that the collapse of puppet tyrants who had ruled for decades would transform their countries into an endless breeding ground for extremism, violence, and terror. Nor did the United States and its allies anticipate that the collapse of their pet tyrants would create a political vacuum in the region. It is also doubtful that the West anticipated that a minority of ultraviolent extremists would fill that vacuum with such ease.

Other new twists followed in rapid order. Millions of refugees flooded Europe and other stable countries. The Saudis and their Gulf allies suddenly found themselves running out of money. More startling was the United States' abandonment of Israel and Saudi Arabia on the issue of Iran's development of nuclear power. Not only were the prospects of war in the Middle East mounting but their consequences were becoming ever more threatening to the future of the region.

Much as in the past, the weapons of choice in the drama of the new Middle East are faith, force, and finance. Faith rules by promises of hope and escape from a life of total despair. Religion is not the only source of faith, but it is the most enduring form of faith in the Middle East today. Force rules by fear of death, deprivation, and despair. Finance rules by meeting people's material wants and using money to shape political decisions. If that fails, it can also buy brute force to keep the masses in line.

Of the three weapons, which is the most likely to succeed in the unending struggle for the Middle East? This is a difficult question to answer. Faith, force, and finance have scored victories in different times and circumstances. All have also failed as times and circumstances have changed.

This is because faith, force, and finance each possess a fatal flaw. *Faith* is far from being a panacea for those who would rule by faith alone. The Koran warns that there will be seventy-three visions of Islam, only one of which will provide entry to heaven. As a result, those who would rule by faith must convince their followers that their path to salvation is the right path. Mainline religious leaders can rely on traditions and formal institutions as the foundations for their authority, but all have been tainted by their attachments to tyrannical governments. By and large, they are on the side of the tyrants rather than the people. They have also been criticized for excessive theological formality that isolates them from the masses in search of a spiritual oneness with God.

The situation is far trickier for leaders of religious cults, such as al-Qaeda and the Islamic State of Iraq and Syria (ISIS), who must convince their followers to accept their absolute authority based on claims that they possess the gift of grace. Personal charisma may get the ball rolling, but faith requires repeated proof of God's blessing. One cannot risk an eternity in heaven on words alone. Victories must mount as signs of God's continued faith in their leader. Doubters and competing prophets must be disposed of, just to be on the safe side.

Force breeds fear, hate, hostility, vows of revenge, and a sycophant culture in which people pretend to support the regime while simultaneously engaging in silent sabotage and offering support to the opponents of the regime. Leaders become frustrated and ratchet up their use of violence in hope of stifling resistance and forcing people to give their all for king and country. The cycle continues as passive resistance turns into armed rebellion. Violence by panic becomes inevitable because the leaders struggling for dominance in the region have boxed themselves in by their reliance on force. The only way out for those dependent on rule by force is to destroy everything in their path. The moderate Islamic leader of Tunisia stated the case cogently when he suggested that the choice is either political reform or ISIS (Ghannouchi, 2016).

Using *finance* to satisfy the wants of the people seems like the most effective means of ruling the peoples of the Middle East. In reality, however, it could be the most difficult to implement. Most countries in the region are poverty-stricken and lack the resources to provide their citizens with a reasonable standard of living. The money that is available is hoarded by the ruling elite who careen through filth-littered streets in their elegant roadsters, inciting the hate and envy of the masses. The oil kingdoms have money to provide their subjects with cradle-to-grave welfare but refuse to provide for freedom of expression, freedom of religion, and freedom from fear, which may indicate that the oil kings are afraid of their own pampered subjects.

The same principles apply to all of the unfolding crises outlined above. The message is clear. Standing alone, faith, force, and finance cannot provide a solution to the terror and chaos reigning in the Middle East. To prevail in the long run, the contenders for power in the region must rule with a reasonable balance of faith, force, and finance.

What, then, is the most effective combination of faith, force, and finance that the United States and its allies can draw upon to bring peace and stability to the region? To state the question in reverse, what is the deadly combination of faith, force, and finance that the United States and its allies are likely to encounter during the coming decade?

As a first step in answering this question, we examine which balance of the three weapons is most powerful and why. Without answers to this question, discussions of balance will be meaningless.

Intuitively, *force* would seem to be the most powerful of the three weapons. All of the countries in the region are armed to the teeth, and their saber rattling dominates the press.

The argument for *finance* is also strong. Saudi Arabia has been able to place itself at the top of the Muslim power pyramid by using its vast wealth to buy the subservience of its neighbors if not the entire Sunni Islamic world. Perhaps finance should also come first for, as the Saudis have demonstrated, finance can buy the most advanced arms in the world and the mercenaries to use them.

This would seem to place *faith* in last place on the Middle Eastern power pyramid. Reality, however, suggests otherwise.

Why, for instance, has the United States, the most powerful nation on earth, found it so difficult to curb the soaring threat of Islamic extremism by force? Why is the tyrant in Egypt, having built the world's thirteenth largest army in the world, unable to defeat the Muslim Brotherhood, not to mention a small spin-off of ISIS on its Sinai Peninsula? Why has Israel been unable to crush the Hizbullah threat and stifle Islamic extremism in the Occupied Territories despite force so brutal that the Jewish state has been condemned for war crimes against humanity? Why have the Saudis with vast sums of money and billions in the latest American weapons fought a losing war in Yemen at the same time that they offer covert support to ISIS in the name of crushing the spread of Shia Islam?

The critical point to be noted is that the weaker combatants in the above and similar conflicts all relied heavily on faith to parry force and finance. This doesn't mean that faith can defeat force and money, but it does mean that force and finance are finding it difficult to defeat faith.

How, then, do we compare the relative power of faith, force, and finance? Unfortunately, we can't compare them quantitatively because each has different indicators of power. It would be would be like comparing apples and oranges.

To make matters worse, *faith*, *force*, and *finance* are such elusive terms that they are difficult to pin down with precision. *Faith* is elusive because it has hundreds of different definitions. *Force* is elusive because quantitative studies equate it with tanks, aircraft, and the size of standing armies. Morale, dedication, loyalty, and other intangibles that separate the winners from the losers are not figured in the power equation. Neither is the deep distrust that the leaders of the Middle East have for their military personnel. The guns may be there, but who will they be aimed at when the next military coup occurs? *Finance* is elusive because, in addition to being largely invisible, it comes and goes with the blink of an eye. Also elusive is the ability to buy love, loyalty, and patriotism. Even if you can buy people, how long do they stay bought?

Given the above problems, the best approach to identifying the dominant weapons for derailing the doomsday script currently threatening the Middle East is to evaluate the effectiveness of faith, force, and finance in eleven radically distinctive stages in the unfolding dramas of the modern Middle East. These stages and their main features are provided in table 1.1 at the end of the chapter.

Curiously, this approach seems to have much in common with the game of rock, scissors, paper that I used to play as a kid. Each could trump the others depending on the circumstances. Paper covers rock, scissors cut paper, rock breaks scissors. And so it is with faith, force, and finance in the quest for dominance in the Middle East and the war against terror. As we shall see in later chapters, the Saudis have money but fear visions of Islam other than their own. The United States has force, but fears Islam. ISIS relies on an extremist version of Islam but might be curbed by an alliance of force and money.

I am not suggesting that we reduce the struggle for control of the Middle East to a game of rock, scissors, paper. It does, however, make a useful metaphor for focusing on how faith, force, and finance may defeat each other. This is particularly the case because none of the contenders for dominance in the Middle East has shown the ability to control all three vital weapons for dominance in the region.

THE POWER OF FAITH

Coming to grips with the power of faith is particularly elusive because its meaning often varies from person to person and time to time. According to its most common psychological definitions, faith boils down to the unwavering belief in something or someone that gives you confidence, hope, and trust. Without belief in something, there can be no hope, trust, or confidence in anything. As most people find it difficult to navigate life's traumas without belief, confidence, hope, and trust in something, faith is often assumed to be a universal need.

This certainly appears to be the case in the Middle East. It is difficult to find another region of the world in which the fear factor is deeper, oppression more brutal, poverty and despair more pervasive, instability and uncertainty a way of life, foreign meddling more frivolous, hate and revenge justified by scriptures, or concern for human life and the environment more fragile. Just for the record, these are also the causes of religious extremism and terror.

Robin Meyer's theological definition of faith is remarkably similar, noting that "we use the word *Faith* to describe an unwavering, unquestioned allegiance to some doctrinal proposition" (Meyer, 2015, 45). He goes on to wonder whether faith is being placed in God or in doctrines about God that are constantly being revised by humans. This, too, is part of the unfolding drama of the Middle East, a region that worships the One God but has multiple doctrines about how to serve God and an abundance of false interpreters of those doctrines.

Donald Crosby, making an extensive review of the philosophical literature, defines faith as that "mysterious inner strength, resolve, and power, that enables one to live in the face of bewilderments, insecurities, frustrations, failures, sorrows, or tragedies" (Crosby, 2011, 1). This, Crosby elaborates, makes faith "an indispensable component of

thought, feeling, volition, action, and thus the whole of human life"
(Crosby, 2011, 2). Crosby also cautions that faith is not limited to religion.

At least six diverse types of faith play a key role in the unfolding
drama of the Middle East: religious faith, faith in kinship bonds, faith in
charismatic leaders, faith in nationalism, faith in political institutions,
and faith in secular ideologies such as socialism, communism, and democracy. Sometimes they work together and sometimes they pull in
opposite directions. Sometimes they surge for a moment and then fade
away.

The definitions of faith discussed above will suffice to highlight the
characteristics of faith that make it a powerful force in shaping the
drama of the Middle East. How could something that is an indispensable component of thought, feeling, volition, and action not be a major
factor shaping the unfolding drama of the Middle East?

The deep appeal of each of the three Abrahamic faiths begins with
the promise of an eternity in paradise for those who will obey its doctrines as portrayed in its scriptures and elaborated by the interpreters of
those scriptures. What other solution is available to people locked in the
human tragedy of the Middle East described above? If you take away
faith, you are taking away the one ray of hope that most people in the
Middle East possess. Hope certainly doesn't come from governments
that are as rapacious as they are brutal.

Perhaps Meyer's wonderings should be modified to ask if people's
faith is in God or in the *interpreters* of God's scriptures. This is because
the land of the prophets is rapidly becoming the land of the false prophets.

In addition to the assurance of an eternity in paradise for believers,
faith in the Middle East provides a sense of belonging and group solidarity while on earth. Faith is security, economic ties, political influence, social status, marriage links, and just about everything else individuals need to survive in this tormented region. Motivation for supporting faith, accordingly, is not merely life in the hereafter. It is also a
vital matter of life in the here and now.

One might also add pride and self-esteem to the joys provided by
faith in the Middle East. Muslims, while defeated and humiliated by
decades of colonial rule, are members of a religion that ruled much of
the world and led the world in science and philosophy. The colonialists

ruled the Islamic world by crushing the self-esteem of their subjects. As a Muslim friend said, "They taught us that we were inferior toads incapable of resisting our colonial masters." The glories of Islam eased the pain of their humiliation but also left a psychological void that could only be filled by an Islamic revival that promised the glories of old. Only then could Muslims fully restore their pride and self-esteem. Until that time, the pain would remain and their holy mission would be incomplete. Much the same can be said of Jewish pride in being God's chosen people and the heirs of the Promised Land.

Beyond addressing the practical and emotional needs of its believers, faith provides individuals with an identity. It tells them who they are and how they fit in the universe that surrounds them. Knowing how they fit in their universe is vital because people in the Middle East invariably assess each other as members of a religious faith. Like it or not, they are branded by their faith and cannot escape it. This is a plus if you are surrounded by members of the same faith in a crisis or need a favor from a government official. It can be deadly if you are viewed as a threat to others' faith or existence. Bear in mind that most conflicts in the Middle East are faith-based.

Because Islam is so ingrained in the culture of the Middle East, it becomes the lens through which people view the world. Faith also shapes how people evaluate what they see in terms of good and bad, right and wrong, and friend and enemy. Evaluations, in turn, trigger fear and other emotions that often lead to conflict. This is all the more the case because memory, too, is part of the cognitive process. Memories of the glories of all faiths are not an artifact of history but a living reminder of what could and should be.

All of the above explanations for the power of faith in the Middle East predispose the peoples of the region and beyond to be easily offended by the humiliation of their faith. To humiliate faith is not only to force believers to defend their faith but to threaten their security. This explains why a few cartoons scorning the Prophet Mohammed unleashed riots throughout the Islamic world. It also explains why the vast array of Jewish organizations throughout the world are devoted to countering anti-Semitism and slurs against Israel.

Commentators on the Middle East often use the phrase *political Islam* to refer to Islamic extremist groups attempting to seize control of the government. Somehow, they would have the United States believe that pure Islam is free of politics. Nothing could be further from the truth, for the Holy Koran, the word of God as revealed to the Prophet Mohammed, was a guide to all dimensions of human life, including politics and economics. It was largely the same for all of the Abrahamic faiths upon which Islam drew so heavily. The Prophet Moses, Jesus Christ, and the Prophet Mohammed were all reformers attempting to lead their followers to a better world by using faith to promote justice, tolerance, and equity.

As might be expected given the above discussion, it is hard to find any dimension of the political process in the Middle East that is not touched by faith. Faith is the dominant political ideology in the Middle East. Many countries in the region use the Koran as their constitution. Israel refers to itself as a Jewish state, but long did without a constitution because it couldn't decide who was a Jew. Religious symbols and slogans are the most powerful symbols in the Middle East. Of these, the most potent is, "God is the solution." This is also the message of religious programs that often top the popularity list.

All countries in the region are engaged in religious wars of one form or another. All use religion to motivate their troops and to justify the killing of innocent populations. The United States military refers to this as "faith-force motivation."

Most leaders in the region use faith to legitimize their regimes. As late as 1986, for example, the Saudi king began referring to himself as "His Majesty, the Guardian of the Two Holy Shrines." The more domestic tensions rise throughout the region, the more religious symbolism soars. Some even claim the special blessing of God.

Faith is also a key factor in the international relations of the Middle East. Recruits for the Salafi-jihadist terrorists come from some sixty countries. Much of the United States' support for Israel is based upon the key role that Israel plays in biblical prophecy. When the Reagan administration attempted to force Israel to withdraw from Lebanon during an earlier war, Prime Minister Begin responded that "Jews bow but to God." In his view, divine law topped international law.

THE POWER OF FORCE

Force, in the context of our discussion, refers to the use of arms to conquer, acquire, defend, crush, punish, cripple, destroy, compel, threaten, humiliate, and constrain. In modern security jargon, the force used in the Middle East is now described as "hard power." This is opposed to "soft power" that achieves its objectives by persuading, attracting, using cyber warfare and psychological warfare, and making your enemy part of the winning coalition (Nye, 2011).

The distinction between hard power and soft power is important because it determines what you can do, when you can do it, where you can do it, and how fast you can do it. Salafi-jihadist bases can be bombed, but how do you use hard force against suspicious Muslim populations in the mega cities of the Middle East, Europe, and North America? A candidate in the 2016 presidential debates suggested what boiled down to search-and-seizure operations in Muslim communities in the United States. A US military publication suggested that all women wearing a heavy veil should be considered terrorist subjects. This view ignores the fact that, in addition to being a sign of piety, the heavy veil is also a sign of religious opposition to the brutally oppressive leaders of the region.

Each type of force also has radically different consequences in the way that it shapes behavior. Hard force, as we have seen in our introductory comments, fuels terror by stimulating hate, anger, vows of revenge, and frustration. Soft power is user-friendly but takes time to produce results. How much time does the United States have in the war against terror?

Hard force prevails in the Middle East because the conflicts in the region take the form of a zero-sum game in which the winner takes all. Losers don't get a second chance. It is all or nothing at all.

This, in large part, is the result of centuries of tribal, sectarian, and ethnic conflicts that have created a reservoir of hate, suspicion, and revenge so deep that it may remain for centuries. This makes the Middle East a poor environment for soft power. The pervasiveness of fear, hate, revenge, and distrust in the region is discussed at length in my book *The Arab Psyche and American Frustrations*. One might also ask just how soft power can defeat fanatical extremists. This topic will be addressed in the final chapter.

Just as the leaders and occupiers of the Middle East rule by fear and force, so do the same leaders and occupiers live in constant fear of attack and rebellion. This puts an emphasis on striking first to prevent attacks. The Israelis are famous for their preemptive strikes against their Arab neighbors. Tribal kings and tyrants are trigger-happy because they fear a new Arab Spring. Signs of weakness are an invitation for sedition, and warnings of revolt are everywhere.

Because of their pervasive fear, the tyrants and tribal kings rule out peaceful reconciliation of conflict such as democracy and accommodation. For example, how can the tyrants and tribal kings allow fair elections when they will lose and faith and despair will win? This means that there are no avenues for peaceful change in much of the Middle East. Violence is the only option.

Finally, a common attitude during the colonial era was that Arabs only understood force. This attitude remains pervasive today and is particularly visible in Israeli defense policy and America's War on Terror. This predilection for force blends well with the panic and fear factor now sweeping the world.

THE POWER OF FINANCE

The power of finance in the Middle East is so varied and pervasive that it includes everything from bribes to boycotts. Provided below are examples of the most common uses of financial power to control the events of the Middle East. This does not mean that finance can be the determining weapon in the struggle to control the Middle East. But finance can, however, be lethal if used to support faith and force.

Arms Purchases as Power

Saudi Arabia and other oil-producing countries attempt to manipulate the major powers by making huge arms purchases so vast that they become a vital economic necessity to the economies of the major powers. Britain, for example, concluded a secret agreement with Saudi Arabia in 2015 that made it the largest arms supplier to Saudi Arabia. The British Parliament, intimidated by the British press, demanded that the secret agreement be made public and the arms deal cancelled. Just how much was cancelled remains vague.

The United States isn't far behind, supplying the Saudi monarchy with billions of dollars in weapons including cluster bombs. These bombs are used against largely Shia Islamic targets.

It could be argued that the vast arms purchases of the Saudis and other oil kingdoms make them military powers. This view ignores the reality that military power rests heavily on the capacity to apply force effectively. The oil kingdoms, for all of their massive arms buildups, have yet to demonstrate this capacity. The Saudi-led war in Yemen launched in 2016 was a disaster, while Saudi-Gulf activity in Syria during the same period has been minimal. Arms purchases by the oil kingdoms provided the illusion of force and the prestige of force but not necessarily the application of force that is provided by dependency on the United States, Britain, and other arms suppliers. If these countries do not comply with the oil kingdoms, they will lose their arms sales.

Gifts as Soft Influence and Image Building

It is supposedly the mission of liberal think tanks to alert the American public to harmful foreign influences on American policy. It seems that this may not be the case. According to a study by the *New York Times*, America's main liberal think tanks are generously funded by the Saudis and other Gulf kingdoms. So are numerous American and European universities. I am not making any accusations, but the recipient organizations that I am personally familiar with seem to have a Saudi fixation. The Saudis also believe in the American adages that there is no free lunch and that the one who pays the piper calls the tune. The more budgets are dependent on Saudi donations, the more these principles come into play.

Finance as the Key to Regional Control

One of the ironies of the Middle East is that the richest countries in the region are also the weakest. Saudi Arabia, the richest of the rich, has long lived in fear of Egypt, Syria, Iraq, and Iran. In the 1960s the Saudi monarchy was nearly destroyed by Abdel Nasser, Egypt's charismatic champion of Arab unity. With Nasser's passing, it became Saudi policy to keep Nasser's uncharismatic successors dependent upon Saudi hand-outs. This remains a foundation of Saudi policy.

Finance as Alliance Building

Saudi Arabia is well aware of its military weakness and is desperately funding alliances focused on stemming Iran's efforts to surround it with a Shia triangle that will choke it to death as Iran takes over the Gulf. One such alliance was the Saudi-led alliance to overthrow the Houthi Shia rebellion in Yemen. This was followed by the Saudi-led Sunni alliance to fight terror and Iranian expansion. Pakistan and some other members were not even aware that they were members of the alliance until they received the necessary Saudi financial support. Such was the case when a Saudi deposit of $68 million suddenly appeared in the Swiss bank account of an Indonesian leader.

Finance as a Social Contract

Domestically, the oil kingdoms use finance to buy the docility, patience, and symbolic loyalty of their subjects. This includes cradle-to-grave welfare and jobs that don't require work. I use the word *symbolic* because the matter isn't put to the test by elections, free speech, or the right to join organizations such as political parties or religious movements not approved by the monarchy.

Popular support for the tribal kings was tested by the sharp decline in oil revenues that occurred in 2016. Sharp cutbacks on welfare rattled the social contract, as did the king's demand that Saudi citizens stop relying on expats and actually do some work. This was not part of the social contract that traded docility and obedience for a free economic ride. It is important to note that it was this social contract that helped the tribal kings avoid the Arab Spring revolutions. The future of oil revenues will be a key indicator in predicting the future of the tribal kings.

Using Finance to Promote Faith and Force

The Saudis well understand the power of faith in Middle East, as well they should. From its origins, the Saudi regime has blended tribal monarchy with the extremist Wahhabi doctrine of Islam. It is the Wahhabi clergy who provide religious legitimacy to the Saudi regime and run its schools, Islamic outreach programs, mosques, and religious police. It is a safe bet that the Wahhabi clergy are a major force in attempting to stamp out the Muslim Brotherhood and other forms of moderate Islam throughout the region. Saudi Arabia also uses its vast financial resources to control Sunni Islam in the Middle East, to promote the Wahhabi version of Sunni Islam throughout the world, and to forge a Sunni alliance against Iran and its efforts to create a Shia crescent hostile to Saudis and the Sunni faith. Strengthening Sunni faith is the goal, but the Saudis are attempting to control faith by footing the bill.

The United States' Soft Power in the Middle East

Two key elements in America's efforts to achieve its objectives via finance are foreign economic aid and economic boycotts. US foreign economic aid is designed to improve the well-being of the poor and destitute of the world. At the same time, it builds friendship with the United States, reduces the causes of terror, and props up puppet tyrants controlled by the United States.

Economic boycotts, by contrast, are designed to force the leaders of uncooperative countries to bow to the wishes of the United States by punishing their people. Hopefully, their people will revolt and the leaders of the country will capitulate to the demands of the United States.

The record of both foreign aid and boycotts is dismal. Most foreign aid goes to shoring up puppet regimes, and most boycotts have failed in their objectives.

The pros and cons of finance as a weapon for control of the Middle East will be discussed throughout the book, as will its ability to trump faith and force.

Information presented in this book is based upon fifty years of studying the Middle East, including working with Muslim scholars on some twenty relevant research projects, spending thousands of hours drinking coffee and conversing with Middle Eastern friends and colleagues, coding the materials from the Middle Eastern press over a ten-year period, teaching courses and guiding graduate students on politics and international relations in the Middle East at the Florida State University and the American University of Beirut, serving as a consultant for various organizations, and serving as a senior fellow at the Al-Ahram Center for Political & Strategic Studies and as director of the Middle East Centers at AUB and FSU. The book also draws on commentaries in the Gulf/ 2000 Project as well as in my earlier books, including *The Arab Psyche and American Frustrations*, *Politics in the Middle East*, and *Islamic Extremism* (with Princess Palmer).

TABLE 1.1: STAGES IN THE EVOLUTION OF THE STRUGGLE BETWEEN FAITH, FORCE, AND FINANCE

Stage 1 (1914–1940):	World War I sets the stage for the struggle between faith, force, and finance in the modern Middle East.
Stage 2 (1940–1967):	World War II sets the stage for the struggle between secular faith and religious faith in the era of independence and secular nationalism.
Stage 3 (1967–1980):	The 1967 Arab-Israeli War triggers the decline of secular faith and the surge of religious extremism.
Stage 4 (1980–1990):	Iran's Islamic Revolution exemplifies the struggle between faith, force, and finance.
Stage 5 (1990–2000):	The end of the Cold War pits hard force against hard faith.
Stage 6 (2000–2010):	The role of faith, force, and finance intensifies during the US War on Terror.
Stage 7 (2010–2013):	Rule by religious faith becomes the new order in the Middle East.
Stage 8 (2013–2015):	Force and finance are used to defeat moderate Islam and turn back the clock in the Middle East.
Stage 9 (2015–2017):	The ultraradical Islamic game plan prepares the road to Armageddon.
Stage 10 (Post-2017):	Efforts to use force and finance to defeat the ultraradical Islamic game plan result in a stalemate.
Stage 11 (Solutions):	Can moderate faith, force, and finance defeat extremist faith?

2

WORLD WAR I SETS THE STAGE FOR THE MODERN MIDDLE EAST (1914–1940)

The turmoil besetting the Middle East today finds its origins in World War I and the era of European colonialism that preceded it. The critical point came at the end of the war when the victorious Allied Powers dismembered Turkey's Ottoman Empire. Turkey had sided with Germany in the war and was to be punished accordingly. France and Britain were also covetous of adding Turkish possessions to their own empires. Whatever the case, a Turkish empire that had ruled most of the region for five hundred years was fragmented. When all was said and done, there remained only the modern state of Turkey and a multitude of independent countries.

Most of the new countries were little more than a hodgepodge of diverse ethnic, religious, and tribal groups controlled by either Britain or France. They couldn't be called "colonies" because the United States demanded that the new countries be mandates assigned to the European powers for guidance toward democracy and economic development.

The European powers smiled at this quaint idea and treated their new possessions much as they treated their other colonies. A semblance of democratic institutions did appear, but most were controlled by carefully selected native elites consisting of wealthy merchants, tribal leaders, large landowners, bureaucrats, and security personnel. As long as this emerging elite enjoyed the support of the colonial power, they were free to pillage at will.

The masses, beset by disease, hunger, insecurity, and illiteracy, could do little about their plight because they were clustered in scattered villages or nomadic tribes, each an island unto itself. Their isolation, however, was far more than a matter of wretched roads and sparse communications. Even if communications had been better, it would not have mattered much because the masses were fragmented by class, caste, religious, ethnic, tribal, and linguistic cleavages.

In addition to carving up the region in a haphazard manner, two prophetic promises were made by the victorious powers. The Jews were promised a national home in Palestine, and the Kurds were promised a national home stretching from Turkey to northern Iraq.

The assault of colonialism didn't transform the Middle East into a modern society patterned on Europe. Rather, it transformed it into a transitional society that incorporated conflicting features of both tradition and modernity. The exact mix varied from country to country, but all countries in the region were torn by intense struggles between ties to tradition and the lure of European modernity.

To make matters worse, the borders of the new and transformed countries were drawn without concern for the ethnic, tribal, and sectarian backgrounds of the populations affected. As a result, ethnic and sectarian wars multiplied.

The Middle East continues to be a transitional society that is being pulled in opposite directions internally, regionally, and internationally. It is impossible to understand the role of faith, force, and finance in today's struggle against terror without this realization.

As a first step in this direction, the present chapter illustrates how and why the events of World War I transformed the uses of faith, force, and finance as key weapons in the struggle for control of Middle East. Force and finance retain their customary meanings, but faith blossoms into a variety of forms including religious faith, nationalism, and personal charisma. Sometimes they blend together. Other times they are at odds.

In the process, the seeds of all of the major conflicts besetting the region today were sown. We begin by examining Turkish efforts to use force to stamp out Islam as an obstacle to modernity. This is followed by a discussion of the explosion of populist Islamic faith in Egypt as a contrary response to westernization. Next comes a discussion of the use of a blend of faith, force, and finance to transform the British mandate of Palestine into a homeland for the Jews. This study in modern nation building, in turn, gives way to a study of Britain's use of faith, force, and finance to establish a puppet kingdom in its mandate of Iraq. We close the chapter by examining the lessons learned from these diverse examples of using various combinations of faith, force, and finance to shape the affairs of the region.

TURKEY: FORCE VERSUS ISLAM

Turkey's Ottoman Empire emerged in the early fourteenth century as a band of border raiders on the fringe of the Byzantine Empire. One hundred years later, the empire born of this band of raiders had captured Constantinople en route to becoming a global superpower that stretched from Algeria to the gates of Vienna. All of Eastern Europe, as well as parts of Greece and Italy, had fallen under Ottoman sway as had virtually all of the Middle East with the exception of Iran.

The strength of Ottoman Empire was its ability to incorporate Muslims, Christians, and a multitude of diverse nationalities into the ruling elite that served the sultan. Turkish nationalism was minimal, and Muslim doctrine was readily sacrificed for the greater glory of the sultan-caliph who reigned supreme in all matters of state, secular and Islamic. The lesson to be learned from the Ottoman experience is that it is possible for diverse faiths to work together if all are incorporated in the ruling apparatus.

The decline of the Ottoman Empire from a major power in the closing years of the seventeenth century to the "sick man" of Europe in the decades preceding World War I was the result of an absolute monarchy that had failed to keep pace with the industrial, political, and military revolutions sweeping Western Europe. Power struggles within the sultan's household became commonplace, as did rebellions in the provinces.

The 1908 revolt of the Young Turks, a blend of military officers and enlightened bureaucrats, forced the reigning sultan to accept a constitution limiting his power. It might have ended the monarchy altogether but stopped short of a coup as the result of a bitter struggle within the ranks of the Turkish nationalists. While some were intent on modernizing Turkey, others gave priority to returning the empire to its former glory. Each stymied the efforts of the other as the sick man of Europe lumbered on and the clouds of World War I drew ever closer.

The sultan made futile efforts to save his empire by forming an alliance with Britain and France, but they had other ideas. And so he turned to the Germans to save his throne. The Germans agreed to save the sultan and his empire with the intention of making it a puppet empire under German control. World War I ended with the defeat of the German-Turkish alliance. A new Middle East was born.

Mustafa Kemal, a young general who had been active in the Young Turk Revolution, rose to the top of the military in 1919 with dreams of forging a new and modern Turkey. His more pressing task, however, would be saving Turkey itself. No sooner had Kemal taken power than the Greeks invaded the port city of Izmir as part of a broader plan for adding much of the Turkish heartland to Greece. The British occupation of Istanbul followed in 1920 with avowed support for the Greek expansion into Turkey. The Kurds and the Armenians, anxious to settle old scores, were also intent on claiming their share of a dismembered Turkey.

It was not to be. The Greeks were defeated by Kemal-led forces on August 30, 1922, a date now celebrated as Victory Day. The British occupation of Istanbul and the straits remained, but France, Italy, and the Soviet Union were hostile to this expansion of the British Empire. A peace treaty was hammered out at Lausanne in 1923, and British troops evacuated Istanbul later in the year. There was no mention of Kurdistan or Armenia, but tensions between Greece and Turkey were addressed by the exchange of populations. Some nine hundred thousand Greeks moved from Turkey to Greece in return for about four hundred thousand Greek Muslims who moved to Turkey (Zurcher, 2004, 164). The Ottoman Empire was stripped of its Eastern European and Arab provinces with marginal exceptions, but the Turkish heartland of Anatolia emerged as an independent and sovereign state.

The new Turkey was a far different entity than the sprawling empire that it replaced. The sultanate had been replaced by a parliamentary republic, the capital had been shifted from Istanbul to Ankara, and the population had become about 98 percent Muslim, the vast majority of whom lived in rural areas. The change in the composition of the Turkish population was reflected in both its economy and its culture. Much of the empire's commerce had been in the hands of the Greeks and

Armenians, both now reduced to small minorities. As a result, the economy of Turkey had become largely agricultural. Socially and culturally it had become a model of the traditional society outlined above.

Such, then, was the challenge facing Mustafa Kemal, later to be called Ataturk or "father of the Turks," as he endeavored to transform traditional Turkey into a modern military industrial society on par with the most powerful states of Europe. His views appeared to have been shaped by the Turkish philosopher Gokalp who applied European social thinking to the situation of the Ottoman Empire. In Gokalp's view, the purity of Turkey's unique national identity had been lost by the Ottoman's dilution of Turkey's national soul with the infusion of Byzantine, Arab, and Islamic culture. For Gokalp, Islam was the spiritual part of Turkey's national soul, and it was the Byzantine and Arab influences that had to be eliminated. This had to be done by replacing the Arab and Byzantine influences that had shaped the Ottoman's medieval civilization with the modern industrial civilization of the West.

Ataturk's views paralleled those of Gokalp with one major exception. Unlike Gokalp, Kemal rejected Islam as being part of Turkey's national soul. For him, Islam was merely another backward-looking Arab influence that had to be eliminated from Turkey's national soul if it were to regain its position as a world power.

Though hardly a coherent ideology, Kemalism, or Ataturkism, consisted of six principles: republicanism, secularism, nationalism, populism, statism, and reformism. The terms were never clearly defined and so they meant what Ataturk said they meant (Zurcher, 2004, 181).

For our purposes, suffice it to say that each of the six key principles played a vital role in Ataturk's effort to crush Islam in Turkey. Republicanism simply meant that Turkey was no longer a monarchy ruled by the heirs of the Ottoman throne. Henceforth, a president elected by the parliament would rule with the guidance of the parliament. As Ataturk's party had total control of the parliament, he possessed the legitimate right to pursue whatever policies he believed were best for the country. It also meant that his control of the security and bureaucratic apparatus enabled him to attack Islam with both force and financial deprivation.

Secularism, in turn, justified a policy agenda that legally separated church and state. Ataturk wasn't attempting to totally destroy Islam but to shift it from the political to the spiritual realm.

The first step in Ataturk's attack on Islam occurred with the abolition of the caliphate in 1924. Henceforth, Islam would be without a
political and spiritual leader capable of challenging Ataturk's program
or his personal authority. A year later dervish (Sufi) orders were out-
lawed and their schools, shrines, and mausoleums closed. If formal
Islam had been attacked by the abolition of the caliphate, the banish-
ment of Sufi orders attacked mystical spiritual Islam that had enjoyed a
strong popular base in Turkey. The fez and other symbols of Islam were
banned, and veils were discouraged and also later banned. In 1926 an
Ottoman legal code, heavily influenced by Islam, was replaced by the
Swiss legal code. As time went on, religious instruction was eliminated
from both public and private schools and the Turkish constitution was
amended to delete Islam as the official religion of the state. The Arabic
script, the language of the Koran, was subsequently replaced with the
Latin script of the West, and the Islamic calendar gave way to the
Georgian calendar. In the process, Sunday replaced Friday, the Muslim
holy day, as the official day of rest. Mosques did remain open, but
Islamic dress was not allowed.

Nationalism was to be the new faith of the Turkish masses. Rather
than faith in God, they were urged to place their faith in their nation, its
unique cosmic soul, and Ataturk, who had become the high priest of
Turkish nationalism. The foundation for a cosmic Turkish soul was the
Turkish historical thesis described by Zurcher as the thesis "that Turks
were the descendants of white (Aryan) inhabitants of Central Asia, who
had been forced by drought and hunger to migrate to other areas such
as China, Europe, and the Near East. In doing so, Turks had created
the world's great civilizations. In the Near East, Sumerians and the
Hittites were really proto-Turks" (Zurcher, 2004, 191).

As the goal of nationalism was to give Turks faith in themselves and
their country, this theory clearly filled the bill. It also placed modern
Turkey above the mystique and Islamic aura of the Ottoman Empire.
While generally debunked by foreign scholars, the Turkish historical
thesis was taught in Turkish schools after 1932, when it became government doctrine.

This meant that Armenians, Greeks, and Kurds were not part of the
Turkish nation. The Greeks and Armenians had been reduced to a
small minority by the closing years of World War I. The Turks rejected
Armenian accusations of ethnic cleansing and attributed the Armenian

deaths to treasonous efforts to carve out an independent Armenian state on Turkish territory. The Kurds still constitute about 20 percent of the Turkish population and are heavily concentrated in southeastern Turkey. Presumably this region would have constituted a major part of the independent Kurdish homeland promised by the Allied Powers at the conclusion of World War I. Kurdish nationalism began to emerge during the World War I era and has become a rebellion that plays a major role in the politics of Iraq and Syria.

Populism, in turn, gave expression to the will of the masses, who were swayed by hero worship of Ataturk and his carefully orchestrated cult of personality. This process of hero building was personified in his thirty-six hour speech that glorified his accomplishments while debunking other heroes of Turkey's salvation as "doubters, incompetents, and traitors" (Zurcher, 2004, 175). If populism and nationalism were to serve as the new faiths of Turkey, there could be only one nationalist hero: Ataturk. This fact was consecrated in the crowning of Mustafa Kemal's family name with "Ataturk," father of the Turks.

Statism simply meant that the government would use all of its resources to finance and stimulate economic growth. Not incidentally, it also gave Ataturk control of the country's financial resources in his struggle against Islam.

Reformism was designed to modernize Turkish society and culture. These reforms included women voting, family names, and the outlawing of fortune-tellers, soothsayers, and similar superstitious practices. Not only were these and similar reforms designed to modernize Turkey but they were also intended to weaken the social traditions in which Islam had thrived.

Did Ataturk succeed in crushing Islam? This is not an easy question to answer. He was successful in crushing the outward symbols and institutional power centers of Islam that might have challenged his authority, but not the spiritualism prevalent among the masses. This said, Islamic spiritualism remained dormant only to make a political resurgence in the post–World War II era. As we shall see in later chapters, Ataturk's success in modernizing Turkey assured that the Islamic revival in later decades was not hostile to modernity.

Ataturk's legacy was a blending of Islam and modernity similar to the blending of Christianity and modernity in the West. Both could prosper as long as one didn't reject the other. Democracy also played a role in forging a link between Islam and modernity by allowing the representation of each and by bringing an end to decades of military rule by force alone. This thought should be kept in mind as we later search for ways to bridge the gap that is now devastating the region: the gap between Islam and modernity.

EGYPT: THE MUSLIM BROTHERHOOD PITS POPULAR ISLAM AGAINST COLONIALISM

European efforts to colonize Egypt began in 1798 when Napoleon, who was sitting out the chaos of the French Revolution, decided to add Egypt to the French empire. Britain feared a power play by its longtime adversary and rushed to the aid of an Ottoman throne too weak to defend itself.

The Turkish sultan dispatched an expeditionary force of three hundred men from his European provinces to assist the British. The Turkish expedition force played a minor role in defeating the French, but its second in command, an Albanian named Mohammed Ali, seized control of Egypt upon the British withdrawal. Mohammed Ali had become so powerful that he twice threatened to invade Turkey. The British stifled Mohammed Ali's ambitions to become the new sultan of Turkey but crowned him king of Egypt as a consolation prize. Mohammed Ali's family would reign with ever-increasing incompetence until it was overthrown by a military coup in 1952.

Once in place, the Egyptian monarchy bore a strong resemblance to the feudal systems of Europe in which an aristocracy of large landowners provided financial support to the monarchy in exchange for the right to exploit their fiefdoms with little regard for the health and welfare of their fellah (peasants). As time passed, the opulent lifestyle of the royal family squeezed the lifeblood of the peasants until they had nothing left to give.

Fortunately for the royal family, the construction of the Suez Canal in 1869 poured money into their coffers. Their opulent lifestyle was insatiable, and so they survived on loans from European banks. When the monarchy couldn't repay the loans, the British and French simply took control of Egypt's customs office, its most reliable source of taxation. The banks got their share and the royal family got what was left.

The seizing of the customhouses sparked a brief military rebellion in 1882, but to no avail. The British simply invaded Egypt under the pretext of protecting the canal. Rather than ruling Egypt directly, they made it a protectorate. The royal family remained, but so did the British troops.

Reaction to the British occupation took a variety of forms. Westernized intellectuals, many of whom had been educated in Europe, bitterly criticized Egyptian culture as being retrogressive. To the dismay of the educated classes, their aspirations for equality with the British were stifled by Western arrogance. Few were allowed to enter the plush British hotels and sporting clubs by the front door. The result of this situation was that the more modernized Egyptians learned nationalism from the British. If they couldn't be British, they would drive out the *kawaga* (foreign master) and rule Egypt for themselves.

Nationalist hostility toward the British was shared by devout Muslims, most of whom were deeply offended by British disregard for Islamic morality. The Muslim clergy, in particular, feared that Western tastes would spread among the masses much as they had among the educated classes.

Faced with the lethal combination of religious and nationalist hostility, the British granted Egypt its independence in 1922. However indirectly, mass protests had forced the retreat of the British occupation of Egypt, the only catch being that Britain had the right to station troops on Egyptian soil. This is not to suggest that the British lacked the military force to continue its occupation but merely that faith-based turmoil had made the cost of occupation so high that the better part of valor was the concentration of British troops in the strategic Suez Canal Zone rather than in Egypt's tumultuous cities. This said, the British ambassador remained a major power broker in competition with the king and the *Wafd*, the leading nationalist movement.

It was not until 1928 that mass resentment of both the British and the monarchy found its voice with the emergence of the Muslim Brotherhood. Populist Islamic faith had always been present in Egypt, but it had never become an organized political movement on a national scale. That changed as the influence of the Muslim Brotherhood soared.

Hasan al-Banna, the founder of the Brotherhood, would later describe his organization as a "Salafite movement, an orthodox way, a Sufi reality, a political body, an athletic group, a scientific and cultural society, an economic company, and a social idea" (cited in Husaini, 1956, 15). In sum, there was something for everyone.

Al-Banna, an instructor of Arabic, was very much a popular preacher in the Sufi mode. Like popular preachers before him, he offered his followers pride in their religion, a clear path to paradise, and the confidence that they could achieve paradise by resisting the foreign master. While the religious elite regaled the masses with the finer points of doctrine, al-Banna spoke to their hearts. In the words of one of his followers:

> People are arguing back and forth, theologians theorizing, would-be philosophers philosophizing, and cultured people are delving in all fields; but Hasan al-Banna does not believe any of it, no matter how the ulema [religious scholars] and the specialists plunge themselves into it. He cites for you a verse from the Koran and the matter is settled and decided, . . . people wear themselves out searching hither and yon, while al-Banna with his Koran has no need for these. (Cited in Husaini, 1956, 31)

Al-Banna began his mission by holding discussion sessions in nearby mosques. Eventually, he and his disciples opened their own mosques. Al-Banna himself visited village after village speaking of pride, honor, hope, dignity, salvation, oneness with God, and the mutual caring of a brotherhood family. He even spoke of nationalism and social justice, for all were one in Islam. It was one-to-one and heart-to-heart, and the urban poor and rural peasants listened intently. So did a growing number of educated Muslims. Branches and newsletters followed, paving the way for the spread of the Brotherhood throughout the Arab world.

The masses were looking for a Mahdi (messiah) to guide them, and al-Banna fulfilled that role by combining Sufi mysticism with a practical program of social and political action that guaranteed dignity on earth with an eternity in paradise.

Did al-Banna have the gift of grace? Husaini describes al-Banna's charisma as that of a prophet.

> His mastery over his followers was a complete, total mastery approaching wizardry. For each person he had a special story, a special manner and a special logic. . . . The mastery of al-Banna over these different groups, the way he attracted constantly supporters in Egypt

and abroad, and the rapid growth of his movement in steadfastness and stability are manifestations of his intelligence and resourcefulness. (Husaini, 1956, 33)

But the Brotherhood was about more than talk. Emulation is deeply rooted in the Islamic world, and members of the Brotherhood were to serve as models for others. Al-Banna also built houses for the wretched, opened schools for the illiterate, and established health and welfare programs for the poor. Preaching and welfare, in turn, led to political activism. Morality, according to the Brotherhood, did not lie in passive acceptance of immoral leaders who emulated the godless ways of their foreign master. He even wrote to presidents and kings, imploring them to change their ways. When they refused, the Brotherhood turned against them. The model of today's political Islam had been born.

Beyond his charisma, al-Banna was a master of organizational skills. "Members were divided into grades; first and second class and supporting and active members. They could not advance to a higher grade until they had passed certain examinations. . . . Active members were divided into spiritual units: nuclei (nawah), cells (khaliyah), families (usrah), and phalanxes (katibah)" (Husaini, 1956, 90). The above, in turn, were combined into branches, many of which contained military, or "rover," units. Various councils guided the affairs of the larger units but lacked the authority to challenge the power of al-Banna. So, for that matter, did King Farouk. The Brotherhood had become so powerful by the end of its first decade that al-Banna merely smiled when a nationalist admirer informed him of the king's plot to ban the Brotherhood. "He can't" was the essence of al-Banna's response; "we are too powerful" (Nasr, 1988, 198).

When al-Banna was assassinated in 1949, the ruling advisory council selected a new supreme guide. Al-Banna's charisma didn't disappear; rather, it became the guiding spirit of the organization and its mystical link to God. By killing a leader, the assassin had created a saint. Although al-Banna has passed from the scene, his Muslim Brotherhood remains a major faith actor in the unfolding drama of the Middle East. So much is this the case that it is tempting to consider the Muslim Brotherhood as a distinct Islamic sect. Force may kill, but faith lives on.

ISRAEL: PALESTINE BECOMES A HOMELAND
FOR THE JEWS

In 1917 the British War Cabinet made a strategic decision to declare Palestine a national home for the Jews. Its goal, as the documents of the era indicate, was to "carry out extremely useful propaganda among the large Jewish communities in America, Russia, and elsewhere throughout the world" (Fraser, 1980, 17).

Supporting this logic was the surge in Zionism triggered by the publication of Theodor Herzl's *The Jewish State,* in 1896. His message was simple: The history of pogroms and violent anti-Semitism in Europe made it clear that Jews could only find true security in their own state. The first Zionist conference was held the following year. Zionism wasn't a religious issue but an issue of survival. It was Jewish nationalism rather than a religious crusade.

This didn't mean that Herzl and the early Zionist leadership were unmindful of the importance of faith in forging a Jewish homeland. Britain's leaders had initially suggested Uganda and Argentina as sites for a Jewish state. These suggestions were rejected by Zionist leaders on the grounds that they lacked religious appeal for the vast majority of Europe's Jews who were religious. This was a vital point for the Zionists who insisted that their Jewish state be a state of Jews, by Jews, and for Jews. Only British-occupied Palestine, the Promised Land, would do.

Far from being a purely strategic document, the Balfour Declaration that made Palestine a homeland for the Jews also reflected the Christian religious view of its authors, who believed that the creation of a Jewish state in Palestine was a requirement for the Second Coming of Christ (Fraser, 1980; Pappe, 2006). Beyond a Christian bias, it was likely that British attitudes were shaped by a view that Muslims were inferior to modern Westerners. Whatever the case, the British saw little wrong in giving occupied territory to Jews as a homeland.

This attitude of compassion toward the Jews reflected a paradigm shift in Christian theology, from the traditional view that Christians had replaced Jews as God's chosen people to the view that God had two plans for his human creations. In one of God's plans, Jews remained God's chosen people based on his promise to Abraham. In God's second plan, Christians, with the advent of Christ, became God's spiritually chosen people. In the new view, referred to as "dispensation theology," Jews were to perish with the end of time while devout Christians would ascend into heaven. Jews who accepted Christ as their savior at this point would ascend into heaven. In the meantime, Christians were to accept Jews as God's chosen people and support the prophetic return of Jews to the Holy Land. The Second Coming of Christ demanded it (Brog, 2006).

Dispensation theology is mentioned at this point for two reasons. First, its influence on American policy toward the Middle East has increased steadily with time. Second, dispensation theology placed Jews in a quandary. Were they to let bygones be bygones as they coveted Christian support for the security of Israel? Or were they to view Christian support for Israel with a skepticism that warns of betrayal when Christian interests are placed at risk?

One answer to this quandary was not long in coming. For all of their bias in favor of the Zionists, the British cabinet was reluctant to offend the Muslims in a region they would soon rule. Their solution was to be a partition of Palestine into Jewish and Palestinian sectors.

The Zionist leadership rejected this suggestion as something akin to treason. In their view, making Palestine a homeland for the Jews meant that Jews had the right to settle Palestine and the Arabs were to leave Palestine. Faith, force, and finance all played their part, a process described in painful detail by Ilan Pappe, an Israeli historian at Haifa University, in his book, *The Ethnic Cleansing of Palestine* (Pappe, 2006).

The rebirth of modern Israel had been facilitated in 1880, when the Ottoman Empire lifted the ban on Jewish immigration to Palestine, which was then part of the Ottoman Empire. Approximately twenty-four thousand Jews had remained in the ancient Holy Land during Islamic rule, and the new arrivals added from twenty thousand to thirty thousand Jews to their numbers. By the beginning of World War I, the end of the era under discussion, Jews only constituted some 12 percent of the Palestinian population. Thoughts of a Jewish state remained largely theoretical (Rodinson, 1969) but the foundation of a Jewish state had been established.

The role of faith in laying the foundation for an eventual Jewish state in Palestine was so formidable that there would not have been a Jewish state today without it. The very concept of Zion and Zionism gave expression to the dream of an ideal Jewish nation in which the Messiah would rule.

Jewish force during this period was largely provided by the *Hagana*, a paramilitary organization developed in 1920 to protect the settlers. It soon became the military arm of the Jewish Agency, the Zionist governing body in Palestine. With time, it received training from the British military and would play a major role in Zionist plans to drive the Palestinians from Palestine. At least part of this training included lessons on how to use bayonets to ethnically cleanse Palestinian villages.

Cooperation between the Hagana and the British forces became a virtual alliance during the Arab revolts of 1929 and 1936 protesting the Jewish takeover of their country. The 1936 Palestinian uprising flared for three years and saw Hagana units attached to British force. In the process, a Jewish paramilitary organization received vital training as it began its transition into a national army (Pappe, 2006).

The Jews used the period between the two world wars to transform large areas of Palestine into a virtual Jewish state with its own government (*Yishuv*) that included a parliament with the power to levy taxes and a labor union that served as an investment company, insurance company, and social security agency. The transition was relatively easy because the Jews who settled Palestine were modern in the European sense. The Palestinians, by contrast, remained locked in the traditional format of the Ottomans and, divided by family and religious conflicts, found coordination difficult.

Finance entered the picture as supporters of the Zionist program bought land from large Palestinian landowners for the purpose of settling Jewish immigrants in Palestine. This process was later taken over by the Jewish Agency and became rushed in the mid-1930s with the advent of Hitler's efforts to eradicate Germany's Jewish population. By 1936, Jews comprised 30 percent of the population of Palestine as opposed to 12 percent in 1922. Rather than protecting Jewish settlers, the Hagana then focused on expelling Palestinians from the Jewish lands that they had once cultivated.

It was this coordinated balance of faith, force, and finance that laid the foundation for a Jewish state in Palestine. The future of Israel continued to rely on this same coordinated balance.

The success of this stage of the building of a Jewish state in Palestine had much to do with the cohesion of the Jewish community in Palestine. The settlers could either work together as a community or they could perish. The Jewish success in Palestine also had much to do with a European view of society that was heavily socialist in nature as well as the technological and organizational skills of the settlers. To these was added a global Zionist support base intent on making Palestine the pillar of Jewish survival in a hostile world.

The Palestinians enjoyed none of the above. By and large, much of the Palestinian population remained rural and traditional in nature. Their technical skills were minimal, and their organizational capacity was fractured by internal conflict and mutual distrust. The large land-owners who had put their tenants in jeopardy by selling land to the Jews took their money and moved to Beirut. External support was minimal and no match for the global support available to the Jews.

All, however, was not well in the Jewish community. Its rapid expansion in Palestine sparked a bitter Palestinian revolt against the British that endured for three years before being suppressed by British and Hagana forces. The cost of suppressing the revolt was horrendous for the Jews; they suddenly found themselves abandoned by their British allies, who had suddenly become more concerned with a looming war with Germany than with the fate of the Jews. The Germans were wooing the Arabs in a bid to put Britain's Middle Eastern oil and route to India in jeopardy.

Strategy took precedence over Christian religious concerns, and the British government issued a 1939 white paper that sharply curtailed Jewish migration to Palestine and the selling of land to the Jews. It also promised the establishment of an independent Arab state in Palestine. It was World War II that would determine the fate of the Jews and their homeland in Palestine.

IRAQ: BRITISH CONTROL OF THE IRAQI SHIA

With the defeat of the Ottoman Empire in World War I, the British assumed control of the three Turkish provinces that constitute the present state of Iraq, then referred to as the "land between the two rivers." Much like other former Turkish territories occupied by the British in World War I, Iraq was to be a mandate that the British guided to democracy and development before granting it formal independence as a full member in the world community.

The British complied with the form of the mandate system by making Iraq a parliamentary monarchy but largely ignored its spirit by selecting a son of the governor of Mecca to be the king of Iraq. This wasn't in the spirit of the mandate system, but it was very much in the spirit of colonialism that had seen the British make Palestine a homeland for the Jews.

Actually, the British had promised to make the governor (sharif) of Mecca the king of a large portion of the eastern Arabian Peninsula and make Fysal, his son, the king of Syria. The French, who had conquered Syria, sent Fysal packing when he rode into Syria to claim his kingdom. Fate thus dictated that the British would fulfill their promise to the governor of Mecca by making Fysal the king of Iraq. A second son of the sharif of Mecca was made king of Jordan when the British created the country of Jordan several years later.

Iraq's Sunni population was supportive of Fysal's kingship, as well it should have been. Not only was he a direct descendant of the Prophet Mohammed but, as a Sunni, his sympathies would incline toward Sunni rule of Iraq. This was very much the case as a Sunni elite dominated by former Iraqi officers in the Ottoman army became the power behind the throne. They were joined by a cadre of Sunni officers who had marched with Fysal into Syria before being repulsed by the French. Whatever the case, the Iraqi administration was Sunni from top to bottom. Bureaucratic affairs were managed by British civil servants, and security was assured by British troops.

This combination of Sunni faith and British force pleased the Sunni Arabs, who constituted 20 percent of the Iraqi population, but was deeply offensive to the Arab Shia, who constituted about 60 percent of the population. The remaining 20 percent were Kurds. Deep suspicion about Shia opposition to British rule pushed the British even closer to the Sunni elite who dominated the monarchy and parliament.

Some authors felt that British worries about the Shia were exaggerated. It is true that some Shia clerics had incited Shia tribes to fight with the Turks against the British, but it was much ado about nothing. The Shia tribes had expected just another tribal war, but they were stunned by the superior firepower of the British forces and so they fled. I mention this story because the Shia tribes were the main source of force available to the Shia clerics at the time.

It was assumed that the Shia clerics feared the negative influence of British culture on their flock, but this was not necessarily the case. As things turned out, the Shia clerics themselves were having a hard time agreeing about what to do about the British, as were other Shia notables. To further confuse matters, each time a dominant ayatollah (grand marjah) would die, his successor seemed to have a different attitude toward the British. Slightly lower clerics often had their own views and didn't always follow the dictates of the grand ayatollah. This said, the views of the grand ayatollah had a profound influence on the Shia populations, as they continue to have today.

Particularly disconcerting to the British were the strong links between the Iraqi Shia clerics and Iran's Shia clerics, each of whom influenced the other. Iran's clerics were hostile to British influence in their country, and the British were worried that this hostility would contaminate the Iraqi Shia.

In 1920 the Shia revolted against direct rule by the British. The Shia revolt, however, was more of an economic revolt than a religiously inspired revolt. The British had raised taxes on the already despairing peasants to pay for their administrative expenses. The tribal chiefs were made tax collectors, which turned the peasants against their sheikhs, who kept their share of the taxes as a reward for keeping their tribes under control. At least in this case, finance had trumped both tribal and religious faith. The victims of the taxes were largely Shia because they populated the more fertile tribal lands controlled by their sheikhs. The Sunni, in contrast, occupied less fertile areas and were largely small farmers.

Adding to the Shia drama was the British reliance on former Sunni officers—those who had served in the Ottoman army—to manage their local affairs. In their view, Iraq was going to be ruled by the Sunni minority whatever the cost.

Did religion play a role in the Shia revolt? This question remains a matter of debate. Whatever the case, the Shia, given their earlier revolt and concentration in the slums of Baghdad, were the most immediate threat. If joined by the Shia clergy and the Shia tribes, the fate of the new monarchy would be in question. Fears that the Kurds would use a

Shia revolt to launch their own revolt would place the new kingdom at war with 80 percent of its population.

As the post–World War I era drew to a close, the main clouds that remained on the horizon were the revolts by the Shia and the Kurds. Both were oppressed, and neither had representation in the newly formed government of Iraq.

This very real threat was confronted by a combination of force and finance. Force was used to keep order in the politically sensitive urban centers and to exile or imprison Shia clerics suspected of fomenting hostility toward Iraq, which served as a British military base. Finance, in turn, was used to convert Shia tribal sheikhs into supporters of the monarchy by making them the owners of what had traditionally been the collective property of the tribe. In the process, the tribal sheikhs became landed barons and the dispossessed members of the tribe be-came peasants. To make matters worse, peasants who borrowed money from the tribal sheikhs—and that was most of them—could not leave the land without their permission. Those who did would find their dwellings destroyed and their families forced into the slums of Baghdad and other major cities already festering with revolt.

The slums of Baghdad continued to grow throughout this era, as did the exile and imprisonment of Shia clerics who were capable of trigger-ing future slum revolts. Fear emerged among the political leaders of the region over the profound influence of Iranian clerics in Iraq, Lebanon, and other areas with large Shia populations, including the oil-rich East-ern Province of Saudi Arabia and many of the Gulf sheikhdoms.

The broader regional influence of the Shia clerics started with the observation that the main holy places of the Shia were located in Iraq and that many of the most powerful Shia clerics had been Iranians who studied in the seminaries of Iraq's holy cities. Many stayed in Iraq. Others returned to Iran or Lebanon. Islam was not and is not con-strained by national borders.

LESSONS LEARNED

The events described in this chapter happened so long ago and under circumstances so different from those prevailing today that it could be argued that they are no longer relevant to the current crises facing the

Middle East. On the other hand, it could be argued that they initiated a pattern that is very much in evidence today, a pattern that might have been avoided had the lessons listed below been heeded. You can be the judge as these and parallel lessons are traced through the unfolding drama of the Middle East, until we reach the final stage of examining solutions to the horrendous crises facing the Middle East and world in the future.

Faith

1. The three Abrahamic faiths cannot be removed from the Arab-Israeli conflict that has played such a dominant role in the drama of the Middle East.
2. Religious faith knows no boundaries when it comes to the affairs of the Middle East.
3. Faith that blends charisma, nationalism, and ethnic identity with religious authority is more powerful than either faith or religious authority alone.
4. To be powerful, religious emotions have to be organized and directed. When that organizational direction fades, so does the power of faith.
5. Faith alone did not trump force or finance during the era under discussion, but it made occupation difficult and costly to the point that it was more logical for the occupying colonial powers to leave rather than stay.

Force

1. Force can trump religious faith with relative ease if force is dominant and the religious establishment is weak.
2. The appeal of religious faith becomes latent but doesn't disappear with force.
3. Religious faith increases when force weakens and when despair increases.
4. Force in the form of occupation by an alien religious faith generates Islamic religious unrest among the occupied population. This

is all the more the case if the occupation imposes financial burdens of the indigenous population.

Finance

1. Finance can trump religious and tribal traditional faith by influencing religious and tribal leaders to avoid inciting the masses distraught by economic despair.
2. Financial limits imposed by an occupying power result in increased nationalism and religious faith.
3. Economic despair prepared the ground for the emergence of the Muslim Brotherhood.
4. Populist religious faith and restrictions on the economic elite may combine to make nationalism an irresistible force.

The Balance of Faith, Force, and Finance

Effective control of the Middle East requires the combination of faith, force, and finance. It is doubtful, for example, that faith, force, or finance individually could have achieved the goal of preparing the ground for the Jewish state that emerged at the conclusion of World War I.

3

WORLD WAR II RESHAPES
THE MIDDLE EAST (1940–1967)

The devastation in Britain and France during World War II left them too weak to resist the nationalist revolutions exploding in the Middle Eastern countries that they controlled under one pretext or another. For better or worse, the United States and the Soviet Union would shape the future of the Middle East in the post–World War II era. The Middle East was new territory for both the United States and the Soviet Union. The mistakes of the past awaited both. They also awaited some twenty-two newly independent countries attempting to dodge the crossfire of the global struggle between the United States and the Soviet Union.

Virtually all countries in the region were forced to join this epic struggle between democracy, freedom, and capitalism, on the one hand, and communism and forced economic development, on the other. The United States allied itself with the tribal kings, Turkey's military tyrants, and Israel. The Soviet Union became the supporter of Egypt, Algeria, Syria, and Iraq, all of which had revolted against their colonial masters in the name of freedom, democracy, socialism, and equality.

The dependence of the Middle Eastern regimes on a major power for their survival during the post–World War II era didn't mean that they were compliant puppets. To the contrary, most were using the support of the major powers to pursue their own interests and plot against their regional foes. In the process, they were drawing the United States and the Soviet Union ever deeper into the conflicts of the region.

Whatever the case, faith, force, and finance played a prominent role in all dimensions of the complex struggles reshaping the region in the aftermath of World War II. The role of faith in this stage of the drama was particularly interesting because the power of religious faith was challenged by power of charismatic faith and various blends of nationalism, socialism, and communism.

Charisma as defined by Max Weber is the gift of divine grace that makes a few exceptional individuals appear to have superhuman, supernatural, or other extraordinary powers. They are followed as leaders, if not saviors, because people have faith in the ability of their exceptional powers to work miracles (Weber, 1947, 328). The key point here is that charismatic faith flows from the people to a leader. A leader may solicit faith, but it is up to the people to decide who or what is worthy of their faith. If the leader's appearance of superhuman power fades, so does the support among the masses. The present chapter examines how diverse combinations of faith, force, and finance shaped the post–World War II era in Egypt, Israel, Saudi Arabia, and Iran.

EGYPT AND ARAB UNITY: USING CHARISMA, NATIONALISM, AND SOCIALISM AS FAITH ALTERNATIVES TO ISLAM

The power of charismatic faith as a weapon in shaping the events of the post–World War II era was dramatically illustrated by the reign of Abdel Nasser, the leader of the 1952 coup that overthrew King Farouk, who was arguably the most decadent and incompetent of Egyptian monarchs.

Farouk had sealed his doom by sending Egypt's ill-equipped and poorly led army to liberate Palestine from Jewish control in the 1948 Arab-Israeli War. According to Hasan Youssef Pasha, the head of the Royal Diwan (cabinet), Farouk assumed that the Jews couldn't fight and that he would add Palestine to his kingdom in a day or two (Pasha, 1983). The Jews humiliated the Egyptian forces and Nasser and his Free Officers overthrew Farouk a few years later. Prophetically, Farouk quipped as he sailed for Italy on his private yacht, "There will soon be only five kings left in the world, the king of England and the four in a deck of cards."

Nasser put Farouk on his yacht rather than dragging his body through the streets as the Iraqis would do with their prime minister a few years later. His leniency was dictated by the prevailing international environment. Colonialism was alive and well, and Nasser didn't want the murder of Farouk to provide the British with a pretext for reinvading Egypt.

Much like Ataturk before him, Nasser's goal was no less than the total transformation of the Arab world into a unified industrial military power on par with the countries of the West. Only then, in his view, could the Arabs regain their former glory and be free from the scourge of occupation.

The British tolerated Nasser's coup on the assumption that he would abide by existing treaties giving the British control of the Suez Canal. That illusion passed when the United States, peeved by Nasser's refusal to join its anti-Soviet alliance, cancelled promised aid that Nasser needed to build a grandiose dam on the Nile. Nasser had boasted that the dam would provide the electric power needed to transform Egypt into a major industrial power. To back down in the face of the US financial threat would be to lose the faith and respect of the Egyptian public. A young leader who had only assumed full power a year earlier, Nasser needed all the respect that he could muster. And so, Nasser responded with force by seizing the Suez Canal in 1956. Canal revenues, he vowed, would build the dam.

The British, French, and Israelis joined together to design a plot to seize the Suez Canal and overthrow Nasser. The show of Israeli force was effective as the Israel Defense Forces (IDF) seized the canal with little difficulty. Nasser had been humiliated, and his future appeared dim. It was at this point, however, that the United States, for all of its faith-based support for Israel, forced a withdrawal of Israeli forces from the canal. As it had in the waning years of the World War I era, faith-based support for Israel gave way to the strategic interests of a Christian power. It wasn't fear of a Muslim uprising that was the culprit in the US case but fear that the Soviet Union would use Egyptian hostility toward the United States and its European and Israeli allies to take over Egypt. Nasser, in the eyes of Egyptians and much of the Arab world, had scored a miraculous victory over the combined forces of the British,

French, and Israelis. It was a political victory rather than a military victory, but a victory is a victory, especially when it was the first Arab victory since the era of Islam.

Was Nasser the new Saladin? How could there be any doubt? In addition to nationalizing the Suez Canal and thwarting a joint Anglo-French-Israeli attempt to seize the Suez Canal, Nasser awed the Egyptian public by evicting the British from their Egyptian military bases. He also liquidated foreign control of the Egyptian economy, distributed land to the peasants, and shattered US control of the Middle East by purchasing weapons from the Communist Bloc. These miraculous achievements were followed by the construction of the Aswan Dam, a massive undertaking that would tame the Nile's legendary floods and provide electrical power for Egypt's industrial revolution. This was breathtaking, miraculous stuff for an Arab psyche trampled by centuries of decay. If Arabs were looking for a superhero, they had surely found him. In mystical circles, rumors soared that Nasser was the new Mahdi (messiah). Nasser denied these claims, but they persisted. Religious faith, however unintentional, had been added to Nasser's soaring charisma. Surely the Egyptians would follow their superhero to the ends of the earth. Nasser knew that it would not be easy, for as he had lamented shortly after seizing power,

> Every leader we came to wanted to assassinate his rival. Every idea we found aimed at the destruction of another. If we were to carry out all that we heard, then there would not be one leader left alive. Not one idea would remain intact. We would cease to have a mission save to remain among the smashed bodies and the broken debris lamenting our misfortune and reproaching our ill-fate. . . . If I were asked then what I required most my instant answer would be, "To hear but one Egyptian uttering one word of justice about another, to see but one Egyptian not devoting his time to criticize willfully the ideas of another, to feel that there was but one Egyptian ready to open his heart for forgiveness, indulgence and loving his brother Egyptian." (Nasser, 1955, NP)

If Nasser's victories were awesome, so were the problems he faced in his dream of transforming Egypt and the Arabs into a global military-industrial power on par with the powers of the West. Colonialism had divided the Arabs into twenty-plus states, each with a narrow elite intent on clinging to power, whatever the costs. Their populations remained largely rural, illiterate, wedded to the past, and fragmented into a multitude of religious sects and kinship networks. As Abdel Nasser would lament, the British had their revolutions one at a time. First came the industrial revolution, then the social revolution, and finally the political revolution. The Arabs were fated to have all of their revolutions at once.

The former colonial powers didn't make things easier for the new hero of the Nile. To the contrary, they had no interest in seeing the Arabs unified. The Western powers no longer ruled the Arab world, but they remained dependent upon its oil resources and covetous of its strategic location. The plot thickened with the deepening Cold War between the Communist Bloc and the United States. The nationalistic slogans of Nasser smacked of socialism and hostility toward the West. To the US strategists of the time, a unified Arab nation allied with the Soviet Union could well tip the balance in global politics toward the latter. For many Americans, the line between socialism and communism was too thin to be tolerated.

Islam also proved to be a problem. Much like Ataturk, Nasser viewed Islam as a cultural obstacle to his modernization plans and a potential source of political opposition. Unlike Ataturk, who had launched a devastating attack on Islam a few decades earlier, Nasser chose to use Islam as a faith asset by bending it to his modernization program. If Islam could not be divorced from Arab culture, Arab faith and culture would have to be modernized. To achieve this goal, Nasser simply incorporated Egypt's Islamic institutions into the revolutionary government. This accomplished, he used Egypt's mosques to preach the Islamic virtues of freedom, national unity, equality, and Islamic socialism.

Problems arose when the Muslim Brotherhood and other traditional groups saw the hand of the devil in Nasser's modernization program. Particularly offensive to the traditionalists were the mingling of the sexes and the glorification of Western values. Unlike the colonial era in which Islamic fundamentalists and modernizers had joined forces to defeat the colonialists, Nasser's charge for modernity placed the two visions of the Arab future on a collision course.

It was the fundamentalists who struck first, when an extremist branch within the Muslim Brotherhood attempted to assassinate Nasser in 1954. Nasser's response was swift and brutal as he set about crushing the Brotherhood by force. Nasser had used Islam when it served his purpose but not when it posed opposition to his rule.

Despite resistance from Islamic fundamentalists, the Arabs had cause for optimism. United, they could have everything the modern world had to offer, including wealth, military power, and industrialization. Divided, they had nothing. Surely, Nasser believed, the Arab masses would seize the moment by putting their shoulder to the wheel of industrialization and overthrowing their decaying tribal monarchies.

Enlightened leaders, for their part, would allocate the resources of the state, however meager, in a wise and egalitarian manner. Revolutions in education and health care would fuel an industrial revolution, which, in turn, would provide jobs and prosperity for all. Economic democracy would, with time and education, lead to political democracy. Force would be necessary to crush reactionary opponents of the revolution, but only as a last resort. When everything was in place, powerful Arab armies would crush what remained of the tribal kingdoms and restore Arab pride by pushing the Israelis into the sea.

Such was the dream of Nasser and the other Arab revolutionaries of the era. It was all summed up in their slogan "unity, socialism, freedom." The order of the words varied from country to country, but the basic concept was the same.

Dream on, sweet prince. How was there to be a political revolution in the Arab world when the existing political institutions were controlled by landowners, aristocrats, and other elements linked to the past? How could there be unity when the existing political parties caused dissension by inflaming ethnic, religious, and class differences? How was there to be mass education when there were few teachers? How was there to be an industrial revolution when there were few factories, little technology, few resources, and a workforce that consisted of peasants with little appreciation of time or discipline? How was the state to allocate what meager resources that existed in a wise and judicious manner when what passed for a bureaucracy consisted of the corrupt sons of the aristocracy? How was there to be a powerful army when the generals were aristocrats and the only weapons available were hand-me-downs from the colonial powers? And the cruelest question of all was, how could the masses be harnessed to the wheel of moderniza-tion when the prevailing Arab psyche was overwhelmed with passivity, petty jealousies, and distrust of the government?

The only solution was to rebuild everything from scratch, including Arab society and Arab culture. Nothing was to be gained by changing the bottles if they were to be filled with the same old wine. What would this new Arab culture look like? Nasser wasn't terribly clear on the topic, but a reading of his collective speeches called for the pride and courage of a Bedouin warrior, the moral discipline of the Prophet Mo-hammed, the zeal of the Islamic invasions, and the discipline and re-spect for the laws of the British. All were part of the Arab experience. All that remained was to put them together (Palmer, 1973). The ques-tion was, how?

Nasser's efforts to rebuild everything from scratch under the most adverse of circumstances relied heavily on three basic assets. First, as commander-in-chief of the security forces, he had a monopoly of coer-cive force. He could crush his opponents and force the masses to carry out his orders. His Soviet allies were experts on the subject and had done wonders in developing his secret service.

Second, Nasser controlled the Egyptian economy. Having national-ized most businesses of any size, finance was used to guarantee all Egyptians a job, health care, and a free education. Surely they would be grateful and support his program.

Finally, Nasser's charisma soared. At last, a true Arab hero had ar-rived to lead the Egyptians to the Promised Land. The long-awaited Mahdi or not, his victories conveyed unequivocal signs of God's bless-ing. His victories became their victories and he their father and guide. It was their obligation to follow and obey as Arabs had always followed and obeyed their patriarch. Such are the demands of charisma, at least as long as it lasts.

These were powerful weapons, but each had a fatal flaw. Military power, alone, could not force people to buy into Nasser's vision of an Arab revival. Arabs knew how to deceive their tyrants with appearances of conformity while they subverted them by playing the fox. Nasser knew the drill and also had doubts about the loyalty of his own security forces.

It was the same in the economic sphere. Nasser controlled the econ-omy, but it was a bankrupt economy shattered by erratic efforts to

impose socialism on a largely rural population. Massive Soviet-style factories were built in an effort to transform Egypt into an industrial power, but they consumed more wealth than they produced. Jobs were
provided for the masses, but the pay was pathetically low. It was the
same in the bureaucracy. Things were to be sorted out with time, but
that time never arrived.

Charisma also had its weaknesses. Nasser was a product of his culture and understood the power of heroes and holy men to sway the
masses. He also knew that this power required an endless series of
victories and miracles. One slip and their aura would fade, and the
masses would abandon them in search of a new savior.

With the economy in a shambles, finance was a weapon of little
utility to Nasser. To the contrary, finance was a glaring weakness that
made him dependent upon aid from the major powers for his survival.
The United States offered aid but only in exchange for Nasser's toning
down his nationalist rhetoric that focused on socialism and hostility
toward Israel. The more Nasser's demands for money increased, the
more the United States put pressure on him to join its anti-Soviet alliance that consisted mainly of the tribal kings. From Nasser's view, this
was just another Western effort to colonize the Arabs. The Soviets, by
contrast, offered money and weapons in return for little more than a
few bases on the Mediterranean.

The deal was struck; the Soviets financed Nasser's Aswan Dam and
made the Egyptian army the most powerful in the Arab world. The dam
and Nasser's soaring military power, when added to his earlier feats of
wonder, so infatuated the international press that it crowned him "Man
of the Year." What more could a leader seeking glory as a superhero ask
for?

Nasser's charisma continued to soar as his promises of food, jobs,
health care, housing, and education became a reality with dazzling
speed. Promises of democracy were finessed by the formation of a
single political party to be dominated by the workers and peasants.
These tangible accomplishments were buttressed by five-year development plans that blended hope and faith in the future with demands for
patience, sacrifice, and hard work.

Development plans gave hope but were largely invisible to a population seeking immediate and dramatic proof of their savior's power. No
problem: the development plans were spiced with dazzling mega pro-

jects, the most dazzling of which had been the Aswan Dam, a project so grand that Egyptian pundits referred to it as Nasser's pyramid.

Not one to rest on his laurels, Nasser's glory born of his domestic accomplishments was soon reinforced by international glory as he joined forces with several other newly independent leaders to form the Third World Alliance. This alliance of former colonies vowed to bring peace to the world by replacing the Cold War with African and Asian solidarity. Rather than seeing the world destroyed by war, the members of the Third World Alliance vowed they would all refuse to become involved in a war between the United States and the Soviet Union. This road to peace was called the doctrine of positive neutrality. No one was quite sure what "positive neutrality" meant and there was little African and Asian solidarity, but it all made for great headlines as Nasser and other third-world leaders lectured the UN on the need for peace and traveled the globe to attend third-world conferences. This was powerful stuff for populations long humiliated by their colonial masters.

Nasser's charismatic strategy at the regional level focused heavily on Arab nationalism and dreams of an Arab and Islamic revival that would see the Arabs and Muslims return to their historic role as leaders of global civilization. The Arab and Muslim revivals from the perspective of many Arabs were one and the same. It was the Arabs who had received God's message, and Arabic was the language of the Koran. The logic of Arab nationalism was compelling: there was a common history, a common language, a common culture, a contiguous territory that stretched from sea to sea, massive oil resources, a common hostility toward colonial domination, and a common sense of humiliation owing to defeat at the hands of a small Israeli state. All that was needed for an Arab revival was a powerful leader to unify them and mold them into a modern military-industrial power. And so Nasser preached that the Arabs could either stand together or fall together. Unity and development were their only hope. The tribal kings who had become lapdogs to the United States would have to be overthrown as traitors to the Arab nation.

Such was the nature of Nasserism, the ideology of a brave new Arab world. It was also an ideology that possessed much in common with the nationalist Baathist ideologies that dominated in Syria and Iraq. They, too, advocated unity, socialism, and freedom, although not necessarily in that order. They also looked to Nasser as the spearhead of the Arab

Nationalist movement, albeit with their shared leadership in a unified Arab state.

In addition to the above charismatic strategies, Nasser was careful to assure that no other members of his leadership organization shared his glory. Nor were competing sources of power allowed to take root. When things went wrong, however, others took the blame. He also encouraged mass participation in sustaining his rule by creating an atmosphere of permanent crisis in which the enemies of Egypt were constantly attempting to overthrow him. This included the United States, the old Egyptian regime, and the Muslim Brotherhood.

For a while it appeared that the dream might become a reality. Factories mushroomed, as did mass education and health services. Huge armies marched in lockstep, their mighty Soviet weapons striking fear throughout the region. Egypt and Syria were unified briefly in 1958 with Iraq and Yemen promising to follow suit. I lived in Egypt as a young student during the early 1960s and was terribly impressed by it all. A new era was at hand.

Then the dream started to unravel. Rural peasants rushed to the cities in search of work, only to find themselves living in squalid slums, many without basic utilities. The government bureaucracies, mired in confusion and corruption, became an obstacle to modernization rather than its guide. Nasser even spoke openly of forming an alliance with the masses against the rapacious officials who filled the administrative and political bureaucracies that he had created to serve as the foundation of his development program.

Mahmoud Fawzi, an Egyptian journalist who interviewed the remaining members of the Nasser regime in the mid-1980s, dated the end of Nasser's dream with Egypt's 1962 war in Yemen. In hope of adding Yemen to Egypt's union with Syria, Nasser committed his massive military machine to the republican side in a Yemeni civil war. His Soviet tanks controlled the cities but were of no use in Yemen's mountainous terrain. It was in this impenetrable terrain that tribes funded by Saudi Arabia with the United States' blessing reigned supreme. Egyptian troops became demoralized as casualties mounted and defeat became inevitable. Nasser's charisma born of victory faded as the agony of Yemen signaled the end of Nasser's mystical powers.

Those powers continued to fade as the union between Egypt and Syria collapsed in the midst of the Yemeni war. Iraq never did join in.

The worse things became, the more Nasser relied on force and ever more dazzling portrayals of a future that would never be.

The death knell to Nasser's divine guidance came with Israel's devastating defeat of the Arab armies in the June War of 1967. Labeled the Six-Day War, the grizzly defeat only took about four days. The Israelis occupied the Sinai Peninsula, what remained of Palestine, and Syria's Golan Heights. Once again, a tiny Jewish state had humiliated the Arabs.

How did Nasser's powerful charisma desert him? Aside from the defeats discussed above, almost every dimension of his charismatic strategy was flawed. Nasser's grandiose dreams created hope, but they also began a revolution of rising expectations that the government lacked the money or capacity to meet. Filling the gap with smoke and mirrors merely added to the problem. Nasser had also become a one-man show as he used his charisma to forge a cult of personality in which he and only he made all of the key decisions. A sycophant culture thus emerged in which praise for Nasser and the shouting of nationalist slogans became the recipe for survival and silent sabotage. It was dangerous to tell Nasser the truth, and so the power structure avoided it. Thus Nasser cut himself off from the main political currents in Egypt and lost touch with the masses.

For all of his woes, Nasser became the model for a seemingly endless line of would-be charismatic leaders in the region, many of whom will figure prominently in later chapters.

ISRAEL REBORN: WAR, PEACE, AND BIBLICAL PROPHECY

The Jewish revolt against the British outlined in the preceding chapter raged until 1947, when the British, throwing up their hands in despair, dropped the fate of Palestine in the lap of the UN. The UN resolved the issue by dividing Palestine into two independent states, one Arab and one Jewish. Neither party was satisfied, giving way to Israel's War of Independence. It would be the first of an unrelenting series of Arab-Israeli wars.

The Jewish forces were far better organized than a hodgepodge of Arab forces from diverse countries. As a result, the war's end found the

Jews in control of most of Palestine with the exception of the Gaza Strip, the West Bank of the Jordan River, and much of Jerusalem.

On May 14, 1948, the date of the final withdrawal of Britain from Palestine, David Ben-Gurion proclaimed the rebirth of Israel. The Zionist dream of a Jewish state had become a reality. Jews and Evangelical Christians were euphoric. For the Zionists, the rebirth of Israel had everything to do with the present and a secure future. For the Evangelical Christians, it had everything to do with Biblical prophecy, Armageddon, and the Second Coming of Jesus Christ.

There was, however, a catch. Israel had been reborn, but it was not whole. The biblical lands of Judea and Samaria remained in Arab hands, as did large parts of Jerusalem. Many Arabs, both Christians and Muslims, continued to live in Israel. Those who had been driven from their lands by Israel's War of Independence were granted the right of return by the UN. How could there be a Jewish state if a large share of the population were non-Jews who wanted their own country? How was Israel to be a secure homeland for all Jews when the driving time for the new state was about ten minutes at its narrowest point, and forty minutes at its longest?

Of the challenges facing the reborn Israel, none was greater than security. If Israel didn't survive, everything else would be moot. Ultimately the survival of Israel would depend on a lasting peace with the Arabs. This could be accomplished by sacrificing land for peace, or it could be accomplished by force. A bitter debate on the topic roared between David Ben-Gurion, Israel's first prime minister, and Moshe Sharett, his foreign minister. Ben-Gurion argued that Arabs only understood force, and he demanded an iron-fist approach to dealing with Israel's hostile neighbors. Sharett, by contrast, argued that force would only prolong and intensify Israel's defensive woes (Sheffer, 1996).

History has proven Sharett right, but no one knows what might have happened if Israel had pursued peace in a hostile environment. The argument for force, however, was compelling. Israel needed more land, not less land. The survivors of the Holocaust had to be settled, as did the Jewish refugees fleeing from Arab lands during the first Arab-Israeli war. Land was also security. How could Israel be secure with even more Arabs within its borders, and how could it be a Jewish state when they weren't Jewish?

Force also had its virtues. Israelis had to have faith in their own power if they were to remain in Israel. Jews in the diaspora also had to be confident of Israeli security if they were to migrate to Israel. Migration to Israel was vital for numbers translated into the ability of Israel to defend itself from the constant threat of attack. Land was needed to settle Jews required to return to Israel by the prophets of old. Only then would Israel be whole, a goal far from attained by the War of Independence. Biblical prophecy was also an issue of vital importance to many Christians, who saw it as a guide for the return of their messiah.

Israel's reliance on force was bolstered by its success in the 1948 War of Independence and by the growing supply of weapons provided by the United States, Britain, and France as part of the Cold War strategy in countering the spread of Soviet bases to Egypt and Syria. In the military jargon of the time, Israel had become a land-based aircraft carrier. Israel stunned the world by becoming a nuclear power in 1955–1956. Both the French and the United States were presumably assisting Israel in acquiring the ultimate weapon, but the details remain vague. Israel denied possessing nuclear weapons in order to avoid efforts by the UN to create a nuclear-free Middle East. A proxy war between the United States and the Soviet Union was manageable, but a proxy nuclear war in the Middle East could well be the trigger for a feared nuclear showdown between the Soviet Bloc and the North Atlantic Treaty Organization (NATO).

This was a very dangerous trend in a bipolar world dominated by two nuclear superpowers locked in a war to the death. The Soviet Union had already committed to Nasser and his Arab allies in an effort to gain a strategic advantage on its US adversaries. Given the stakes in the global conflict between the United States and the Soviet Union, it was entirely possible that the United States would again sacrifice Israeli interests for its own. This was a scary thought for Israelis locked in a situation over which they had little control.

Given the dire nature of the global realities, Israeli policy focused on controlling what Israel could control. It would control the Arabs by force. It would control the United States by faith and finance and by becoming a reliable ally in an unstable region. This, however, was a tricky proposition. Israel had to control US Middle Eastern policy without being controlled by the United States. Israeli survival interests would have to come first, and it would have to be the Israelis who defined their survival interests. Israel couldn't let the United States decide what was best for Israel. This required a special relationship with the United States in which the United States was responsible for Israel's survival, but Israel was not responsible for the vital interests of the United States.

Distrust, paranoia, or logic? All three were possible. Long and painful experience had convinced Jews that they could only trust themselves. The Holocaust was too fresh in the Jewish memory to be ignored as an ever-present danger. This was particularly the case in an era in which Israel had become the epicenter of the conflict between the United States and the Soviet Union. America was at war for its own survival, and that was dangerous for Israeli survival.

In the final analysis, Israel's defense during the era was based upon the coordinated application of faith, force, and finance to the single and all-consuming goal of security. Israel's special relationship with the United States was key to that goal.

Faith came from Jewish organizations formed to lobby for the Israeli cause in a US political system particularly vulnerable to the pressure of political lobbies and public opinion. Some Jewish organizations, such as the American Israel Public Affairs Committee (AIPAC), played a key role in providing financial and electoral support to politicians in favor of a pro-Israeli foreign policy. Others, such as the Anti-Defamation League, concentrated on eradicating anti-Semitism and countering negative attitudes toward Israel. These largely Jewish groups would eventually be joined by Evangelical Christian groups supporting Israel as a Christian obligation dictated by biblical prophecy. Many liberal groups supported Israel in hope of bringing democracy to a largely authoritarian region. This curious mix was also to be joined by US war hawks who applauded Israel's growing military power as the solution to peace in the Middle East. It was all legal, and it fit the American way of doing politics.

Force was vital because force alone could protect Israel from the Arabs and Muslim allies. Diplomacy was available, but only at the price of trading land for peace, a price that Israeli leaders at the time were unwilling to pay. Reliance on force, in turn, required military, financial, and diplomatic support from the United States.

The Arabs, by contrast, had few supporters in the United States. As a result, this burgeoning coalition of Israeli supporters had the field to themselves. American politicians had everything to gain from support-ing Israel and everything to lose by opposing it. This didn't mean that Israel could dictate to US presidents, but they could make a stink in Congress if a president opposed Israel.

Israeli propagandists also did their part in shaping US public opinion by casting the young Jewish state as a frail and fragile David pitted against the Goliath of Arab hordes. CIA estimates didn't agree, indicat-ing that Israeli strength was far superior to that of the Arabs.

The forging of Israel's special relationship with the United States was slow at the beginning but continued to pick up speed as the drama of the Middle East unfolded. Ironically, so did complaints that Israel's special relationship with the United States was a one-way street.

Such complaints came to a head when President Kennedy was de-nied access to Israel's nuclear facilities. Irate, he openly demanded that the Israeli-US cooperation be a two-way street. Ben-Gurion's terse de-fense of Israel's one-way relationship with the United States was based on his fear that Israel would vanish without it. As Ben-Gurion framed the issue: "Mr. President, my people have the right to exist, both in Israel and wherever they may live, and this existence is in danger" (Tyler, 2012, 129).

The Israeli goal of survival was exceptionally effective in balancing faith, force, and finance, yet each had its problems. Force turned Israel into a garrison state in which the military played a dominant role in shaping policy. According to Israeli authors on the left, Jewish humani-tarian and democratic values suffered accordingly.

Faith, too, proved problematic. Although a Jewish state, Israel found it difficult to define who was a "Jew." This problem resulted in Israel having an unwritten constitution that gave all Jews the right to return to Israel without specifying who was a Jew.

Jewish financial support for Israel became mixed with US politics as both Israeli and American Jews worried that the harshness of Israeli anti-Palestinian military procedures would weaken Israel's special rela-tionship with the United States.

There were other faith disappointments as well. The hope for a rush of American and Western European Jews to Israel proved to be little more than a steady trickle. Reverse migration also became frequent during times of crisis. By and large, the US Jewish population has re-mained roughly the same size as Israel's. This raised the question of which Jewish population would guide the policies of Israel. American Jews were at the core of the special relationship and of Israel's financial structure. Both populations demanded that they be listened to. The faith problem became even trickier when Christian Zionists (mostly Evangelicals) entered the picture and wanted a voice in Israeli policies in return for their financial contributions and political support.

SAUDI ARABIA: TRIBAL FORCE, ISLAMIC FAITH, AND THE COUNTRY'S CREATION

The use of faith, force, and finance in Saudi Arabia in the post–World War II era was far different from that in either Egypt or Israel. Perhaps this was because there was no Saudi Arabia as we know it today until the sabers of World War II had begun to rattle. Until 1936, Saudi Arabia was simply a remote area of the Arabian Peninsula, a vast area stretching between the Red Sea and the Persian Gulf. The region was so desolate that only nomadic tribes and oasis dwellers could survive in its harsh climes. Even the Turks, who ruled most of the Middle East for some five hundred years, ignored much of the Arabian Peninsula.

What did concern the Turks were the holy Islamic cities of Mecca and Medina. It was in Mecca, a pagan religious and trading center, that the Quraysh, the tribe of the Prophet Mohammed, dwelled. It was there that Islam was born, and it was from there that the Prophet Mohammed was forced to flee the hostility of pagan priests and the merchants who feared that Islam would destroy their lucrative business of selling pagan idols to the pilgrims who flocked to Mecca in search of spiritual redemption. The Prophet Mohammed was welcomed in Medina, and it was in Medina that the Prophet Mohammed ruled before conquering Mecca and eliminating its decadent ways. When Salafi-jihadists yearn for a return to Islamic rule, it is to the Prophet's rule in Medina that they refer.

More than one thousand years later, Saud Ibn Mohammed seized control of the oasis of Ad-Diriyah in the remote east-central region of the Arabian Peninsula and used it as a base for conquering the neighboring tribes. The Saudi dynasty was born. Tribal force alone, however, was unlikely to expand Saud's empire, and so he joined forces with Mohammed Abd al-Wahhab, a traveling preacher who had gained a

large following with his fire-and-brimstone versions of Islamic purity—
that which is referred to as Salafi. It was this blend of tribal force and
Wahhabi faith that enabled them to capture the holy cities of Mecca
and Medina in 1803. Alas, Saudi glory was short-lived before being
forced by another of the region's dominant tribes to seek refuge in
Kuwait. Saudi memories of empire festered until 1901. It was then that
Abd al-Aziz al-Saud, a direct descendant of the founder of the Saudi
dynasty, descended on the fort guarding Riyadh in the dark of night
with a raiding party of somewhere between thirty to one hundred men.
The raiders killed the governor, and a new Saudi dynasty began. The
alliance with the Wahhabis was revived, and by 1913 this combination
of tribal force, Islamic faith, and booty-finance had conquered all of the
east-central (Nejd) and eastern (al-Hasa) regions of the Arabian Peninsula.

It was at this point that the alliance of faith and force began to show
strain. Tribal fighters who were aligned with the Saudis got their share
of the booty as the empire continued to expand, but their main loyalty
was to their own tribe. Rebellions were frequent and one could never
be sure when tribal fighters would bolt at the command of a tribal
sheikh envious of Saudi power.

More dangerous for the Saudi monarchy was the emergence of a
more extreme version of Wahhabi doctrine in 1912 known as the Ikhwan or Brotherhood. Its members dedicated themselves to reviving a
puritanical Wahhabi creed that had grown lax among wandering tribes
of the desert. As Robert Lacy describes these Wahhabi zealots:

> The Prophet condemned personal ostentation, so the Ikhwan
> shunned silk, gold, jewelry and ornaments, including the gold thread
> traditionally woven round the dark bhisht or mishlah, the outer
> robe—and they also cut their robes short above the ankles. This was
> because the Prophet had declared clothes that brushed the ground
> to be an affectation, and the same went for luxuriant moustaches. So,
> the Ikhwan clipped the hair on their upper lip to a mere shadow of
> stubbiness—while adopting a different rule for hair on the chin. In
> this case they argued, it would be affectation to trim and shape, so
> beards must be left to grow as long and to straggle as far as God
> might will them. (Lacy, 1981, 142–43)

Finding it difficult to assure the piety of wandering nomads, the Ikhwan decided to settle them in agricultural communities better suited to indoctrinating the tribes and focusing its energies on God's war against evil. Its most pragmatic of leaders, Ibn-Saud, transformed the Ikhwan into something resembling a standing religious army. As Holden and Jones described this arrangement, "In 1916 he ordered that all the bedouin tribes owing allegiance to him must also give up herding and join the Ikhwan, and their sheikhs were brought to Riyadh in relays for special religious instruction. They were to receive subsidies from the treasury and, in return, respect the King as their Imam and swear to uphold Wahhabist orthodoxy" (Holden and Johns, 1981, 69).

Ibn-Saud's army of religious fanatics had conquered eastern Arabia, the Hijaz, by 1926, and with it the holy cities of Mecca and Medina. For the first time since the days of the Prophet Mohammed, symbolic control of Mecca had passed from the hands of the Prophet Mohammed's Hashemite clan of the Quraysh tribe.

The conflict between the Wahhabis and the Hashemites was triggered by the decision of Sharif Hussein, the governor of Mecca who had conspired with the British to revolt against the Turks in World War I, to declare himself caliph. The thought of the moral and spiritual leadership falling into the hands of the lax governor was more than the passionately puritanical Ikhwan could take. Not only was this a war within Sunni Islam but it was also a war akin to the wars between lax Islam and the puritanical Salafi devastating the region today.

Ibn-Saud was proclaimed king of Saudi Arabia but soon found himself surrounded by Hashemite kings in the recently created British mandates of Jordan and Iraq. Both kings were sons of Sharif Hussein and had been placed there by the British as a reward for his leadership in the Arab revolt against the Turks. Finance entered the picture as the British added seven thousand British pounds annually to Ibn-Saud's annual stipend in exchange for a concession to explore for oil. Saudi's borders with Iraq and Kuwait, a British protectorate, were also adjusted in Saudi Arabia's favor.

Ibn-Saud well understood that vows of loyalty were fragile expedients, as were vows of the Ikhwan to accept him as their imam, or spiritual guide. Tensions between the king and the Ikhwan soon became tense and Ibn-Saud, preparing for the showdown, recruited a new army of townspeople and tribes he considered loyal.

The Ikhwan rebelled in 1929 but were crushed by the king's army. The power base of the monarchy remained an army recruited from loyal tribes and faith based on the traditional alliance with the descendants of the Wahhabi founder. Finance, meager at best, came from the annual pilgrimage Muslims made to the holy cities and the British stipend. The British didn't find oil, but the Americans struck black gold in 1938. Wealth was not immediate, but the US government was more than generous in making loans to the tribal king in constant need of buying the loyalty of his tribal forces.

The future of Saudi Arabia changed with the discovery of oil. So did the balance of faith, force, and finance in the Saudi monarchy. This did not mean that faith and force had lost their importance. To the contrary, Ibn-Saud needed the alliance with the Wahhabi elite to establish the legitimacy of his regime among a largely tribal population whose loyalty to the regime was suspect. Ibn-Saud may have had himself proclaimed king of the country that bore his name, but nationalism had yet to be discovered.

The dependence of the Kingdom, as Saudi Arabia is referred to in the Middle East, on the Wahhabi faith meant that the Wahhabi clerics had free reign to indoctrinate the young Saudis with the same extremist doctrine that had given birth to the Ikhwan. As we shall see in later chapters, it is the perpetuation of that same extremist doctrine that is fueling terrorism in the Kingdom and the region today. And yet the king had no choice in the matter. To turn on the Wahhabi elite was to invite rebellion. In a strange way, the king had become a prisoner of his own faith. He needed faith for legitimacy, but as the Ikhwan experiment had demonstrated, using religious faith to generate force was dangerous and could not be trusted. Could oil wealth do better? This question has yet to be answered.

As in days of old, the preoccupation of Ibn-Saud, the ruling king, was the survival of the Saudi dynasty. Much as then, the old king continued to worry about the revenge of the Hashemite kings in Jordan and Iraq and the ever-present danger of tribal revolts. He also worried about age and the fear of a power struggle within the diverse clans of the royal family. In the best traditions of the Arabian Peninsula, he had attempted to solidify his rule by taking wives from most of the major tribes. The male brood of each wife thus became a separate power center within the ruling elite. Tensions between the mother-based clans threatened the future of the Saudi dynasty, and so the aging and ill king made his sons swear on the Koran to accept the rule of the eldest son. Ibn-Saud died in 1953, and it was his eldest son, Saud, who faced the task of dealing with Nasser's Arab nationalist revolution and the rebirth of the Jewish state on Arab territory.

Sadly, from the perspective of the royal family, Saud was not the best and brightest of Ibn-Saud's progeny. That honor belonged to Faisal, who had also served as the Kingdom's foreign minister. More than anyone else among the senior princes, Faisal understood the regional and international crises facing the monarchy. The royal family was thus faced with the cruel choice between honoring their vow to accept an incompetent king in trying times or risking clan warfare within the royal family by supporting Faisal.

Faisal eased the crisis by swearing allegiance to Saud, but that didn't solve the crisis of Saud's incompetence. Nor did it stop the power struggle between the two brothers, each from a different mother-based clan within the royal family.

Saud, for all of his faults, was adept at survival. His major asset was finance, the flow of the Kingdom's oil revenues having increased some $235 million annually by the time he had ascended to the throne. Support for his struggle against Faisal was purchased by lavish outlays to the dominant tribes and the massive royal family, neither of which was enamored of Faisal's frugality and penchant for order, planning, and discipline. Blatant corruption served as a form of income distribution for those with influence, and wealthy merchants thrived on the lavish spending of this profligate Arabian monarch.

It was much the same at the regional level as Saud attempted to use his newfound wealth to divert Nasser's attention from Saudi Arabia and focus it on the Hashemite kings of Jordan and Iraq. He also attempted to use finance to create the illusion of force by buying sophisticated weapons from the United States, most of which were beyond the capacity of his army to use.

All things considered, Saud had little choice in the matter. What passed for an army was no match for Nasser's forces, and the king was also haunted by questions of the army's loyalty. Some troops were swayed by Nasser's nationalist rhetoric, while others were caught up in the struggle between Saud and Faisal.

Tribute satisfied Nasser for a while, but he needed money for his grand dreams of Arab unity. The Saudis, weak and rich, were no match for Egypt's massive armies. And so it was that the special relationship between the United States and the Saudi monarchy was born. The United States would provide Saudi Arabia with security while the Saudi monarchy would provide the United States with cheap oil and the religious foundation it needed to use the Islamic faith as a weapon against the Soviets.

Inevitably, Saud's behavior was so bizarre that the senior princes of the royal family had no choice but to replace him with Faisal. The special relationship with the United States remained in place and represented the perfect balance of convenience between a global superpower and an archaic tribal monarchy forged at a time when each needed the other. Without this special relationship there would be no Saudi Arabia today.

In the remaining chapters we examine the evolution of this special relationship until it reaches an era of terror and violence in which Saudi Arabia's extremist Wahhabi vision of Islam found itself in direct conflict with the security interests of the United States and Israel. Finance as the key weapon in the Saudi arsenal also evolved dramatically. Rather than being dependent on US loans, the Saudi monarchs began to use their vast wealth to shape policy making in the West. Finance was also used to create the illusion of force through the purchase of a vast arsenal of weapons, but Saudi weakness remained. US force continued to be vital, as did Saudi reliance on the extremist Wahhabi vision of Islam as the foundation of its political legitimacy.

IRAN: THE DANGER OF PUPPET RULERS

Iran had not been colonized but was occupied by the British and Russians during World War I to counter the ruling shah's (king's) pro-German inclinations. With the war's end, the British imposed the leader of the Cossack brigade as the new shah. He possessed many of the authoritarian and modernizing goals of Ataturk. The Shia clergy were curbed, Western legal codes replaced Islamic law, and the vast funds controlled by the religious establishment were simply transferred to the shah's treasury. Traditional rule was replaced by a technological elite designed to transform Iran into a military power capable of fulfilling the shah's aspirations for regional power. Much of Iran's best land became the shah's personal property. The lands that the shah didn't claim for his personal domain were absorbed by a parasitic aristocracy whose function was to support the shah. Force prevailed with the exception of rabble-rousing by a young cleric named Ruhollah Khomeini.

Perhaps the British were confident of their ability to control their new puppet shah much as they had managed to control their puppet kings in Jordan and Iraq. They were sadly mistaken. The shah didn't want constraints of any kind and like his predecessor, he turned to Germany and Russia to counter the heavy hand of the British. With World War II looming, the British occupied southern Iran and deposed the shah in favor of his twenty-two-year-old son, Mohammed Reza Pahlavi. The United States followed suit by occupying the center of the country, and the Soviets occupied the north. At the end of World War II, all three countries withdrew from Iran to avoid another bloody conflict.

All seemed well as the young shah implemented a more democratic political system replete with reasonably fair elections. In an unexpected twist, these were won by a nationalist-communist coalition anxious to be rid of both the British and the monarchy. Stepping in to prevent a Soviet advance into the Middle East, the CIA engineered the return of the young shah to power.

The shah, beholden to the United States, joined the Baghdad Pact, a US anti-Soviet alliance that also included Turkey, Britain, and Pakistan. All, however, was not well. The Shia clergy, fired by the rhetoric of Ayatollah Ruhollah Khomeini, stirred popular hostility toward the shah's subservience to the West. Clerical hostility to the shah's rule became increasingly intense as the young shah launched a White Revolution designed to modernize his kingdom. Key to his White Revolution was a land reform program that gave land owned by the clergy and the aristocracy to the peasants. Both turned against the shah. They were joined by waves of disappointed peasants who didn't receive their anticipated land, frustrated technocrats deprived of their jobs, and despairing urban youth whose dreams of prosperity failed to materialize. It was this blend of frustrated Iranians who surged to the Khomeini-led protests against the shah in 1963. The protests were crushed by the shah's security services and Khomeini was exiled to the holy cities of Iraq (Bill,

1988). Force had brought peace, and the United States had found the island of stability that it needed to consolidate its control of the region against Soviet expansion. Khomeini, however, had learned valuable lessons about using faith to mobilize the masses against a tyrannical leader.

With all vestiges of opposition crushed, the shah had himself proclaimed shah-in-shah, king of kings. It was a grand ceremony worthy of the king of kings that featured planes showering Tehran with roses and the Tehran symphony premiering "You are the Shadow of God" (Mackey, 1996, 230). This display of grandeur faded in comparison to the shah's dazzling celebration of the 2,500th anniversary of the Iranian monarchy. So lavish was the celebration held at the ancient Iranian capital of Persepolis that many world leaders were too embarrassed to attend such a self-serving display of megalomania.

Not content with being the king-of-kings in a poor country, the shah seized upon the rush of oil money precipitated by the oil boycott in the 1973 Arab-Israeli war to transform Iran from an agricultural country into a global military-industrial power based on forced industrialization. The grandiose plan was managed by his incredibly corrupt ruling elite and bureaucracy and sold to the masses under the slogan, "Iran will be Sweden by the year 2000" (Zonis and Mokri, 1991).

The shah's delusions of glory were not shared by the masses. No doubt they inspired awe and fear among the dispossessed, but the fear and awe were not to be confused with charisma. To the contrary, the masses were motivated to search for a faith-based solution to their agony. Islam remained the faith solution for the dispossessed, a solution made all the more powerful by Khomeini's prophetic message that the Hidden Imam could not return and save humanity until a Shia theocracy had prepared the moral path for his return. The shah added insult to injury in 1976 by changing the Islamic calendar to the Iranian imperial calendar based on Cyrus the Great's ascent to the throne. For the more educated Iranian youth, the search for a faith solution sparked a revival of leftist ideologies that inclined toward communism. In some cases leftist ideologies were blended with Islamic morality to reach a broader audience. This lethal blend of Shia Islam and communism unleashed a dramatic surge in urban guerilla violence during the later years of the shah's rule.

Much as the British had earlier lost control of their monarchy in Iraq, the United States was now losing control of the young shah whom it had returned to power during an earlier era. Force and squandered finance had promoted faith rather than crushing it.

LESSONS LEARNED

1. The use of force to control deprived masses stimulates resistance based on religious faith.
2. Both religious and charismatic faith can be transformed into force.
3. Charismatic faith is less enduring than religious faith and requires constant testimony to its power.
4. Charismatic leaders are idiosyncratic and difficult to control.
5. Charisma leads to a cult of personality and authoritarianism.
6. Religious faith can be used by small countries to draw the major powers into the conflicts of the Middle East.

4

A SURGE OF RELIGIOUS EXTREMISM (1967–1980)

The Arab-Israeli War of 1967, often referred to as the Six-Day War, resulted in Israel's destruction of Egypt's Soviet-built army in less than six days. Not only had Israel destroyed Nasser's force weapon but the humiliation of Nasser's defeat deflated the charismatic faith weapon upon which his influence in the Sunni Arab world had depended. For all intents and purposes, the collapse of the Arab armies in the Six-Day War brought an end to popular faith in Arab nationalism.

In addition to shattering the pride of Nasser and other Arab leaders who had participated in the war, the wounds of the war reshaped the boundaries of the Middle East. Egypt's Sinai Peninsula and Suez Canal were occupied by the Israeli's, as were Jerusalem and the remainder of Arab-ruled Palestine. Adding insult to injury, the Jewish state also occupied Syria's Golan Heights. By and large, the Arabs were now at Israel's mercy.

That did not mean that faith had ceased to be a major factor in the conflicts of the Middle East. To the contrary, the void created by the collapse of Arab nationalism was soon filled with what proved to be a more powerful faith: Islamic extremism. Nasser and Arab nationalism had fired Arab spirits with dreams of a glorious Arab revival. Islamic extremists offered an Islamic revival that combined glory and power with an eternity in paradise. A simple slogan said it all: "Islam is the Solution." Our recounting of the surge of religious extremism resulting from the Six-Day War begins in Egypt and then moves to Israel, Saudi Arabia, and Syria.

EGYPT: ARAB NATIONALISM COLLAPSES AND RELIGIOUS EXTREMISM SURGES

Nasser passed away shortly after the debacle of the Six-Day War and was briefly followed in office by Anwar Sadat, his vice president. Sadat was the weakest member of Nasser's inner circle. This may have been why Nasser had appointed him vice president in the first place. Charismatic leaders, as we have seen in the last chapter, don't want competition.

Whatever the case, a bitter power struggle among Nasser's heirs allowed Sadat to remain as president while his more powerful adversaries sorted things out. Their underestimation of Sadat's shrewdness was a mistake, one that the Israelis and Soviets would also make. The United States, by contrast, overestimated Sadat's mental balance and found itself saddled with a megalomaniac tyrant who laid the foundation for the surge of Islamic terrorism threatening the world today.

Fearing a coup by his adversaries, Sadat's primary goal upon becoming the president of Egypt was to remain the president of Egypt. Lacking faith, force, and finance, the odds in his favor were virtually nil. To make matters worse, poverty and hostility toward the government were soaring.

The anticipated leftist coup failed in 1971 largely because of the military's fear of the communist left. Sadat got the message. There would be no more second chances. He had to develop his own base of support or more coups would follow. But how was Sadat, who lacked a power base, to counter his leftist adversaries, who possessed easy access to Soviet arms and money?

Sadat's answer was a revival of the Muslim Brotherhood that had been suppressed but not destroyed by Nasser. Sadat had been a Muslim Brother and knew the drill. Sensing an opportunity to use Sadat as an avenue of power, the Brotherhood did Sadat's bidding by fighting pitched battles with leftist protesters. In the process, the Brotherhood became Sadat's weapon of force and faith for controlling the streets and universities.

The Muslim Brotherhood helped Sadat crush the leftists, but the Brotherhood was not strong enough to keep him in power. He also feared becoming controlled by the Brotherhood. More vital to Sadat's survival in the long run was his need to gain control of the military, by far the most powerful organization in Egypt. Other problems also loomed. Sadat would have to free himself from Nasser's shadow if people were to take him seriously. This meant developing his own persona as a leader worthy of mass respect. It also meant freeing himself from Egypt's dependency on a Soviet Union intent on putting its own people in power.

The solution to gaining control of the army and establishing his own persona was a show of power that eclipsed even the glory of Nasser. Driving Israel from the Suez Canal and the Sinai would crown him a military genius and allow him to succeed where Nasser had failed. The problem was that Sadat couldn't drive the Israelis from the Suez Canal without the vigorous support of the Soviet Union. The Soviets, however, didn't trust Sadat, nor were they anxious to get involved in a risky Cold War venture doomed to failure.

Sadat's solution to Soviet obstructionism was to build a special relationship with the United States. Force and finance for his grand adventure had to come from somewhere, and the Americans had plenty of both. They were also anxious to drive the Soviets from the Middle East. The only difficulty was that the Americans didn't want to get involved in an adventure that was sure to fail—not to mention an adventure that targeted its Israeli ally—any more than the Soviets did.

Left to his own devices, the only option open to Sadat was a surprise attack on Israeli occupation forces stationed in the Suez Canal Zone. Making the best of his lack of stature, Sadat assumed that the Israelis wouldn't take his threats of an attack seriously. If the Americans and Soviets didn't take him seriously, why should the Israelis who had just devastated the Egyptian army in six days?

The ploy worked. Israel didn't take Sadat's buildup for an attack on the Canal seriously, and Israeli forces were driven from the Canal. The Israelis still debate their loss at Suez, but the fact remains that they had been defeated. And if it happened once, it could happen again. The Saudi-Arab oil boycott of the United States and Europe that supported Sadat's October 1973 Yom Kippur War added to Israel's woes and demonstrated the power of Arab finance to turn the West against the Jewish state.

Few gambles in history have been as successful as Sadat's gamble at Suez. He had freed himself from Nasser's shadow by becoming the hero of Suez. This enabled him to consolidate his control over the army, end Egypt's dependency on the Soviets, and establish a special relationship with the United States. He also assured himself of a steady flow of funds from the Saudis by convincing them that the Nasser days were over and they had nothing to fear from his rule in Egypt. His message to Israel was much the same as he signed the Camp David Peace Accords negotiated by President Carter.

Peace, stability, and development were to be the future of Egypt as Sadat pledged Egypt's participation in a global world dominated by the United States. As America's ally, there would be no more wars with Israel. The socialist menace of the Nasser era would also disappear as Sadat traded the socialist welfare programs of the Nasser era for the free market economic vision of the United States, the International Monetary Fund (IMF), and the World Bank. And what a marvelous program it was. Unproductive government-owned factories hurriedly built during the Nasser era were privatized, the swollen bureaucracy was slashed, and the subsidies on food, fuel, and other basic goods were reduced. Sadat warned the Egyptian masses that there would be pain for a while as they bit the economic bullet, but he assured them that Egypt would soon be a robust and prosperous economic tiger.

Unfortunately, nothing worked quite as it should have worked. Faith was the big problem as the Muslim Brotherhood demanded greater influence. Making matters worse was an explosion of a variety of impatient jihadist extremist groups unhappy with the Brotherhood's moderate approach to building an Islamic state and society. They wanted immediate action.

Finance fanned the flames as the rich got richer and the poor even more destitute, as subsidies were cut. Privatization led to fewer jobs and lower salaries. Cuts in the bureaucracy, in turn, eliminated guaranteed jobs for students. One way or another, the social-political contract between the rulers and the ruled established by Nasser was being shattered. This may have made economic sense to the IMF economists, but it made no political sense as protests choked Cairo and other major cities.

Sadat's new persona also became a nightmare as the hero of Suez became a megalomaniac referring to Egyptians as his children and surrounding himself with corrupt sycophants.

The more anger surged, the more Sadat relied on force to keep order and to keep himself in power. Nasser's army had become Sadat's army as the Soviet-armed and trained army of the past became the US-armed and trained army of the future. It was an army designed for domestic security only. The wars of Nasser were a thing of the past, and the well-equipped, well-trained, and very well-paid Egyptian army would fight no more foreign wars.

Nor was the army responsible for routine security. That was the job of the minister of the interior and his intelligence and police units. They had been brutal and corrupt under Nasser, and they became more brutal and corrupt under Sadat.

Egypt's economic despair and police brutality and Sadat's megalomania fueled Islamic extremism, as did latent hostility toward Israel and Egypt's dependency on the United States. As a result of his efforts to survive by becoming an American puppet, Sadat sacrificed his faith weapon. This was evident in the explosion of some ninety diverse Islamic extremist groups dedicated to establishing an Islamic state in Egypt by force (Mustafa, 1995).

The Muslim Brotherhood had also fully revived after Nasser's attempt to eliminate it, and it possessed immense popularity among Egypt's dispossessed. As the vast majority of Egypt's population was dispossessed, anything approaching fair elections would lead to a Brotherhood victory. This meant that there could be no fair elections. It also meant the Brotherhood's control of the street had increased proportionally. The Brotherhood understood its strength and put intense pressure on Sadat to transform Egypt into a moderate Islamic state that blended Islamic morality with modern morality.

Egypt's mainline religious establishment wasn't much help in dampening the influence of either the Muslim Brotherhood or the Salafi-jihadist extremists, because it was the same religious establishment that had been forced by Nasser to justify nationalism, development, and cooperation with the Soviet Union. Sadat now demanded that the official Islamic clergy preach a tougher message of cooperation with Israel, subservience to the United States, and economic sacrifice. It didn't work (Palmer and Palmer, 2008). Salafi-jihadist extremists assassinated Sadat in 1981.

ISRAEL: FORCE GIVES WAY TO EXTREMISM

Israeli's crushing victory in the Six-Day War fulfilled the Jewish state's long-sought goals of security and land. In the mind of many Israelis, land and security were one and the same. The more land that Israel controlled, the more secure it became. Many of the lands occupied by Israel during the 1967 war represented far more than security. They were holy lands whose return to Israel had been predicted by the prophets of old. Israel could not be whole in the biblical sense without them.

All, however, was not well. The holy lands had been occupied, but a large Palestinian population remained there. Not all of the lands occupied by Israel in the Six-Day War were holy lands. This was the case with regard to Egypt's Sinai Peninsula and Suez Canal as well as the occupied Syrian Golan Heights.

A new chance for a lasting peace based on trading land for peace beckoned, but which lands were to be traded? Trading parts of Egypt and Syria for peace posed little problem because they were not holy lands. The thought of trading biblical lands for peace, by contrast, was deeply offensive to religious Jews. The opportunity for making biblical Israel whole again had arrived and could not be squandered by frivolous negotiations.

Making Israel whole again in the biblical sense would require settling the Occupied Territories with Jews and eliminating the Palestinians. Another Arab-Israeli war in which the Arabs were supported by the Soviet Union was threatened, but the threats were minimal. The 1967 war had made it clear that no Arab country had the capacity to defeat Israel. With Arab nationalism dead, none seemed anxious to try. It would be up to the Israelis and the United States to decide between land and faith. Israeli survival was still linked to the United States, and US Cold War concerns could not be ignored.

Strong domestic pressures within Israel argued for retaining the lands occupied during the 1967 war. Among them were right-wing Zionist nationalists, military hawks, and Jewish fundamentalists demanding fulfillment of God's promise to Abraham. In their view, trading holy land for peace would be a sacrilege. Added to Israel's domestic coalition was an American Evangelical community that was vocal but not politically organized.

Ironically, Israel's overwhelming victory in the 1967 war resulted in a surge of Jewish extremism in Israel much as it had led to Islamic extremism in Egypt. As Ian S. Lustick writes in his *For the Land and the Lord: Jewish Fundamentalism in Israel*, "After more than eighteen centuries of dormancy, the distinctive blend of messianic expectation, militant political action, intense parochialism, devotion to the land of Israel, that characterized the Jewish Zealots of Roman times caught the imagination of tens of thousands of young religious Israeli Jews and disillusioned but idealistic secular Zionists" (Lustick, 1988, 2).

Much of Lustick's book is devoted to the fanatical activities of the Jewish Defense League founded by Rabbi Meir Kahane. The inside cover flap of Kahane's *Our Challenge* warns, "OUR CHALLENGE is not a Jewish MEIN KAMPF, though some readers are sure to think so. But it is nothing less than a battle plan for the creation on the ancient model of a new Jewry and the reshaping of the Jewish destiny" (Kahane, 1974, book flap).

Whatever the visions of the Jewish fundamentalists, the strategic interests of the United States, Western Europe, and the Soviet Union forced Israel to relinquish its claims to the Occupied Territories in exchange for peace. Israel signed a treaty accepting UN Resolution 242 that established a "Green Line" separating Israel and the Palestinian-controlled territories. Once again, the interests of the Christian powers had trumped the faith-driven policies of the Israeli government.

Israel signed UN 242 under duress, but there was no need to relinquish its Occupied Territories to the Palestinians. Who was going to make them do so? In a clever twist of words, the Israeli government said that they had agreed to Palestinian rule of the Palestinian people but not to Palestinian control of the holy land they resided on. More than ever, Israel's special relationship with the United States would require US acceptance of Israel's use of force and finance in its relentless ethnic cleansing of the Occupied Territories.

Israel continued to occupy Palestinian territories under the pretext of Israeli security. The Palestine Liberation Organization turned to terror in order to force an end to the Israeli occupation. At least in terms of international law, the Green Line remained valid and Israel's occupation of Palestinian territories was illegal. The critical legal question for any settlement of the Israeli-Palestinian conflict, from the Israeli perspective, hinged on which law had priority: international law or God's law? From a pragmatic perspective, the critical law was the law of possession.

The Green Line remained as a glaring symbol that Israel, for all of its past victories, had only acquired partial control of the Promised Land of ancient Israel. This reality led to a surge in the fervor of Jewish fundamentalism that paralleled the mounting Islamic extremism in Egypt, Iran, and Saudi Arabia. So much had Jewish fundamentalism surged that Menachem Begin, the former leader of the terrorist Irgun that had helped to drive the British from Palestine, was elected Prime Minister in 1977. His election was assured by the strong support of Israel's religious parties, and no sooner had Begin been elected than he visited an extremist settlement on the West Bank with a Torah in his hand and called for more settlements (Lustick, 1988).

Much to the dismay of the Israelis, the surge in Islamic extremism was supported by the United States in hopes that Islamic extremism would stem the Soviet expansion into Afghanistan and other areas of the Middle East.

The United States' pursuit of a special relationship with Israel at the same time that it was stoking Islamic extremism to counter Soviet expansion cast a quixotic hue to US foreign policy that has never been completely resolved. Perhaps more pressing for the Israelis at the time was the Saudi oil boycott of the United States and other major industrial countries during the 1973 Yom Kippur war. If the Arabs used their financial oil weapon to pressure the United States to create an independent Palestinian state, what option would Israel have? Its faith and force weapons would be washed away by oil.

SAUDI ARABIA: FINANCE TO THE FORE

The Saudi monarchy was not known for taking risks, but it chose the 1967 war to use the Arab oil weapon against Israel for the first time in the modern history of the Middle East. Perhaps it made this decision in response to searing criticism that the monarchy had become a traitor to both Arabism and Islam. Other views suggested that the monarchy feared Israeli domination of the region, while still other views simply gave them credit for being good businessmen. The world was starving for oil. A boycott of Saudi oil was a sure bet to send oil prices soaring. And so it did, as Saudi Arabia became the richest of the rich. So great was its new wealth, that the Kingdom was almost instantly catapulted into the role of a major Arab power. The Kingdom wasn't a powerful military force, but its financial and faith weapons made it a formidable power. If Israel was the holy land of Judaism and Christianity, Saudi Arabia was the holy land of Islam.

There had been Saudi fears that the United States might overthrow the monarchy as punishment for its oil boycott, but these fears eased with the United States' decision to use Islamic extremism as a faith weapon against the Soviet occupation of Afghanistan. The Saudi Wahhabi vision of Islam was vital to the United States' project because of its similarity to the religious doctrine of the Taliban in Afghanistan. The Saudis knew the Taliban and could serve as an intermediary in channeling support to them. The Saudis shared the United States' hostility toward Soviet encroachment in the Middle East and seized the opportunity to mend its special relationship with the United States. They also relished the opportunity to use their soaring oil wealth to spread the extremist Wahhabi doctrine throughout the Islamic world while the United States smiled knowingly.

The Saudi-US special relationship was far different from an American special relationship with Israel based largely on biblical faith. In addition to Saudi cooperation in using extremist Islam against the Soviets in Afghanistan, the United States wanted bases in Saudi Arabia for both strategic reasons and to protect the monarchy and its oil from rapacious predators and future oil boycotts. The Saudis were reluctant on both counts. American bases ran counter to the Wahhabi refusal to allow infidels on Saudi soil that was considered sacred. From the Arab and Islamic perspective, US bases on Saudi soil smacked of neocolonialism and would result in the American occupation of Saudi Arabia. The Saudi traditions of restraining females and child marriage also were an embarrassment for a US government that was attempting to counter Soviet propaganda with vows of democracy, human rights, and religious freedom, none of which existed in Saudi Arabia.

Things were worked out with various mixes of faith, force, and finance. The Saudis used finance to buy billions of dollars' worth of US weapons combined with subtle hints that the oil weapon would not be used again. Faith entered the picture as a young Saudi of Yemeni origin played a dominant role in organizing Islamic extremists against the Soviet occupiers of Afghanistan. His name was Osama bin-Laden. The United States, for its part, undertook Saudi defenses at the regional level.

A sticking point in the special Saudi-US relationship was an Israeli concern over the massive sale of US weapons to an Arab country. Israeli security officials were less worried about the Saudi capacity to use the arms than they were about the weapons falling into the hands of hostile countries and terrorist groups. An awkward situation thus arose in which Israel used its faith-based influence in the United States to impose a limit on US arms sales to Saudi Arabia. The Saudis received billions of dollars in weapons, but not the most sophisticated US weapons. They were reserved for the Israelis. It was a humiliating arrangement, but what choice did the monarchy have when its security depended on the United States? The faith-based special relationship between America and Israel had trumped the financially based US special relationship with Saudi Arabia. Faith didn't stop the finance weapon of Saudi Arabia, but it modified it.

On the domestic front, the monarchy's reliance on tribal force faded as oil revenues soared. Unlike earlier eras in which Saudi Arabia was a poverty-stricken backwater, domestic tensions eased as surging oil revenues trickled down to the masses in a variety of ways. Foremost of these was a social contract in which the monarchy traded cradle-to-grave welfare programs for subservience and political docility. These were abetted with the provision of government jobs that paid well but required little if any work. Foreign expatriates were hired to do most of what got done. Fellowships for foreign study were readily available, as were housing loans that didn't get repaid. Saudis who found the Wahhabi faith enforced by the religious police too restrictive spent their time in London.

SYRIA AND IRAQ: MINORITY RULE

The fall of Nasser brought a sigh of relief in Israel, Saudi Arabia, and the United States, but new and unexpected dangers were in the making in the post-1967 era. Syria and Iraq fell under the rule of brutal tyrants, the scars of whom are still haunting the Middle East. Ironically, both claimed to rule in the name of the Arab Renaissance or Baath party.

The ideology of Baathism had emerged with the end of World War II, when two Syrian students at the Sorbonne proposed a new secular ideology designed to return the Arabs to their historic glories with a blend of Arab nationalism, communism, socialism, modernity, unity, democracy, and the elimination of religious and tribal conflicts.

This dream was to be achieved by a political, social, and industrial revolution that assured jobs, education, health care, and justice for all. Democracy would have to wait for the social and economic revolutions, for the political revolution would be impossible without economic and social equality. Full democracy would come once modernity had been achieved and the Arabs had returned to their rightful place in the world community.

The Baathist dream had so much in common with Nasser's dream of a unified Arab state that it had been the Baathist leaders of Syria who joined Egypt in forming the United Arab Republic. It was also the Baathist leaders who plotted the coup that destroyed the United Arab Republic three years later over conflicts of leadership. Unity was important to the Baathist leadership, but so was the equal sharing of political power. Nasser, his charisma at a peak, simply shunted the Baathist leaders into symbolic positions without power while he ruled both Egypt and Syria.

And yet, for all of the conflicts between Nasser and the leaders of the Baath over who should rule the unified Arab state, Syria joined Egypt's 1967 war with Israel, as did Jordan. Both paid the price. Syria lost its Golan Heights, and Jordan lost its control of the West Bank. Both remain under Israeli occupation and are still threatened with Israeli annexation.

Blame for the splintering of the United Arab Republic and the loss of the Golan Heights to Israel were only two of problems confronting the leaders of the Baath Party in Syria at the climax of the 1967 Arab-Israeli War. The Baathist leaders also found themselves increasingly challenged by the Syrian branch of the Muslim Brotherhood that, having been established in 1935, had developed deep roots among Syria's predominantly Sunni population. The Syrian Brotherhood found Baathist ideology to be an affront to Islamic law and vowed to force Syria's Baathist leaders to accept Islamic law or face the consequences.

Far more damning than Baathist ideology, from the perspective of the Muslim Brotherhood, was the 1980 takeover of the military wing of the Baath party by Hafez al-Assad, a member of the Alawi sect. The Alawi were a small Shia sect so exotic in their beliefs that even many Shia doubted that the Alawi were true Shia. So touchy was the situation that Hafez al-Assad, the leader of the Alawi cabal in the military wing of the Baath Party, couldn't have himself proclaimed president of Syria until the grand ayatollah of Lebanon, also a predominantly Shia country, certified that the Alawi were Shia. Assad had the force to make himself the president of Syria, but faith trumped force until a powerful ayatollah intervened.

The stage was thus set for a confrontation between a secular Baathist regime headed by an Alawi general and the Syrian branch of the Muslim Brotherhood. The Brotherhood's rebellion began in 1982 with the seizure of Hama and other Sunni cities.

Assad had no intention of waiting for the revolution to spread and slaughtered an estimated twenty thousand citizens of Hama, regardless of their religious affiliation. Force had trumped faith and Assad ruled supreme.

The Assad rule in Syria was based on a unique and carefully integrated combination of faith, force, and finance that was dedicated almost exclusively to the goal of keeping Assad in power. Faith was vital because Assad's rule was dependent upon a complex series of faith alliances without which Assad could have little confidence in his force and finance weapons.

First and foremost, Assad's faith was placed in his family, clan, and sect. It was they who headed the faith order of confidence and mutual survival. If Assad fell, they would pay the price for his brutality. Next in Assad's pyramid of faith came Sunni friendship, consisting of Sunni officers who had stood by him in the traumatic days of his rise to power. It was they, referred to as the robber barons, who, along with his relatives, controlled his security apparatus. Then came faith by marriage as the Assad clan gained stature by marrying into prestigious Sunni families, especially the rich merchant families who controlled much of the Syrian economy. Finally, Assad had been impressed by the tremendous power of Nasser's charisma and attempted to transform himself into a mythological figure with mystical powers. The trouble was that Assad was not a charismatic figure by nature. Nor had he accomplished any of the dazzling feats that had transformed Nasser into a legendary figure.

What Assad did do was establish a cult of personality that made him the sole and absolute leader of Syria whose every whim became law. His power was based on fear and the need of the masses to praise and applaud his every move as a safety measure for avoiding suspicion and arrest by one or more of Assad's security organizations. This gave the illusion of mass popularity and conveyed the illusion that he was beloved by all. This may have dissuaded people from revolting, but that is conjecture. What isn't conjecture was the people's mass fear of their leader.

It was the perpetuation of this fear that made force such a vital weapon for Assad. Force as it evolved under the Assad regime consisted of the military, the police, the elite presidential guard, a variety of intelligence (secret service) organizations, and Baathist militias. All were commanded by close confidants of Assad. All were watched by Assad and his special intelligence agencies. One way or another, everyone was watching everyone else.

Faith and force, in turn, were softened by finance as the Sunni military, the business community, the bureaucracy, and the police all used blatant corruption to line their pockets. Socialism also provided at least a moderate level of survival for the masses.

The clients of Assad had to weigh the financial and security gains of supporting Assad against risking the chaos of his overthrow. This was a tricky proposition because those who had supported Assad would be the target of revenge with his downfall. All in all, Assad had brought security and stability to Syria, something that Syria had not possessed in the World War II era.

IRAQ: SAME FORMULA, DIFFERENT FAITH

In 1968 the Baath Party in Iraq seized power in a coup led by military officers from the poor Sunni region of Tikrit. It was they, much like the

Alawites in Syria, who had sought their fortunes in the military. Also in common with the Assad clan, the Sunni of Tikrit were a minority group in Iraq with few options for advancement other than the military. They weren't a tribe in the formal sense of the word, but the region was clearly inbred and shared a common hostility toward the dominant landed aristocracy that had seized power under the monarchy. Also in common with the Alawite cabal in the Syrian Army, the Tikrities worked their way into key positions in the military, joined the Iraqi Baath Party, and seized power in the immediate aftermath of the Arab debacle in the 1967 Arab-Israeli War.

The 1968 coup, the tenth successive coup in Iraq, was led by Ahmed Hassan al-Bakr, the head of the military wing of the party. The civilian wing of the party was soon to be headed by Saddam Hussein, al-Bakr's relative and talented protégé. By the end of the era it was Saddam who ran everything.

It would be the last coup in Iraq, much as Assad's coup was the last coup in Syria, and Nasser's overthrow of the monarchy had been the last successful coup in Egypt.

Something had clearly changed, but what? The answer was outlined in the balance of faith, force, and finance designed by Assad and copied to the letter by Saddam Hussein.

It would be tempting for the leaders of the West and their intelligence and military advisors to believe that this magic formula could work forever. It couldn't, but Arab tyrants kept trying.

LESSONS LEARNED

1. Tyrants who develop cults of personality can't get along with each other regardless of ideological similarities.
2. Combinations of religious faith, charisma, and nationalism are more powerful than any one element by itself.
3. Faith in leaders created by illusions leads to cynicism and hostility.
4. Special relationships based on faith are more powerful than special relationships based on finance.
5. The ability of force to contain faith among the dispossessed is temporary.

6. Reliance on puppet regimes as a force strategy is risky business.
7. Finance in the hands of tyrants leads to waste and oppression rather than development.
8. The IMF model of free-market economics increases political instability unless it is paired with free-market politics.

5

RELIGIOUS VIOLENCE UNLEASHED
(1975–1990)

The shattering defeat of the Arabs in the Six-Day War of 1967 unleashed a surge of religious extremism throughout the region and was
then transformed into the religion-based violence that now threatens
the world.

The era of religious extremism in turn unleashed a series of events
that merged to send the region into a cauldron of unprecedented violence. The first of these events, listed chronologically, was the 1977
election of Menachem Begin, the leader of the former Irgun terrorist
group, as Israeli prime minister. A champion of the Israeli extremists,
his goal was to make Israel a thoroughly Jewish country. On route to
achieving this goal, Israel occupied southern Lebanon and Beirut in the
name of destroying the Palestinian Liberation Organization. This, in
turn, led to a bitter showdown between Begin and President Reagan,
crowned by Begin's statement that Jews bowed but to God. Begin was
voted out of office for threatening Israel's special relationship with the
United States. Israel subsequently withdrew to a forty-kilometer security zone in occupied southern Lebanon.

Next in line came the 1979 overthrow of the shah of Iran by the
Ayatollah Khomeini. Faith had defeated the most powerful tyrant in the
Islamic world and his US sponsor.

The same year saw the Soviet invasion of Afghanistan. The United
States, in the midst of the Cold War and suffering from the pangs of
guerilla war in Vietnam, decided to counter the Soviet expansion into

the Middle East with the same guerilla warfare. Islamic faith would counter Soviet force. All that was required was pumping Salafi-jihadists, the most violent strain of Sunni fanatics, into Afghanistan to fight the Soviet devil who was now occupying Islamic land. Much of the work would be done by the Pakistani Intelligence Services, an organization that possessed strong ties with the American CIA. Pakistan, a Muslim country, also had an oversupply of Salafi-jihadist fanatics. The ground operations were headed by a prominent figure in the Jordanian branch of the Muslim Brotherhood and seconded by a young Osama bin-Laden (then in his twenties).

The United States and Salafi-jihadists' war against the Soviets in Afghanistan coincided with Saddam Hussein's launching of an eight-year war against Iran and Khomeini's Islamic Revolution. The United States and Saudi Arabia became active supporters of Saddam Hussein's war in an effort to crush faith with force and finance.

Hardly had the dust settled on these events when, in 1981, Egyptian President Anwar Sadat, the pillar of US policy in the Arab world, was assassinated by Salafi-jihadists.

In the following discussion we examine the parallel surge of Sunni Salafi-jihadist violence and Shia extremist violence that soon dominated the unfolding drama of the Middle East. In particular, it was this dual unleashing of Sunni and Shia fanaticism that marked a shift from wars fought between secular armies to wars fought between secular armies and religious extremists. The differences between the Salafi-jihadists and the far more moderate Muslim Brotherhood as well as the differences between Salafi-jihadist and Shia extremism are also noted.

EGYPT: THE RISE OF SALAFI-JIHADIST TERROR AND THE MUSLIM BROTHERHOOD

The assassination of Anwar Sadat by Salafi-jihadists in 1981 gave way to thirty years of rule by Hosni Mubarak, Sadat's vice president and former air force general. Mubarak's mission was to perpetuate the regime that Sadat had put in place following the death of Nasser. That included strengthening Egypt's ties with the United States and Israel, as well as the perpetuation of a rapacious elite that blended the old royal aristocracy of the Farouk era with the generals of the Nasser era and a new capitalist elite intent on acquiring greater wealth at the expense of the poor and destitute. Mubarak performed his duties admirably while enriching friends and grooming his sons to follow in his footsteps.

The major obstacle facing Mubarak during his rule was the threat of an uprising by the Salafi-jihadists who had assassinated Sadat. Not far behind was growing pressure from the Muslim Brotherhood to make Egyptian politics more Islamic and less secular. Tensions between the Muslim Brotherhood and the Salafi-jihadists were intense. The Brotherhood was intent on making an Islamic state viable in the twenty-first century while the Salafi-jihadists were intent on returning the world to a replica of society and politics during the reign of the Prophet Mohammed in seventh-century Arabia.

The Salafi-jihadists are the focus of the present discussion, the Muslim Brotherhood having been discussed at length in earlier chapters. Both, however, remain critical to the unfolding drama of the Middle East: the Salafi-jihadists as the major agents of terror in the world today and the Muslim Brotherhood as a weapon for fighting the Salafi-jihadists with faith. In order to elaborate this point, the discussion of the Salafi will be followed by an examination of key differences between the Muslim Brotherhood and the Salafi-jihadists.

The Peaceful Salafi and the Salafi-Jihadists

The Salafi are a subsect of Sunni Islam who believe that paradise can only be achieved by following the way of the founders of Islam. For all intents and purposes this means returning a corrupted and sinful world to the purity that prevailed during the era of the Prophet Mohammed's rule.

By and large, the Salafi fall into three categories. The first of these are the nonviolent Salafi who believe that the goal of returning Muslims to the ideal purity of the Prophet Mohammed's rule can be achieved by promoting virtue and eliminating vice by means of indoctrination and social pressure.

The second variety of Salafi is the Salafi-jihadists. For the Salafi-jihadists, promoting virtue and eliminating vice mean the violent eradication of sin, much as it did to the Prophet Mohammed and the Prophet Moses. "How," they ask, "can sin be eliminated by indoctrination and social pressure in a political and social environment dripping in sin and perversion?" In their view, indoctrination and social pressure are necessary but insufficient tools for combatting sin. Violence is vital because only violence can eliminate environments of sin and force people to conform according to Islamic principles. Al-Qaeda and ISIS clearly fall into this category.

A third and growing variety of Salafi is the political Salafi. While both violent and nonviolent Salafi are hostile to regimes that incline toward secularism or become clients of foreign powers, many nonviolent Salafi living in the West are now cooperating with secular governments in hope of keeping their dream of Islamic purity alive in Western culture. This process has posed a problem for multiculturalism in France and other countries with large Muslim populations despite the fact that most Muslims do not adhere to Salafi doctrine.

A different version of political Salafism follows the Saudi model of partnership between a tribal monarchy and the Salafi-Wahhabi clergy, a topic to be elaborated shortly.

While the nonviolent Salafi and their violent Salafi-jihadist brethren differ in their inclination toward violence, it would be a mistake to draw a sharp line between the subtle and violent Salafi. All forms of Salafi doctrine share the goal of returning the Islamic world to the purity of a far distant era. Differences between the diverse varieties are a matter of strategy, not doctrine. A shared Salafi doctrine, in turn, makes nonviolent Salafi potential allies of the Salafi-jihadists. As such, they are the most likely support group of the Salafi-jihadists. It is also possible that rejection of violence by some nonviolent Salafi may be little more than expediency.

The line between the violent and nonviolent Salafi is also blurred because both are fragmented into a multitude of diverse organizations that continually splinter and regroup under different leadership.

As both nonviolent and Salafi-jihadist groups are headed by a charismatic leader assumed to have God's blessing, matters of violence and nonviolence may be dependent upon the leader's religiously inspired assessment of the prevailing situation. Sheikh Omar Abdel Rahman, known as the "blind sheikh," who designed the Islamic Group's 1993 attack on the World Trade Center, for example, later urged the Islamic Group to follow a more peaceful political strategy. He was in an American prison at the time, but God's inspiration cannot be limited by stone walls. Indeed, prisons have become prime indoctrination centers in which the Salafi convert innocent Muslims jailed by oppressive leaders into violent jihadists.

Soaring Islamophobia in Europe and North America may also incite nonviolent Salafi to violence. Salafi-jihadists do form sleeper cells masquerading as peaceful Salafi. This fuels fear and Islamophobia in the West. It also plays into the hands of the Salafi-jihadists by focusing hostility toward all Muslims in the West, the vast majority of whom are productive and peace-loving citizens. This is precisely what the Salafi-jihadists want. It may also be what some Western Christian and Jewish extremists want.

The discussion of the Salafi has focused on Egypt because Egypt tends to be the spark plug for most political movements in the Arab world. With this thought in mind, the remainder of this section focuses on the primitive Salafi-jihadist model that threatened a civil war in Egypt during the 1980s, and tracing the evolution of Salafi-jihadist organizations in the Middle East over the ensuing decades. It will also provide a comparison of Salafi-jihadist organizations with the Muslim Brotherhood, a far more moderate organization that is advocating Islamic rule compatible with twenty-first century expectations. The world can live with the Muslim Brotherhood far more easily than it can live with the Salafi-jihadists or even the nonviolent or political Salafi for whom nonviolence may be a matter of temporary expediency. This topic will be discussed in the final chapter of the book when weighing the choices between eliminating religious extremism and dealing with moderate extremism.

Most of the Salafi-jihadist violence during the period occurred after the assassination of Sadat in 1981 and remained constant throughout the 1990s, as the Salafi-jihadists pushed Egypt to the brink of civil war. Beyond question, the assassination of Sadat had given the Salafi-jihadist movement a strong shot of adrenalin by demonstrating that their sacrifices were not in vain. Faith, with the grace of God, could defeat the US-supported tyrants who ruled by force.

The two largest groups, the Islamic Group and the Islamic Jihad, were responsible for most of the violence during the period. The Islamic Group was responsible for the lion's share of the violence during the second half of the 1980s and the dawn of the 1990s. The success of the two larger groups demonstrated both their greater organizational power and the blend of charisma and rectitude possessed by their leaders. The smaller groups couldn't keep pace, and their members migrated to the two more active groups.

The core of the Salafi-jihadist groups, large and small, was a charismatic guide believed to possess divine inspiration, or baraka. This blend of charisma and baraka blended faith in Islam with faith in the leader and faith in his interpretation of the message of the Prophet Mohammed. The power of the guide of Salafi-jihadist groups is well illustrated by the defection of Rahman from the Islamic Jihad to the Islamic Group in 1990. The influence of the Islamic Jihad faded while that of the Islamic Group soared.

The recruitment appeal of the Salafi-jihadist groups in Egypt began with the ubiquitous slogan, "God is the solution." This slogan was shared by all Salafi groups. It was also the slogan of the Muslim Brotherhood. Added to the "God is the solution" appeal was the use of partial truths designed to convince the masses that Salafi violence was approved by the Koran and offered the surest path to paradise (Crosby, 2018).

Many of the Salafi-jihadist groups also found a responsive chord among the masses by attacking the corruption and lack of morality in their society. This they blamed on a ruling elite whom they accused of conspiring with the United States and Israel to destroy Islam.

This theme was followed up with Muslim moral-majority attacks on nightclubs, video outlets pushing porn, drug sellers, and the mixing of the sexes in "inappropriate" ways. Morality attacks also spilled over into sectarian conflicts and included both attacks on Christians and hostility toward Egypt's small Shia minority.

It is probable that support for violent Salafi-jihadists also contained a strong revenge motive against an oppressive government and its support for Western attacks on Islam. Far from enforcing morality, Salafi-jihadists also stress the obligation of true Muslims to protect their faith. Martyrdom was the surest path to paradise.

These appeals were particularly successful in recruiting members from the lower middle class and upper level of the lower class. They also found support among the dispossessed struggling to survive in marginal areas of cities with high immigration from poor rural areas in which there was hardly any chance for upward mobility. The squalid slums of Cairo and other major cities offered little in the way of hope for a better life, but it did bring migrants into direct contact with the Salafi-jihadists.

The twenty- to thirty-five-year-old age group was particularly active, especially among students and unemployed graduates of universities. The sociological and psychological predispositions of this group led them toward resistance to the regime and membership in resistance groups calling for change, including groups in the Islamic extremist movement. They also gravitated toward leadership positions in the Salafi-jihadist groups.

The middle class was also pushed toward the Salafi-jihadists by psychological, sociological, and economic pressures. The aspirations of the middle classes, having been fueled by the gaudy lifestyle of the elite, were also being squeezed by the greed of the elite they were trying to emulate. Only the rich could play the elite game, and the middle classes could only dream as they struggled in vain to keep up appearances.

As a whole, the dispossessed of Egypt were pushed toward the Salafi-jihadists by emotional states that included anger, fear, loneliness, helplessness, hopelessness, humiliated pride and honor, and lust for power, money, and influence, all of which accrued to smaller groups that were often little more than gangs. Sexual pressures due to delayed marriages may also have been involved. Who would want to marry a student with no hope for the future?

Many of the recruits to Salafi-jihadist groups also seemed to share the psychological traits of authoritarian submissiveness. As seekers of mystical salvation they placed unquestioning faith in rightly guided leaders while simultaneously demanding the same submissiveness from their inferiors.

Given these psychological predispositions, it is easy to understand how recruits were pulled to the Salafi-jihadists by appeals that offered an escape from the despair of the present, gave hope for a glorious eternity, and provided immediate gratification of the needs for belonging and security in a culture founded on collective belonging and security.

This was all the more the case because the Salafi-jihadist appeals offered gratification of cultural values that stressed pride, honor, status, piety, wealth, and power. These appeals also offered slum migrants a new identity and a new persona. This new identity often included a sense of efficacy that gave them a stake in their own future and in the future of the country and their religion.

The push-pull appeal of the Salafi-jihadists is vital to understand the perpetuation of the Salafi-jihadists in the world today, for as long as people are pushed toward violence they will find a charismatic guide to lead them. The success of the new guide will depend upon the same principles that were discussed earlier with regard to Nasser's charisma and that will be discussed shortly in examining the mystical power of the Ayatollah Khomeini.

Thus, the Salafi-jihadist groups were able to push the Mubarak regime to the edge of civil war. Other factors, however, were also involved. Among these were the use of more powerful weapons and better networking between Cairo and Salafi-jihadist strongholds in the rural areas. Strategies also improved. The Salafi-jihadists learned from earlier disasters.

Particularly important in explaining the success of the Salafi-jihadists was the sharp increase in labor activism in 1989–1992 resulting from the implementation of new laws nationalizing the state-owned enterprises that had formed the core of Nasser's socialist economy. Fear and anger soared as salaries and jobs declined at the same time that the Mubarak government attempted to please the IMF by reducing social security and government subsidies on vital goods including food and fuel. Mubarak assured Egyptians that things would work out in the end and encouraged them to bite the bullet in the meantime. The Salafi-jihadists couldn't have asked for a better scenario. It all made sense to the global financers and the Egyptian elite, but not to Egyptian youth who couldn't get married because they didn't have jobs and couldn't afford a place to live. Even those with jobs saw their salaries decline at the same time that prices soared.

Why, then, did Salafi-jihadists fail to overthrow the Mubarak regime when such a broad array of social, political, and economic pressures was pushing a growing wellspring of recruits in their direction? Or, to express the question differently, why were the Salafi-jihadists able to push Egypt to the brink of civil war but not able to complete the job?

The answer begins with the observation that the early Salafi-jihadists had lost touch with reality. Most were small vanguard groups that believed their violence would trigger a mass uprising. There was no mass uprising, and the Salafi-jihadists were left vulnerable to the repressive violence of the security forces. Many fanatics were killed, and many more were stuffed into Egypt's overflowing prisons. Families also suffered.

Not only were the Salafi-jihadist groups small but there was little unity or coordination among them. A large share of this problem was that charismatic leaders possessing God's blessing simply couldn't get along. They also suffered from splintering caused by the loss of a popular leader, the disillusionment with replacement leaders, and power struggles within groups.

Even the most powerful Salafi-jihadist groups were not organizationally equipped to fight a long war, manage a mass revolution, or provide an effective government capable of ruling the country. This forced them into a strategy of gratuitous violence that included the killing of civilians and tourists. This, in turn, posed a hardship on the masses and made Salafi-jihadists the enemy. At the very least, it dulled support for them. In the final analysis, the masses feared both the government and the Salafi-jihadists. As a result, many people steered clear of both.

The Mubarak regime also chose to fight faith with faith by allowing the Muslim Brotherhood, a far more popular movement than the Salafi-jihadists with an overlapping constituency, to operate as an illegal political party. This curious deal allowed the Muslim Brotherhood to consistently gain about 15 percent of the seats in fraudulent parliamentary elections to a fabricated parliament totally controlled by Mubarak's ruling party. The 15 percent figure made the Muslim Brotherhood the leading opposition party and provided it with a platform for criticizing the plight of the poor, the gross ineptitude of the bureaucracy, the greed of the rich, and the failure of the Egyptian education and health care systems.

In the process, the deal with the government enhanced the Brotherhood's populist resistance image while allowing it to expand its program of preaching, teaching, welfare, and investment with minimal repression.

The government, in turn, could claim to be democratic and Islam-friendly. Intentionally or not, the martyrdom image of the Brotherhood was enhanced by the brutal harassment of Brotherhood supporters at the polling stations. This illusion was part of a game whose deeper message was power. The Brotherhood was demonstrating its hold on the masses and the Mubarak government was demonstrating the power of its security services. What would prove to be an inevitable battle of faith versus force between two hostile contenders would be delayed for two decades while they conspired to stop a common Salafi-jihadist enemy.

The Salafi-jihadists accused the Brotherhood of weakening Islam by the pursuit of its own interests. The Brotherhood countered by accusing the Salafi-jihadists of perverting Islam by their needless violence. Both were confident that Islamic rule was imminent, and the Brotherhood wanted to make sure that its moderate vision of Islam would rule.

SALAFI-JIHADISTS VERSUS THE MUSLIM BROTHERHOOD: HOW THEY DIFFER

Supporting the Muslim Brotherhood may be the most effective way of fighting the Salafi-jihadists with faith. With this thought in mind, the following list of critical differences between the Muslim Brotherhood and the Salafi-jihadists may prove helpful.

- The Muslim Brotherhood claims to be a Salafi organization that uses the founding fathers of Islam as a moral guide and inspiration. It also claims to be a Sufi organization that embraces mystical concepts rejected by the mainline Salafi. To make matters worse, it pursues Islamic unity with the Shia, an apostate sect in the eyes of the Salafi. This makes the Brotherhood far more flexible and inclusive than the Salafi-jihadists' rigid doctrine.
- Unlike the Salafi, the goal of the Brotherhood is to save Islam by making it relevant to the twenty-first century. This places a forward-looking and realistic Brotherhood at odds with the backward-looking and questionably realistic Salafi. The Salafi-jihadists reject this view by claiming that violence is the only viable path to salvation for Islam in the twenty-first century. That battle between two conflicting views is the dominant theme in the unfolding drama of the Middle East.
- The realism of the Brotherhood requires cooperation with the West to the extent that it preserves Islam by making it relevant to the needs of Muslims now accustomed to modern lifestyles. The Salafi-jihadists find this view akin to ending sin by making a deal

with the devil. Expressed differently, the Brotherhood is dealing with present realities while the Salafi-jihadists are attempting to revive the distant past.

- The Brotherhood is in a better position to achieve its objectives because it was founded by a charismatic leader intent on establishing an organization capable of continuing his mission with his passing. In this way he was able to attain sainthood by transferring his personal charisma and baraka to the institution that he had created. The same institutionalization of charisma and baraka was achieved by the Ayatollah Khomeini in Iran. The Salafi-jihadists are still struggling with this issue.
- The above differences have given way to a variety of sharply different behavioral characteristics between the Brotherhood and the Salafi-jihadists. While the Brotherhood inclines toward patience, practicality, pragmatism, nonviolence, realism, and inclusiveness, the Salafi-jihadists are pursuing a vision of Islam that is guided by urgency, exclusiveness, ideological rigidity, and frantic efforts to create new realities in a world of sin. These differences are also expressed in their respective strategies. While the Brotherhood is attempting to use a strategy of welfare, teaching, and political involvement to build a strong base for its rule, the Salafi-jihadist strategy is based on force and imposed conformity with their rigid version of Islam.

SAUDI ARABIA: THE EXPANSION OF SALAFI DOCTRINE

The tumultuous chain of events outlined in the beginning of this chapter placed the Saudi monarchy in greater peril than it had faced during the days of Nasser's nationalist revolution. Voracious predators surrounded the Kingdom on all sides, not the least of which were the tyrannical regimes in Syria and Iraq.

Far more frightening was the Ayatollah Khomeini's Islamic Revolution, whose sights were set directly on Saudi Arabia. And what a wonderful prize it was with the holy cities Mecca and Medina and its vast oil reserves. If Khomeini's plans for Iraq were added to the picture, he would control most of the region's oil and both its Sunni and Shia holy shrines. With faith and finance in his control, force would follow. The

Saudi monarchy could only cringe at the thought of the force at Ayatollah Khomeini's disposal if he succeeded in blending faith, finance, and a huge military establishment in one package.

The thought of a Salafi-jihadist victory in Egypt also rankled. If the Salafi-jihadists took over Egypt, their next target would presumably be Saudi Arabia, the homeland of the virulent Salafi Wahhabi cult hostile to the monarchy's strong ties to the United States. These fears were not fantasies. The success of the ayatollah's Islamic Revolution spawned a 1979 seizure of the Holy Mosque of Mecca by Salafi zealots demanding the overthrow of a decadent monarchy and its replacement with the Islamic Republic. The monarchy couldn't handle the crisis itself and had to call in foreign security forces to dislodge the rebels. The following year witnessed an uprising in Saudi Arabia's predominantly Shia Eastern Province. The uprising was crushed by brutal force, but suspicion of Saudi Shia deepened, as did the toll of the ayatollah's attacks on immoral behavior of the Saudi monarchy and its subservience to the American devils. Other problems also loomed. The king of Jordan was on shaky ground, and the fall of one king would likely trigger a chain reaction. Israeli expansionism also proved touchy for the tribal monarchy that proclaimed itself the protector of Islam.

As in the past, the survival of the Saudi monarchy would depend on the mustering of its faith, force, and financial assets to parry the mounting threats to its survival.

All were tricky but none more so than force. The monarchy was strong enough to keep recalcitrant tribes in order and to defeat border scrimmages with Yemen, but little more. Domestic protection of the monarchy rested heavily on a National Guard recruited from loyal tribes. A less reliable Saudi army was largely responsible for border security. Each branch of the military was headed by a different powerful clan within the royal family. This assured the ability of each of the powerful clans to check the other.

The weakness of Saudi military forces was demonstrated by its reliance on foreign forces to recapture the Holy Mosque in Mecca from Salafi-jihadist rebels. The hidden question was the loyalty of Wahhabi-indoctrinated forces to deal with a rebellion defending core Wahhabi principles. Wahhabi-indoctrinated forces had no trouble crushing the Shia uprising in the Eastern Province, for the Wahhabi forces considered the Shia apostates worthy of death.

The same hostile attitude toward the Saudi Shia led to the monarchy's assumptions that the Saudi Shia were covertly supporting the Ayatollah Khomeini's Islamic Revolution. Invariably, such faith-based fears led to greater oppression of the Saudi Shia, which in turn inclined some of the rebellious Saudi Shia to support the ayatollah. Most of the Saudi Shia displayed support for the monarchy, but were they sincere? The monarchy had its doubts, because Shia religious practice allowed oppressed Shia to feign support for their Sunni oppressors as a means of protecting the Shia faith. The United States would do well to keep this policy in mind in its reliance on Shia forces or any other Islamic forces to do its bidding. As the drama of the Middle East unfolds, the manipulation of faith is risky business.

Faith was a strong point as long as the monarchy could count on the Salafi-Wahhabi clergy to provide it with religious legitimacy, justify its policies, and preach that it was the duty of Muslims to obey Muslim leaders.

Things, however, were not quite that simple. The relationship between the Saudi monarchy and the Wahhabi religious establishment was an alliance between two independent power centers that had been forged during the first Saudi dynasty and revived with the reemergence of the Saudi monarchy in 1901 and 1920. Each maintained its own independent objectives. The monarchy's objective was survival and expansion, while the goal of the Wahhabi establishment was to propagate the Wahhabi vision of Islam. The Wahhabi clerical establishment pursued these objectives through its control of the Saudi religious, educational, and judicial systems. It also controlled the religious police. The monarchy controlled the military, treasury, and just about everything else. The monarchy's enforcement of strict Wahhabi doctrine was part of the bargain.

The monarchy and Wahhabi clerical establishment depended upon each other for their survival, but tensions were inevitable. The clerical establishment was hostile toward cooperation with the United States and its allies, whom they perceived as enemies of Islam. Both entities were hostile to the growing Westernization of the Kingdom, which they deemed threatening to both Sharia law and the piety of Saudi culture.

Presumably the monarchy could rely on the United States for protection, but this was not assured. How could the United States protect the Saudi monarchy if it couldn't protect the shah of Iran, a critical US ally strategically located on the Soviet border? The monarchy became even more worried at the end of the era, with Saddam Hussein's invasion of Kuwait in 1990 and the prospect of a civil war in Egypt. More than ever the monarchy needed the Wahhabis, but did the Wahhabis need the monarchy?

Given the complexities of faith and force, it was finance that remained the strong suit in the Saudi arsenal. It was a suit that grew stronger as oil prices soared with the growing instability in the Middle East. On the home front it was used to bolster the legitimacy of the Saudi regime by expanding the Kingdom's cradle-to-grave welfare programs that made Saudi citizens among the most pampered in the world. By using money to buy love, the monarchy reduced its dependence on the Wahhabi clergy as a source of legitimacy. The clergy was still vital, but the monarchy's use of finance to build popular support gave it more leeway in curbing some of the clergy's excessive extremism. The increasingly educated sector of Saudi society was particularly upset by the intrusive policies of the religious police, such as its seeking assurances that all couples in restaurants were married. By pitting financial legitimacy against religious legitimacy, the monarchy was also creating a growing divide in Saudi society between younger Saudis—many educated in the West—and the hard core of traditional Saudis who clung to their religious and tribal traditions.

It also posed a curious question for the monarchy. Which of the two sources of legitimacy was most likely to sustain the monarchy in times of crisis: financial legitimacy or religious legitimacy? The monarchy hedged it bets by pursuing both. Welfare expanded at the same time that the king changed his title to "His Majesty, the Protector of the Two Holy Shrines." Henceforth all mentions of the king in the media would start by saying, "His Majesty, the Protector of the two Holy Shrines," said this or did that.

On the regional front the monarchy used finance to support a war that Iraq's Saddam Hussein had just launched against Khomeini's Islamic republic. The war endured throughout the decade, and billions of dollars were poured into Iraq by Saudi Arabia and the Gulf sheikhdoms to keep the war alive. They had no choice. Saddam Hussein was their only hope of surviving the ayatollah's Islamic Revolution. The United States did its part by providing Saddam with aerial data on Iranian targets. It was all in vain. Iran did not fall, and Saddam Hussein became an even greater threat to the Saudis than the ayatollah did as he invaded Kuwait in 1990.

It was also during this period that the monarchy decided to control Sunni Islam all over the world through its global outreach programs. Not only did Saudi outreach programs demonstrate the religiosity of the monarchy but they also enabled the monarchy to keep tabs on the Salafi-jihadists. At the same time, it pleased the Saudi clergy by spreading the extremist Salafi-Wahhabi doctrine throughout the world.

At the international level the monarchy used finance to maintain its special relationship with the United States and the EU by making vast weapons purchases and funding a huge array of think tanks and universities. Finance couldn't buy love, but it could surely buy political influence. It was during this period, for example, that the Saudis made a $25 million grant to the University of Arkansas, the major university in President Clinton's home state.

Ideally, the ability of the Saudi monarchy to survive the challenges facing it would be based on striking a balance between and coordinating faith, force, and finance. However, doing so did not seem to happen during this era. Each had its uses, but they weren't coordinated or balanced. Rather, they seemed to pull in conflicting directions. The Saudi monarchy would have to rely heavily on US forces for protection, but Wahhabi faith was not compatible with a US military presence on the sacred sands of Saudi Arabia. Americans and Europeans, by contrast, wondered why their leaders were supporting a tribal monarchy that refused to let women drive, supported slavery, condoned child marriage, beheaded opponents of the regime, whipped professors who communicated with their female graduate students by phone, and propagated an anti-American vision of Islam. Finance, in turn, was polarizing Saudi society and creating tension between the religious and more secular sectors of the Saudi population. One or the other would have to dominate.

IRAN: THE FIRST ISLAMIC STATE IN THE MODERN ERA

The reign of the shah, as we have seen in the preceding chapter, was so bizarre and inept that some form of revolt was inevitable. The beginning of the end came in 1978 with protests by religious students and clergy in the holy city of Qum. Oil workers went on strike the same year, reducing production by some 80 percent and infusing religious protests with labor hostility. Adding to the fray were leftist elements intent on fueling religious turmoil as the quickest way to dispose of the shah. Evidently, leftist faith in Marx and modernity had deluded Iran's leftist intellectuals into believing that they could outmaneuver the quaint clerics with ease. With Soviet help, Iran would become a socialist republic rather than an Islamic republic.

By 1979 the ayatollah was in control of the country and most of the leftists had either died or fled. The shah's elite had also fled, taking much of Iran's money in the process. Without leadership, both the military and the bureaucracy dissolved, leaving the country without political institutions at any level. The CIA had picked up the pieces following the earlier coup, but now there were no pieces left to pick up. James Bill, a leading American expert on Iran, chided the US government for being out of touch with Iranian realities (Bill, 1988).

By 1980 the Ayatollah Khomeini had been elected president of the Islamic Republic of Iran. He had also proclaimed an Islamic Revolution that was to change the future of the Middle East. Implicit in the ayatollah's Islamic Revolution was a Shia revolution against the Sunni tribal kingdoms that ruled the Gulf, all of whom possessed large Shia populations. This accomplished, a Shia crescent would emerge that linked the Shia populations of the Middle East under the control of Iran. The geographic crescent was to begin in Iran, the largest and most powerful of the Shia enclaves in the region, and then absorb the Shia populations of Iraq, the Gulf, and Syria as it wended its way to Lebanon. Afghanistan, Pakistan, and Yemen also possessed large Shia populations and were not to be neglected.

Once established, the Shia crescent would serve the dual purpose of liberating the Shia from the oppression of the Sunni at the same time that it rescued Islam from the scourge of dominance by the United States and the Soviet Union. The two goals were linked, for the same Sunni tribal kings and tyrants who oppressed the Shia were also defiling Islam by becoming puppets of either the United States or the Soviet Union.

For all of his grandiose aspirations, the ayatollah was also a realist. The Shia, who constituted about 17 percent of the Muslim population, could not drive the United States and the Soviet Union from the Middle East without Sunni support. His Islamic Revolution would have to be an Islamic revolution in the fullest sense of the word. With this reality in mind, the ayatollah's Islamic Revolution began to offer financial and military support to the Salafi-jihadist revolutions sweeping the Arab world. Both revolutions shared the same goal of a pure Islamic state, faced the same enemies, and drew upon the same wellspring of mass despair. Differences of doctrine could be sorted out with time.

Whatever Khomeini's grand plans, his immediate task was not revolution but building an Islamic nation from scratch. There could be no Islamic Revolution until Iran had been transformed into a staging ground capable of defeating the enemies of Islam. This would be a daunting task at best. The clerics had no experience in running a county. Nor could they rely on the suspect remnants of the Shah's regime, most of whom had fled for their lives.

To credit the Ayatollah Khomeini's inflammatory speeches with the fall of the shah is not to say that the ayatollah orchestrated or controlled the revolution. Evidence of this was the spontaneous outbreak of revolutionary committees in villages throughout the country. Religious activists dominated the committees and swore allegiance to the ayatollah, but revenge against their former oppressors was also high on their minds. Suspect under the shah, their time had come.

A similar sign of spontaneous chaos was the 1979 seizing of the US Embassy by university students in Tehran. This unexpected twist came as a shock to both the ayatollah and the United States. The ayatollah couldn't back down from a spontaneous act of support for the revolution, nor could the United States ignore the diplomatic hostages seized by the students. The ayatollah, reluctant to capitulate to the threats of what he had branded the American devil, embraced the students. The United States responded by sending special forces to liberate the captured diplomats. The showdown was a godsend for Khomeini, or so it seemed to the faithful as a sandstorm clogged the engines of the US rescue helicopters. What greater proof could they demand of the ayatollah's baraka?

Using Faith to Build a Nation

The ayatollah brought an end to the chaos by holding presidential and parliamentary elections in 1980. An Islamic political party was created

by the clergy and swept the elections. It also orchestrated a new constitution that centered on Khomeini's principle of *vilayat-i-fiqih*, which is
best understood as rule by the dominant religious leader. As Khomeini
was the dominant religious leader, he possessed veto power over both
the popularly elected president and the popularly elected parliament.
The only catch in the elections was the prior vetting of electoral candidates by the senior clergy. All in all, it provided an interesting framework for a theological democracy. Khomeini kept a close eye on events,
and it was he who vetoed the reigning president's decision to free the
US hostages.

Transforming Faith into Military Force

No sooner had the ayatollah stabilized his domestic control over Iran
than Saddam Hussein launched an invasion of Iran in the fall of 1980.
With the shah's much-vaunted army dissolved and the ayatollah struggling to get his act together, the power-hungry Saddam Hussein had
everything to gain and nothing to lose. With a little luck, Saudi Arabia
and the Gulf sheikhdoms would come next.

The ayatollah could either transform faith into a military force capable of repelling the Iraqi invasion or see his control over Iran threatened. This was all the more the case because the Iraqi invasion was
supported by the Arab kings and the United States, both anxious to
destroy the ayatollah and his Islamic Revolution. Saddam Hussein was
worrisome to the United States but not as worrisome as the Ayatollah
Khomeini.

The faith weapon of the Ayatollah Khomeini, in contrast to the charismatic faith of Nasser, was a blend of charismatic hero worship based
on his overthrow of the shah and religious authority based on his status
as an ayatollah whose superior learning placed him in favor with the
Hidden Imam. In some circles, he was viewed as the reincarnation of
the Hidden Imam. This, as long as it lasted, personified the epitome of
faith-based power. All faiths may be partial faiths, but the faith foundation of the Ayatollah Khomeini was clearly more substantial than that of
either Nasser or the earlier Salafi-jihadists discussed above.

The ayatollah's transformation of faith into armed force operated at
several levels. The immediate resistance to the Iraqi invasion fell to the
Basiji. As described by Mackey,

> The Basiji (popular militias) operated from nine thousand mosques, enrolling boys below eighteen, men above forty-five, and women. Primarily the zealous products of poor, devout families from rural areas, they volunteered for temporary duty in God's war. . . . At the front, a Basiji could be identified by his tattered leftover uniform and mismatched boots, the bright red or yellow headband . . . declaring God's or Khomeini's greatness, and the large imitation brass key, the key to paradise, that hung around his neck. (Mackey, 1996, 323)

Mackey goes on to note that boys as young as twelve years old were used as human minesweepers to prepare the way for more advanced troops, such as the Revolutionary Guards. It is interesting to note that Saudi press expresses a deep interest in the continued development of the Basiji as instruments of Iran's surging Islamic Revolution.

Next in order came the Hizbullah (Party of God) militias organized in Lebanon, Iraq, and other Middle Eastern countries with substantial Shia populations. Hizbullah, although operating under different names, was to become the armed wing of the ayatollah's Islamic Revolution, which had begun with flawed ventures to overthrow the king of Bahrain and the ayatollah's effort to destabilize the Saudi monarchy by sending some one hundred thousand faithful zealots branding posters of Khomeini to the annual Haj in Mecca. The demonstrators created havoc by clashing with Saudi security police, but the police prevailed. In both cases, spontaneous outpourings of religious emotions in hostile territory had been crushed by the security police. The lesson was clear. To be powerful, religious emotions have to be organized and directed much as they had been in the ayatollah's overthrow of the shah.

The organizational adjustments came with the formation of the Lebanese Hizbullah by the dominant Lebanese ayatollah shortly after the Iranian Revolution. Beirut, then in a state of civil war and under Israeli occupation, was the ideal place for the formation of an armed Hizbullah organization. Chaos reigned, and the Lebanese Shia, about 40 percent of the Lebanese population, were also its most dispossessed and angry segment of the Lebanese population. Indeed, an earlier Shia cleric had closed down Beirut by forming a Movement of the Dispossessed.

While secret organizations among Shia minorities destabilized Sunni leaders beholden to the United States, the Hizbullah organization in Lebanon was to focus on driving the United States and its Israeli outpost from the Middle East. American concerns with Hizbullah mounted with the bombing of the US Embassy in Beirut in 1983 and the bombing of the marine barracks in Beirut later the same year.

Psychological warfare, in turn, was used to prepare the ground for the Hizbullah militias by accentuating the causes of violence discussed throughout the earlier chapters. This involved playing the Sunni-Shia card steeped in historical religious emotions. It also stressed the despair and deprivation of most Shia populations as well as the oppression of Sunni elites in Lebanon, Iraq, Saudi Arabia, and most everywhere else. Religion and deprivation blended well with the ayatollah's Islamic Revolution.

A final and particularly tricky part of the ayatollah's transformation of faith into force was his efforts to make his Islamic Revolution compatible with Sunni Salafi-jihadist extremism at the same time that he was attacking Sunnis to build Shia solidarity. He succeeded in the early stages of the game because his overthrow of the shah and humiliation of the Americans had sent of powerful message to the Salafi-jihadists that Islamic faith could defeat the United States and its allies. The doubters had been proven wrong by the will of God.

Khomeini's successes were based heavily on his ability to transform faith into force. As we shall see in the next installment of the unfolding drama of the Middle East, finance based on Iran's vast oil revenues would play a critical role in building bridges between Khomeini's Shia-based Islamic Revolution and the Sunni-based Salafi-jihadist revolution sweeping the area.

Ironically, Khomeini's failures were also largely of his own making. Stunned by Khomeini's repulsion of his invasion, Saddam Hussein offered a peace settlement that would have sent the ayatollah's charisma and baraka soaring. The choice was Khomeini's alone, but he was intent on punishing the Iraqi leader who, upon pressure from the Shah, had banished him from his exile in Iraq's holy cities. Personal whim had trumped reality. Khomeini, like Nasser before him, was subdued by pursuit of a war that he could not win. Had he accepted the truce, his pressure on Saudi Arabia and the Gulf sheikhdoms could well have been insurmountable.

As for Saddam Hussein in Iraq, he simply slaughtered the Shia clergy suspected of complicity with Khomeini.

LESSONS LEARNED

1. Shia doctrine contains a higher spiritual and mystical content than the stark rigidity of Salafi-jihadist doctrine. This is a powerful recruiting tool as evidenced by the vast appeal of Sufi mystics in the Sunni world.
2. While Iran and its allies offer official support for Shia extremist groups, Salafi-jihadist groups are bitterly opposed by most Sunni political leaders.
3. Senior Shia clerics are more likely to justify violence by Shia extremist groups than senior Sunni clerics who view them as apostates.
4. Religious faith is more powerful and enduring than secular faith based on nationalism.
5. Faith that blends charisma, nationalism, and ethnic identity with religious authority is more powerful than either faith or religious authority alone.
6. The combination of extremist faith and despair may be unstoppable.
7. As political fear of religious extremism increases, tyrants implement the dual strategy of making unreal promises of the glories to come while at the same time making their police forces larger and more brutal. This combination of faith and force increases both aspirations and despair.
8. The political castration of the religious establishment pushes the dispossessed into the hands of the extremists.
9. Faith-based rulers who possess religious authority, charisma, or a combination of the two are so powerful that their decisions are absolute and cannot be challenged.
10. Faith is easily transformed into force, but force is difficult to transform into sincere faith.
11. Force can buy docility but not sincere faith.

6

THE ERA OF PEACE, STABILITY, AND ILLUSION (1990–2000)

The advent of the 1990s gave hope that the Middle East was entering a new era of peace and stability. Illusion or not, all signs pointed in that direction. Of these, the most dramatic was the implosion of the Soviet Union in December 1991 and the emergence of a new Russia intent on becoming a democratic and capitalist member of the world community. The Cold War that had shaped Middle Eastern politics since the end of World War II was over.

Also over was Soviet support for the Assad regime in Syria, for Saddam Hussein in Iraq, and for Muammar Qaddafi in Libya. Without their Soviet protector, they began to mend their fences with the United States.

The collapse of the Soviet Union had eliminated the United States' need to maintain a base camp for Salafi-jihadist extremists in Afghanistan. Presumably, the thousands of Salafi-jihadists who had gathered there to smite the Soviet devil, the Great Satan, would simply return in glory to the scattered countries from which they had come.

Adding to the mood of optimism were doubts about the ability of Iran's clergy to maintain the Islamic Republic without the presence of Khomeini. When the clergy fell, so would Iran's Islamic Revolution.

Even the Israeli-Palestinian conundrum was showing signs of resolution as peace agreement followed peace agreement.

Finally, the Salafi-jihadist resurgence that had shaken the Arab world during the preceding era appeared to be losing steam. Religious extremism had lost its sting, or so it seemed at the beginning of the era.

The signs of peace and stability traced above were based on hope and illusion rather than reality. Like all signs and illusions, they contained sufficient hints of reality to make them believable, but little more. In the present chapter we discuss each of these illusions and their impact on the unfolding of the drama of the Middle East.

HOW THE COLLAPSE OF THE SOVIET UNION FUELED ISLAMIC EXTREMISM IN THE MIDDLE EAST

The implosion of the Soviet Union in 1991 gave birth to a multitude of new Islamic countries including Azerbaijan, Kazakhstan, Turkmenistan, Uzbekistan, Tajikistan, and Kyrgyzstan. Armenia, while hardly Islamic, also declared its independence from the Soviet Union. The Middle East that had been cobbled together at the end of WWI now had several new members for the United States and its allies to cope with in their search for peace and stability in the region.

Much like the new countries to emerge after WWI, the newly independent countries formed by the collapse of the Soviet Union were chaotic countries in which the preconditions of Islamic extremism soared. This was particularly the case of Chechnya, a small Islamic province that failed in its efforts to break away from the new Russia. Fearing even more secessions by former Soviet provinces, the Russian government chose to crush the Chechnyan rebellion. At first, this appeared to be a mistake, as Russia found itself inundated with a plague of terror. When the rebellion was eventually crushed, many of the intensely motivated and experienced Chechnyan fighters joined bin-Laden's Islamic revolution against the United States in Afghanistan. The lesson was clear. Religiously motivated fighters were easily shifted from one battleground to another. Finance was also a factor, for al-Qaeda was a well-funded organization.

Many of the new countries created by the breakup of the Soviet Union possessed deep cultural links to both Turkey and Iran. Turkey proclaimed itself protector of the countries that were Turkish in culture and language. Iran did the same for the Shia of the region. Christian

Armenia also had deep scores to settle with Turkey over its earlier slaughter of Armenians, slaughters that the Turks heatedly denied.

A more deadly illusion resulting from the collapse of the Soviet Union was the illusion that the United States' victory in the Cold War had ended Russia's role as a key actor in the Middle East. The Soviet Union may have imploded, but the emergent Russia, while still reinventing itself, had inherited 77 percent of the land area of the Soviet Union, 51 percent of its population, more than half of its GNP, some two million troops, and twenty-seven thousand nuclear warheads with the rockets to match. It had also inherited a heavy dose of Russian nationalism and a strategic location on the border of the Middle East. New or old, Russia remained a superpower with little interest in playing second fiddle to the United States. It would be up to the United States to either make Russia a full partner in the new world order created by the end of the Cold War or pay the price. As we will discuss throughout the chapter that follows, the United States is paying that price in the Middle East.

CONTROL OF THE MIDDLE EASTERN TYRANTS

The illusion that Middle Eastern tyrants would become peaceful with the collapse of their Soviet patron quickly vanished. In reality, the reverse appears to have been true. Saddam Hussein, long a Soviet client, invaded Kuwait and thumbed his nose at a US government that had earlier supported him in his war against Iran. The United States' luck in controlling Qaddafi and Assad was little better. Qaddafi supported various terrorist organizations, while Assad supported Iran's development of Hizbullah in Lebanon, a virtual Syrian colony. The United States remained infatuated with the use of military tyrants as a force weapon in the region but found it difficult to keep Saddam Hussein under control following the collapse of his Soviet patron.

Why did Saddam Hussein, his country in a shambles following a long and unsuccessful war with Iran, openly challenged the might of the world's remaining superpower by invading Kuwait? Surely he understood that this threat to the oil kingdoms of the Gulf would bring a brutal US response.

Answers to this question require a curious blend of psychology, culture, and logic, each of which overlaps with the others. From the psychological perspective, Saddam's behavior indicated manifest signs of megalomania and paranoia. Megalomania was evidenced in his speeches that left little doubt that he intended to be the next superhero of the Arab world as he transformed Iraq into the region's dominant military industrial power. This goal accomplished, he would march from victory to victory against the enemies of the Arabs. Of these none were greater than Israel and Iran. His dreams of grandeur also sparkled in his dazzling military regalia suited only to a commander-in-chief who had never served in the military.

Saddam's paranoia reflected the cutthroat nature of Iraqi politics and a culture that pitted clan against clan, tribe against tribe, ethnic group against ethnic group, and sect against sect. Saddam's fear, however, went well beyond logic to encompass threats to imagined glories more at home in the *Arabian Nights* than the reality of global politics.

And yet there was a logic to Saddam's madness. His earlier invasion of Iran appeared to be a sure victory that would place him on the path to regional dominance. Not only had Iran been in a shambles but his invasion was blessed by the United States and Saudi Arabia. He had been their savior, and now it was their responsibility to compensate him for Iraq's horrendous losses of his war with Iran.

Far from being inclined to help Saddam Hussein rebuild his shattered country, Saudi Arabia and Kuwait claimed that the billions of dollars that they had given Saddam during the war were loans that had now come due. Adding insult to injury, Kuwait appeared to be illegally pumping oil from neighboring Iraqi territory. From Saddam's perspective, it was payback time for the treachery of his former allies.

A humiliated Saddam and his inflated ego also faced problems on the home front as domestic adversaries including the Kurds and Shia sensed his weakness. Bluff and bluster had run their course, and the awe and fear of the masses crumbled as rumors of attempted coups flourished. Something had to be done. It had to be easy, it had to be dazzling, and it had to be done in a hurry. It had to be Kuwait with its vast oil wealth. Saddam possessed the force for a lightning strike on a tiny city-state that lacked the power to defend itself. He was also in desperate need of Kuwaiti wealth to finance the rebuilding of his shattered country. Force was the key to finance. If the United States didn't balk, Saudi Arabia awaited.

Saddam Hussein lost his gamble as his massive army was crushed by US forces in about one hundred hours. It seems that Saddam Hussein had believed his own bluster of invincibility, as the lights of the Baghdad airport remained on during the US attack. The lesson was clear. The Arab armies were no match for the force of the NATO armies in face-to-face, symmetrical warfare.

And yet Saddam Hussein was not defeated. Wary of occupying Iraq and wanting to keep Saddam alive to counter the Iranians, the United States imposed a no-fly zone on Iraq to keep Saddam from bombing Iraq's Kurdish and Shia regions.

Saddam Hussein responded by plotting weapons of mass destruction for his next grand venture. In the meantime, he controlled the Shia and the Kurds by pitting the Shia ayatollahs against each other and allowing Turkish troops to pursue Kurdish rebels in Iraqi territory. Saddam was able to control the faith weapon of the Shia clerics by using finance to divide them. This he was able to do because the Shia ayatollahs were in a popularity contest for money and power within the Shia community. The generous donations of the faithful depended upon the ayatollah's access to travel, television, and political influence to aid parishioners. When a reigning grand ayatollah died, Saddam had Mohammed Sadiq as-Sadr appointed as the new grand ayatollah. As-Sadr was an Iraqi Arab ayatollah who disdained politics as dirty business. Only as-Sadr's sermons were carried on Iraqi radio and television and, of all the ayatollahs, only as-Sadr had freedom of movement. The other leading candidates, for their part, complained of being harassed by the regime. Force and finance had trumped faith for the moment. Saddam, however, had guessed wrong, for as-Sadr proved to be so popular that he had to be assassinated. Saddam Hussein fell to US force a few years later. It would be a new ayatollah of Iranian origin who would come to the fore during the period of American control of Iraq.

THE PASSING OF THE AYATOLLAH KHOMEINI AND THE TRANSFER OF FAITH

Expectations that the Islamic Republic of Iran would collapse with the death of Khomeini in 1979, although logical, also proved to be an illusion. It was the unique charisma and religious aura of Khomeini that had enabled him to dominate Iranian politics. He was irreplaceable. There was no second in command or specified successor but merely a void that no single person was qualified to fill. This was because Khomeini, like most autocrats, didn't want the competition of a second in command or a named successor. Making matters worse, Khomeini had played the moderate clergy against the conservative clergy to assure that neither faction would be in a position to challenge his total dominance of Iranian politics.

The passing of Khomeini forced the clergy to select his successor from one of the two hostile factions: the moderates or the conservatives. As the two factions couldn't reconcile their differences, they compromised by selecting Hojjat al-Islam Sayyed Khamenei as the supreme guide of the Islamic Republic. The solution was a pragmatic one that found a hojjat, a lesser member of the clerical hierarchy, named as Iran's supreme religious leader. Hojjats might become ayatollahs, but they weren't there yet. As a result, both the moderate and conservative ayatollahs outranked Iran's supreme religious leader religiously but not politically. Added to the confusion was an elected parliament and an elected president.

The situation became even more complex as the Revolutionary Guards and the Basiji also became institutionalized as independent power centers. This raised questions over which of the competing power centers would become dominant as the drama of the Middle East unfolded. Would it be the faith-based clergy headed by the supreme guide, the popularly elected parliamentary system, or the force-based Revolutionary Guards and fanatical Basiji? Added to the puzzle was the quasi-autonomous power of a growing Hizbullah network that turned faith into forceful militias funded by Iran. Khomeini, for his part, remained the patron saint of Iran's ruling apparatus, a saint who had spoken with the voice of the Hidden Imam. Keep in mind also, that other grand ayatollahs throughout the Shia world are not required to accept the supreme guide of Iran as their leader.

For all of the confusion, Iran survived the passing of the Ayatollah Khomeini. So did the Islamic Revolution. The puzzle of the unfolding drama of the Middle East is, who rules Iran?

THE ILLUSION OF PEACE BETWEEN THE ISRAELIS AND THE PALESTINIANS

Abba Eban, a former Israeli foreign minister, celebrated the implosion of the Soviet Union by declaring, "Israeli security was strengthened a hundred-fold by the Soviet Union going from the 'anti' column to the 'pro' column. After all, it was the Soviet Union and not the Arabs that posed an existential threat to Israel in terms of life or death, or to live or perish" (Eban, 1994).

Israelis also rejoiced at the liberation from Soviet control of some three million Jews, many of whom would seek a new life in Israel. As many of the new arrivals tended to be conservative religious Jews, the gradual shift of Israeli society from the socialist secular left to the conservative right was intensified. This placed Israel's far right prime minister with the dilemma of settling the new arrivals, the cost of which, including housing, health, education, and welfare, was placed at approximately $26.5 billion that Israel didn't have. Land was not a problem for Israel's prime minister, who welcomed a justification for settling more Palestinian land.

It was at this point that Saddam Hussein, suddenly faced with the reality of a US invasion, made a futile call on Arabs to attack Americans. He then unleashed thirty-nine Soviet Scud missiles on Tel Aviv and other Israeli cities. There was no sign of the chemical warheads of which Saddam had boasted and only thirteen direct and indirect deaths. That was a blessing, but Saddam Hussein had made his point. He clearly had the capacity to breach Israeli security, and no one knew what would come next. Saddam's rocket attack, having inflamed Palestinian hopes of repelling Israeli domination, also threatened a Palestinian intifada (uprising) on the home front.

President Reagan, confronted with the prospect of another catastrophic Arab-Israeli war at the same time that the United States was about to invade Iraq, played the finance card by offering Shamir, the Israeli prime minister, money for the settlement of the Soviet immigrants in exchange for making a land or peace settlement with the Palestinians. In one fell swoop, the United States settled the Iraqi crisis, the Iranian crisis, and the Arab-Israeli crisis. The peace negotiations were to take place in Madrid and Oslo.

Prime Minister Shamir promised Reagan good-faith participation in both negotiations while simultaneously telling members of his right-wing Likud party that he would handle this crisis as he had managed the others. The Israelis did make a final withdrawal from southern Lebanon as a demonstration of good faith, one that enabled Israel to withdraw from a costly lost cause. It was a game that the Israelis played with the Americans, an endless game that the Americans never seemed to win. Were the Americans really duped by the Israelis, or did the Americans want to be duped? Whatever the case, it was a dangerous game that made many Israelis nervous. Israel's special relationship with the United States was too vital to be toyed with.

It was in this mood that Yitzhak Rabin, a much-decorated general, won the 1992 elections and vowed to make peace with the Palestinians. Rabin didn't play games, and while Shamir was delaying the peace process in Madrid, Rabin had been holding secret talks in Oslo with Yasser Arafat, the leader of the Palestinian Liberation Organization. Rabin believed that peace was necessary for Israel's survival, and an agreement was reached between the two adversaries on working out an Israeli withdrawal from large areas of the West Bank and Gaza in return for the PLO's recognition of Israel and its right to exist. The details would be worked out, but a land-for-peace agreement had been signed.

Settlement building was suspended in the Occupied Territories, but Rabin was assassinated by a Jewish religious fanatic before the details of the agreement could be worked out. The message was clear: there would be no sacrifice of sacred land for peace as long as religious extremism played a dominant role in Israeli politics. This was all the more the case as Christian Evangelicalism, dedicated to keeping Israel pure, continued to soar in the United States. Islamic extremists, for their part, now had yet another case for claiming that the United States was declaring war on Islam. More than ever, faith was dominating the politics of Israel. Force would follow.

THE FORMATION OF INTERNATIONAL ISLAMIC TERRORIST NETWORKS

Perhaps the most dangerous illusion resulting from the Salafi-jihadist defeat of the Soviets in Afghanistan was the assumption that this vast body of Salafi-jihadist fighters would simply crawl back in the wood-work from whence they came. What made this assumption dangerous was that it led the United States and its EU allies to relax their guard on the terrorist threat. The 1993 bombing of the World Trade Center by Egypt's Islamic Group, for example, was written off as an isolated event. Omar Abdel Rahman, the group's leader, was subsequently arrested and sent to a prison cell, from which he guided the spiritual policy of the Islamic Group.

Bin-Laden had returned to Saudi Arabia for a hero's welcome. Many Pakistanis had returned home to liberate Muslim Kashmir from Indian rule. Chechnyans had returned home to fight for independence from Russia. One way or another, the Afghan Arabs, as bin-Laden's fighters were commonly referred to, were still fighting. Many other Afghan Arabs returned home to establish fundamentalist cells based on the training they had received in Afghanistan. The Taliban fighters simply took over Afghanistan.

The Turabi Terrorist Network

If the assumption that the Afghan Arabs would simply disappear into the woodwork had led the Americans to relax, it had the opposite im-pact on Hassan Abdullah al-Turabi, a brilliant Muslim cleric who, in addition to possessing a master's degree in law from the University of London and a doctorate of law from the Sorbonne, had become the intellectual guide of the Salafi-jihadists. Turabi counted on the willing-ness of the Afghan Arabs to lay their lives on the line to drive the United States and Israel from the Middle East much as they had laid their lives on the line to drive Russia from Afghanistan. This goal, Tura-bi preached, could never be achieved as long as the Salafi-jihadist movement was fragmented into a thousand parts scattered throughout the global Muslim community. Much as Muslims had been unified to fight the Russians in Afghanistan, they would now have to be unified to drive the United States and Israel from the Middle East. Turabi's mission was to provide that unity.

Turabi, judging from his writings, was also aware that his goal of driving the United States and Israel from the Middle East would require an effective blend of faith, force, and finance. Of these, faith was the most important, for only faith in God and the Prophet Mohammed could unite a Muslim nation fragmented by centuries of sectarian bickering. Muslims were brothers in Islam, and faith could bring them together. It was also faith that would provide the motivation for driving the United States and Israel from the Middle East. Finally, faith provided the organizational and cohesive framework for melding the diverse components of the Islamic movement into a coherent and disciplined movement capable of challenging the United States as the Afghans had challenged the Soviets.

Turabi well understood that force and finance would be vital to challenging the United States, but as Khomeini had demonstrated in overthrowing a US-backed shah and resisting a Soviet-armed Saddam Hussein, faith was easily transformed into force and courage.

Faith, as the Muslim Brotherhood had demonstrated, could also be transformed into finance in the form of money, jobs, and community service. Faith-based finance would finance the Islamic movement much as faith-based finance would provide for the Islamic state (Umma) once the United States and Israel had been driven from the region.

Turabi's vision for liberating the Middle East focused on bringing together all of the active Islamic movements intent on establishing Islamic rule in the region regardless of the bitter tensions that divided them. This included the moderate and patient Muslim Brotherhood, the Iranian-sponsored Hizbullah network, bin-Laden's Afghan network of Afghan Arabs, and the vast array of Salafi-jihadist organizations throughout the Middle East and beyond, including Wahhabi currents in Saudi Arabia and the Gulf.

Turabi claimed to know them all, secret as well as public, moderates as well as radical extremists, and Shia as well as Sunni. He also claimed to have met with all of the major heads of state in the region and to have a close relationship with Qaddafi and Saddam Hussein (Palmer and Palmer, 2008).

Turabi was under no illusion about the near impossibility of eliminating the theological, ideological, and personality conflicts between these groups and political leaders, but that wasn't his concern. His concern was driving the United States, Israel, and all former colonial members of NATO from the Middle East. This was doable, in Turabi's view, because it was also the goal of all of the Islamic organizations and political leaders that Turabi intended to weld into his new Islamic movement. Driving NATO and Israel from the Middle East was the common denominator that would unite them. Together they had everything they needed to succeed: faith, force, finance, and a secure launching pad in the Sudan.

They also had the experience and training provided by the United States in Afghanistan, not to mention the lessons learned by the Ayatollah Khomeini in overthrowing the shah and pursuing his Islamic Revolution. Beyond these advantages, they had also acquired a new faith (efficacy) in themselves and in the blessings of God. Paradise and revenge against the enemies of Islam awaited. All they needed was someone to put it all together. That someone was Turabi. Not a man of small ego, it is probable that he viewed himself as the caliph-in-waiting for the new Islamic empire. God would do the rest.

Turabi's path toward the creation of an international Islamic network began with a series of conferences convened in Khartoum between 1991 and 1993 to bring together diverse Islamic groups from approximately fifty Islamic countries. Some meetings focused on predominantly Arab Salafi-jihadist groups while others tried to find common ground between the violent Salafi-jihadists and the more moderate Muslim Brotherhood. Others searched for ways to build cooperation between the Sunni and Shia groups. Councils were formed that met periodically in Khartoum, the capital of the Sudan.

Turabi was able to accomplish this because one of his devout followers, General Omar al-Bashir, had recently seized power in a military coup and proclaimed the Sudan to be an Islamic state of which Turabi was the high priest. The Sudan was a chaotic country in which Turabi's activities would draw minimal attention. It was also the poorest of countries, in which the money brought in by Turabi's partners in faith had a great deal of influence. It was this combination of faith, force, and finance that were to be Turabi's building blocks for transforming the Sudan into the launching pad for his struggle to drive the United States and Israel out of the Middle East. In his view, Muslims had little choice in the matter. Both the United States and Israel had declared war on

Islam. Faith and finance had brought Muslims together. Now it was time for the emphasis of Turabi's network to shift to force.

Turabi, for all of his religious and intellectual credentials, was not in a position to give orders to the groups that attended his conferences. He was the movement's coordinator, but he consulted on key strategic matters with bin-Laden and Iran. Iran was vital because it provided the finance and weapons required for the defeat of the United States and Israel. Its leadership role was limited because Shia would not be accepted as leaders of Sunni Salafi-jihadist troops.

The role of military commander fell to bin-Laden, an engineer, economist, proven leader of Salafi-jihadist fighters, national hero of Saudi Arabia, and leader of a large contingent of Afghan veterans taking refuge in the Sudan. He also had access to the wealthy angels of Saudi Arabia who were anxious to strengthen the Islamic cause. Bin-Laden, however, was not a cleric who spoke in the name of Islam.

Collectively, Turabi had put together an organization that had everything that it needed to succeed. Faith, force, and finance topped a list that included a remote and chaotic region in which to build a base camp for its operation, a strategic location, and political protection from the Sudanese government. The United States and Israel were doing their part by expanding what Muslims perceived as their war on Islam. Everything, or so it seemed, had fallen into place and immediate successes were scored by a surge of Salafi-jihadist activity that would push both Algeria and Egypt to the brink of civil war. In the process, Iran was also pouring money into Lebanon that would make it a base camp for its Hizbullah activities, including support for Hamas and other Sunni extremist groups operating in the Israeli Occupied Territories and Lebanon.

It was not long, however, before things began to fall apart. Turabi wanted to focus efforts on the large Muslim countries in Africa that could easily be transformed into Islamic states. Bin-Laden and Iran were more focused on driving the United States from the Middle East. The Pakistanis wanted the new organization to focus on the liberation of Kashmir from Indian rule. Sunni Salafi-jihadists, meanwhile, were wary of growing Shia influence in Sunni countries, as was Saudi Arabia. The Saudis saw the hand of bin-Laden in Iran's growing influence in the Sudan and, in the mid-1980s, threatened to withdraw its financial aid from the Sudan unless al-Bashir expelled their former national hero from this poorest of countries. Al-Bashir did better than that. He arrested Turabi, who had begun to act as if he were the president of the Sudan. Bin-Laden took the hint and departed for Afghanistan, where he and his Afghan Arabs were welcomed by the Taliban, a Salafi-jihadist organization intent on expanding its control of Afghanistan.

It was in Afghanistan that bin-Laden built upon his Sudanese links to revive his al-Qaeda (base camp), and he plotted his 9/11 attack on the United States. Activities in this period have generated a heated debate about the role of the Saudis and the Saudi monarchy in funding bin-Laden's attack on the United States, a topic best examined after the attack itself is addressed.

LESSONS LEARNED

1. Religiously motivated fighters are easily shifted from one battleground to another.
2. Turabi's experience suggests that full coordination and cooperation between diverse Muslim groups may be impossible for a sustained period of time.
3. Mutual support is possible when it serves mutual goals.
4. Driving the United States and Israel from the Middle East takes center stage in the priority list of Islamic extremist groups.
5. Hostilities toward Israel and the United States are linked because the countries are viewed in much of the Islamic world as the source of a Jewish-Christian conspiracy against Islam.
6. International Islamic extremist movements rely on US and Israeli attacks on Islam to build motivation and unity.
7. Israel is viewed as an American colonial outpost in the Muslim heartland.
8. Success in attacking anti-Islamic targets, including Israel, builds confidence and recruitment.
9. Successful terror causes more terror.
10. Rationality cannot be assumed in dealing with megalomaniac tyrants.
11. Client tyrants make poor puppets who are difficult to control and shift strategies for achieving their goals in line with the changing circumstances of the era.

12. The Arab armies were no match for the force of the NATO armies in face-to-face, symmetrical warfare.

7

THE ERA OF GLOBAL TERROR AND COUNTER-TERROR (2000–2010)

The era of global terror and counter-terror began with bin-Laden's September 11, 2001, attacks on the World Trade Center and Pentagon and the attempted attack on the White House. The United States was at war, and there was no turning back.

The burden of response to the al-Qaeda attacks fell on US president George W. Bush and a supporting cast of conservatives who shared his political views. Pundits of the time referred to them as "neo-cons" because of the intensity of their conservative views on the economy, Christian morality, Israel, and a strong military. All were new to their positions, which made the burden of dealing with the al-Qaeda attacks that much more difficult.

Adding to their woes was the time factor. They had to do something, and they had to do it quickly. But what? The Bush administration faced a global war on terror unlike any war the United States had ever experienced. Rather than a war between massed armies supported by tanks and aircraft, it was a war against Islamic fanatics that, like phantoms, struck at dusk but disappeared at dawn.

Even more difficult was the complexity of their challenge. Logic and urgency dictated that the first step in the War on Terror would be the elimination of bin-Laden and his base camps in Afghanistan before he could strike again. Afghanistan, however, was only one link in al-Qaeda's global operations. All had to be eliminated. Questions about Iran and its Shia version of Islamic extremism also abounded, as did questions about the intentions of Saddam Hussein, who claimed to have weapons of mass destruction. Syria's support for Hizbullah in Lebanon was on the table, as were worries about the spread of Islamic terrorist activities in Africa and Yemen.

Particularly delicate for the Bush administration was the need to protect Israel from Salafi-jihadist terror and threats from Iraq and Iran at the same time that Israeli persecution of the Palestinians was inflaming Muslim hostility toward the United States. Not too far behind was the US desire to protect oil-rich Saudi Arabia from Iraq and Iran at the same time that Saudi Arabia was promoting Salafi-jihadist doctrine. Both Israel and Saudi Arabia, it will be recalled, possessed special relationships with the United States that could not be ignored. Israel's special relationship was based largely on faith, while the Saudi special relationship was based largely on finance in the form of black gold.

The neo-con philosophy of the Bush administration led to the bombing of bin-Laden's headquarters in Afghanistan and wherever else signs of the group could be found. The US administration relied on advice and intelligence from Israel, the world leader in fighting Islamic and related Arab terror. It also needed to prop up its Arab allies in the region, the foremost of whom were Egypt and Saudi Arabia.

Such, then, was the mood as the United States launched a global War on Terror with the strong support of the European Union, Israel, and its Arab allies. The British were the strongest European partners of the Bush administration despite the fact that British prime minister Tony Blair was a member of the Labor Party and shared none of the Bush administration's neo-con philosophy. Britain, too, had a special relationship with the United States and was reluctant to deviate from the Bush program in a time of crisis. It would be Blair's later admissions that revealed just how chaotic the War on Terror had become.

The goal, however, is not to critique US policy but to examine the influence of that policy in reshaping the Middle East and the role of faith, force, and finance therein. The focus will be on five countries that shaped the initial year of the War on Terror: Afghanistan, Iran, Israel, Iraq, and Saudi Arabia.

AFGHANISTAN AND THE RESTRUCTURING OF
BIN-LADEN'S AL-QAEDA NETWORK

The destruction of bin-Laden's headquarters and base camps began immediately following the 9/11 attacks on the United States. Bin-Laden fled Afghanistan, as did his terrorist army. Bin-Laden's Taliban hosts were crippled but not destroyed. This said, it was no longer they who controlled Afghanistan but the United States and allied troops.

It is tempting to say that force had trumped faith, but that would not be accurate. American force had destroyed the military base camp of al-Qaeda and crippled the Taliban's grip on Afghanistan, but the faith-based core of both al-Qaeda and the Taliban remained unscathed. It could well be argued that the faith power of both had been enhanced by the US invasion of Afghanistan.

Bin-Laden escaped from Afghanistan to become a Robin Hood–type of charismatic inspiration to aspiring Salafi-jihadists as he led the United States on an eleven-year cat-and-mouse chase throughout the Middle East and beyond. It was this core of inspired Salafi-jihadists, many of them graduates from his Afghan training centers, that bin-Laden used to restructure his terrorist network throughout the world.

The Taliban, in turn, used hostility fueled by the US-led occupation to launch a seemingly endless civil war against the US occupiers and the rapacious warlords put in place by the United States. The civil war was more tribal than religious, as many of the warlords that the United States put into power in the name of democracy were enemies of all but their own tribe. Tribal battles supported by the United States flared, while finance provided by the United States to its puppet regime became a base for flagrant corruption. Chaos reigned as battles between the United States and the Taliban took a horrendous toll on all sides.

The United States finally decided to talk to the Taliban rather than destroy it. In the meantime, the Taliban had established strong bases among supportive tribes and Salafi-jihadists in neighboring Pakistan, presumably a US ally albeit a favored hideout for bin-Laden. Bombs reigned on tribal areas suspected of harboring either al-Qaeda or the Taliban until the Pakistani government, fearing for its own security, put a damper on US force activities over which it had little control. Like it or not, the Taliban and the United States had made Pakistan another battlefield in the War on Terror.

In the case of both bin-Laden and the Taliban, a Salafi-jihadist leader had used US force to transform faith into terrorist force and direct that terrorist force against the United States and its allies. The message was clear. The War on Terror could not be won without dealing with faith in all of its varieties.

The Salafi-jihadist faith used by jihadist leaders to restructure their organizations in the aftermath of the initial allied strikes in the War on Terror was far different from the casual faith of the average Christian, Jew, or Muslim. As described below with great clarity by the "blind sheikh," who had orchestrated the 1993 attack on the World Trade Center:

Q. by Moderator: What did the Grand Sheikh Abdel-Rahman have to say about the truce declared in June 1997?

A. by Al-Zaiyat: They are youth who believe in who raised them. Only the Sheikhs of the Islamic Group can initiate actions. That is because of the deep esteem in which they are held by their sons (disciples), supporters, and admirers. It is much like a military commander gives orders to his soldiers. . . . It is not a military relationship. . . . It is spiritual. It is spiritual. . . . Maybe it is a relationship of love. It is a relationship of confidence. (Al-Zaiyat, 2002, NP)

The Salafi-jihadist only constituted about 4 percent of the Muslim population, but interviews following the 9/11 attacks indicated a pervasive satisfaction that Muslims had finally struck back against the United States. Most Muslims did not want to live under Salafi-jihadist rule.

Yet another type of faith confronting the War on Terror in Afghanistan was the intense faith that people placed in their tribe and tribal traditions. As elaborated in my *Arab Psyche and American Frustrations*, tribes are the basic social, economic, and security unit of most people in tribal regions. The Taliban were a religious movement, but they were also linked to the Pashtun tribes of Afghanistan and Pakistan. By attacking the Taliban, the United States was also attacking a confederation of Pashtun tribes. This overlap of tribal faith and religious faith was critical to understanding the bitter hostility of the Afghans to US forces. It is also vital to understanding the spread of the Taliban to Pakistan. It was this tribal-based faith that stymied US efforts to create a pro-American democratic government in Afghanistan. Tribal logic dictated that the newly empowered warlords who had been engaged in Afghanistan's civil war would use the force and finance that accrued to them to support their own tribes while crushing their adversaries, including the Taliban as well as Shia tribes on the Iranian border. By bolstering its puppet warlord government, the United States had declared war on the rest of Afghanistan. Casualties on all sides were horrendous as the United States bombed Taliban targets and the Taliban launched attacks on US troops in a nearly impenetrable terrain of peaks and narrow roads winding their way through valleys of death. Frustrated troops took their revenge as they could find it, including urinating on dead bodies and rape. All went viral throughout the Muslim world.

It was this combination of diverse faiths, Christian as well as Muslim, that bin-Laden used to restructure his global terrorist network after being forced to flee from Afghanistan by US forces. On the run and with his base camp destroyed, bin-Laden's role was transformed into that of heroic model, internet teacher, coordinator of terrorist groups, mocker of President Bush, charismatic spiritual leader, financier of terrorist groups, arms dealer, recruiter, propagandist, and defender of Islam against the American and Israeli crusade to destroy Islam. Bin-Laden's war was a psychological religious war that al-Qaeda launched to inflame Muslims throughout the world against the United States. Such was the price that the United States paid for allowing bin-Laden to escape from Afghanistan. The occupation of Afghanistan dragged on for eleven years before US troops withdrew, only to return. Force had disrupted faith, but it didn't destroy it.

After four years of frustration following their dispatch of Taliban rule in Afghanistan, the United States accepted the reality that it had been unable to crush the Taliban resistance. Faced with this reality, communications were opened with the Taliban, and efforts were made to regain the trust and confidence of the Afghans via massive reconstruction projects designed to compensate for the damage caused by the US-led invasion. It was also hoped that making Afghanistan a better place to live would overcome Afghani bitterness at the death and maiming of their loved ones. The reconstruction failed on both counts. US reconstruction efforts were described by Hillary Clinton, then secretary of state under the Obama administration, as "heartbreaking in their futility" (Kessler, 2009). The message was clear. The bitterness caused by force cannot be wiped away by finance. The winner and still champion was the Taliban and its ability to transform faith into force.

THE WAR ON TERROR EXPANDS INTO IRAQ

The invasion of Afghanistan had been dictated by the compelling logic of stopping bin-Laden before he could strike again. There was no compelling logic for the invasion of Iraq as a major goal of the War on Terror, only illusion and confusion.

The justification for linking the invasion of Iraq to the War on Terror, by contrast, was based on two illusions. The first illusion was based on flawed intelligence information indicating that Saddam Hussein had ties to al-Qaeda. The second illusion was that Saddam Hussein possessed weapons of mass destruction that could reach Israel and the oil fields of Saudi Arabia and the Gulf. This illusion was provided by Saddam Hussein, himself, as a bluff to deter an Iranian attack. Neither illusion passed the muster of a rigid examination by the CIA.

A bitter response to the Bush administration's blaming the Iraq war on flawed intelligence was provided by Raymond Close, former head of the CIA in Saudi Arabia, who equated intelligence to the metaphor of the gasoline that you put in your car. The gas doesn't tell you where to drive, it just helps you get where you want to go. The administration wanted to invade Iraq, and so they seized upon the first intelligence that they found to support their ambitions. Along the way, they created the term "actionable intelligence," a term that demanded immediate action by the administration. This, Close warned, turned intelligence into absolute truth with a capital T rather than data that required further confirmation before action was required. This did not happen in the case of Iraq (Close, 2004).

While the intelligence reaching the Bush administration was flawed, it did contain partial truths that would make it believable. Earlier intelligence reports about weapons of mass destruction, for example, had suggested that Saddam Hussein might use weapons of mass destruction against a US invasion. This was a warning for invasion forces, but nothing more (Close, 2004). This was feasible, for Saddam Hussein had earlier used gas to quell a Kurdish uprising. As discussed above, he had also boasted of possessing weapons of mass destruction. As noted in the preceding chapter, Turabi had boasted of good relations with both Saddam Hussein and Qaddafi while forging his international terrorist organization that was the predecessor of al-Qaeda. This didn't make Saddam Hussein a supporter of bin-Laden, but this slim partial truth was enough for an administration anxious to justify an invasion of Iraq.

With unsubstantiated intelligence and no clear plan for fighting the terrorist threat, an inexperienced and frantic president was easily swayed by partial truths about Saddam Hussein's weapons and intentions.

These illusions based on partial truths and questionable intelligence were perceived through the lens of a neo-con Bush administration known for the intensity of its conservative views on private enterprise, Christian morality, support for Israel, and a strong military. Even if the military, CIA, State Department, and United States' Arab allies had raised questions about the wisdom of invading Iraq, the illusions contained enough partial truths to trigger "what if" questions. What if Saddam Hussein were linked to bin-Laden's terror network, and what if Saddam Hussein did have weapons of mass destruction that could reach Israel, and what if bin-Laden had access to these weapons of mass destruction? Adding to the persuasiveness of the administration's "what if" fears were the neo-con illusions of what might be if the United States invaded Iraq. Bush's "axis of evil," consisting of Iraq, Iran, and North Korea, would be put on notice that the United States would and could destroy the evil of terror whenever and wherever it raised its ugly head. Iraq, the weakest country in the axis of evil, would be the easiest to defeat and would serve as a launching pad for the defeat of Iran, a far harder nut to crack. Oil would be secure and Iraqi oil would be controlled by the United States. If "what if" questions had been the stick propelling an invasion of Iraq, the "what might be" illusion was the carrot encouraging it. Such then were the fantasies created by the lure of partial truths and unsubstantiated intelligence.

The cruel irony of the Iraq war is that the United States won the war but lost an occupation that turned Iraq into a base for Salafi-jihadist and Shia terror. The occupation did this by turning Iraq into a cesspool of all of the causes of terror that have been discussed thus far. The initials ISIS stand for the Islamic State of Iraq and Syria. Those who would later decry the Obama administration's reluctance to invade Iran can thank the failures of the war in Iraq for their pain.

With this thought in mind, it might be useful to examine why the balance of faith, force, and finance went so terribly wrong in Iraq. Since more than six hundred books have been written on the war in Iraq, the comments will only focus on the major points to be weighed in fighting a war on terror that has become a tragic stalemate.

Force was the chosen weapon of the Bush administration in dealing with the threat of Saddam's weapons of mass destruction. There was no question that the United States possessed the force to defeat Saddam Hussein. The issues in question were how much force to use and when and how to use it. The memoirs of those in the commanding heights of the administration paint a grim picture of conflict and confusion. Confusion at the top of the administration invariably led to confusion throughout the lower echelons of the chain of command.

Faith entered the picture in a variety of ways. Christian Evangelicals were alarmed that America's failure to counter Saddam Hussein's threat to Israel would bring a curse on the United States for not standing by Israel. Some idea of this pressure is provided by Michael D. Evans, an avowed Middle East expert with strong ties to Israel, in his best-selling book, *The American Prophecies*. Among other things, Evans, the founder of the Jerusalem Prayer Team, to which hundreds of American religious leaders belong, writes, "There is absolutely no question that God's hedge of protection was lifted from America. September 11 was a curse on our beloved nation" (Evans, 2004, 14). The author went on to note that when the Iraqi war was at its lowest, President Bush defied his critics and stood by Israel (Evans, 2004, 263). The author found Bush's decision to be prophetic but was deeply alarmed by his soft treatment of Saudi Arabia and US arms sales to Arab countries.

The Evangelicals were part of a broader Israeli lobby that included the neo-cons, who viewed Israel as the hardcore foundation of US Middle East policy and various Jewish organizations headed by AIPAC. Mearsheimer and Walt conclude in their book, *The Israel Lobby*, that the Israeli lobby didn't cause the war, but they suggest that the war would not have happened without it (Mearsheimer and Walt, 2007, 230). No one seemed to know why President Bush made the decision to invade Iraq, but faith clearly ranked high on the list.

The administration also played the faith card during the invasion by calling on Iraq's Shia to revolt against their oppressor. The results proved disappointing, as the United States had failed to protect the Shia when they revolted during the first Iraqi invasion in 1991. The United States had called for the revolt, only to be a bystander to Saddam's slaughter of those who had placed their faith in US promises. Memories run deep in the Middle East, and this loss of faith in the American occupiers would pose an obstacle to Shia cooperation during the ensuing occupation of Iraq. Saddam was also aware of the Shia revolt during the earlier war and took no chances on a second Shia revolt during the second Iraqi war. Sunni soldiers shot any Shia remotely suspected of supporting the United States and asked questions later. The Sunni were no better off, for they were the primary targets of US bombing attacks leading up to the invasion.

This brings us to the role of faith, force, and finance in a failed occupation. Faith comes first because the United States was faced with the occupation of a country in the midst of faith-based civil war in which Sunni, Shia, and Kurds were fighting for their survival. None had faith in the United States. Even a nod to one of the three groups was sure to alienate the others. The Shia had strong faith ties with Iran, and soon there evolved Hizbullah-type extremist militias. Many of Saddam's Baathist killers, in turn, joined Sunni extremist militias. The picture was much the same among the Kurds who formed militias to stake their claim to the Kurdish areas of Iraq. Seeing that the Kurds were already revolting against the Turks, any US efforts to appease the Kurds threatened a crisis with its Turkish ally. One way or another, the United States found itself in the middle of a complex sectarian ethnic war of religion in which US troops were fair game to all of the combatants.

Lacking a positive faith solution to the dilemma that it found itself in, the Bush administration turned immediately to force to bring order to the country that it now ruled. Force, however, was a problem in itself. A long and bloody occupation that produced only American military casualties but little success would heap nothing but criticism on the US president. A positive force alternative had to be found.

And so it was. Illusion was used to turn "occupation," a negative image, into "transition to Iraqi rule," a positive image. American and British boots remained on the ground, but most of the dirty force was turned over to the private sector. The occupation that was labeled transition to Iraqi rule resulted in the United States employing nearly twenty thousand private contractors performing traditional military roles.

American mercenaries killed and pillaged at will, because no one was in charge or capable of holding them accountable—not the US government and not an illusionary Iraqi government hastily cobbled together by the United States in the name of democracy. If the use of force in Iraq had spawned faith-based violence against the United States, the impact of unregulated, privatized force produced even greater hostility toward the nation.

The picture with regard to the finance weapon was equally complex. The United States had hoped to use finance to ease the economic disaster caused by the war by rebuilding Iraq much as it was using finance to rebuild Afghanistan. The result was the same pageant of corruption and mismanagement, with many of the same US contractors involved. As a result, economic despair fueled violence and religious extremism throughout the battered country. Added to the woes of rebuilding Iraq were attacks on restoration projects by the competing Sunni and Shia militias that had emerged as a result of the war and ensuing occupation.

This assessment of the confusion caused by the invasion and occupation of Iraq is not that of this author, but that of the US government. One of the two major justifications for invading Iraq, for example, was to stop Saddam Hussein's support for bin-Laden and his al-Qaeda organization. As the National Intelligence Estimate for 2007 made starkly clear, the invasion of Iraq had precisely the opposite effect.

> Coalition forces, working with Iraqi forces, tribal elements, and some Sunni insurgents, have reduced al-Qaeda's (AQI) capabilities, reduced its freedom of movement, and denied it grassroots support in some areas. However, the level of overall violence, including attacks on and casualties among civilians, remains high: Iraq's sectarian groups remain unreconciled: AIQ retains the ability to conduct high-profile attacks. (US Government, 2007, 1)

In a similar tone, a 2006 Report to Congress, while praising the increased involvement of Iraqi security forces in controlling their country, lamented the "escalating violence in some of Iraq's more populous regions and the tragic loss of civilian life at the hands of terrorists and other extremists" (US Government, 2006, 1).

The same report placed the number of trained and armed Iraqi security forces at 433,600 but went on to note, "However, the trained-

and-equipped number should not be confused with present-for-duty strength. The number of present-for-duty soldiers and police is much lower, due to scheduled leave, absence without leave, and attrition" (US Government, 2006, 1).

ISRAEL AND THE WAR ON TERROR

Israel shaped the War on Terror triggered by the 9/11 attacks in so many ways that it is virtually impossible to sort them out. Even if it were possible, bitter debates would exist at every turn. This was very much the case in sorting out the role of Israel in the invasion of Iraq. What we do know is that the Israelis were candid in stating that Saddam Hussein was viewed as a threat to the security of the Jewish state, but did that threat exist in reality or was it an illusion?

Israel continues to shape the struggle against terror in diverse ways. Invariably, many of the same points will shape efforts to find a solution to the global crisis of terror and the role of faith, force, and finance therein.

The role of Israel in the War on Terror is not necessarily what Israel did in influencing the war in Iraq or encouraging the United States to attack Iran but the very existence of Israel. In the Arab and Muslim view, it was Britain that created Israel and it was the United States that sustained it with its arms and financial resources, with the objective of making Israel its base for controlling the Middle East if not launching a new crusade against Islam. To wit, Israel and the United States are one.

In this regard, it should be noted that the War on Terror is as much a psychological war as it is a ground war. The emotions swirling around Israel in both the West and the Muslim world are the core of psychological warfare in the War on Terror. They are also the basis of the propaganda cyber war that has surged to the fore in the psychological war for and against terror.

This is not to suggest that Israeli behavior has made things easy for US relations with the Islamic world. Particularly offensive to Arabs and Muslims are the gradual cleansing of Muslims from Palestine via settlement policies and the brutality of Israeli control over land allocated to Palestinian rule following the 1967 Arab-Israeli War. The Palestinians viewed this land as the foundation of a Palestinian state with Jerusalem as its capital. The Israelis viewed the Occupied Territories as a security threat that had to be controlled and as holy land required to make Israel whole. One way or another, every inch of Palestinian-ruled land was vital if not sacred to both sides. A new round of peace talks began at Camp David in hopes of resolving the three key issues separating the Israelis and the Palestinians: the final borders of a Palestinian state, the right of return for Palestinian refugees, and the status of Jerusalem.

The talks were futile and gave way to a prolonged struggle of terror and counter-terror that exploded into a full-scale war with the Palestinian uprising or intifada in September of 2000, approximately a year before the 9/11 attacks on the United States. While the Palestinians fought with terror, the Israelis fought with the latest US weapons, including tanks and US aircraft. So bloody were the Israeli attacks that the European Union accused Israel of using disproportionate force in the Occupied Territories and called on it to dismantle illegal Jewish settlements (Brown, September 20, 2001).

Force was clearly on the side of the Israelis, but the magnitude of that force was so great that it unleashed a hostile reaction to Israel in the West. This was all the more the case as Israel employed the finance weapon by imposing an economic boycott on the Occupied Territories. As a result, the EU complaints of excessive Israeli force were joined by UN warnings of mass starvation if the boycott continued. The United States sent the head of the CIA to try to calm things down.

The Israeli prime minister resigned, giving way to Ariel Sharon, a former general and advocate of force to make Israel whole. This change in the Israeli leadership from moderate to extremist was matched in the United States by Bill Clinton giving way to George W. Bush. Hard-line conservative leaders were now in control of both countries. A warm relationship between Sharon and Bush was bolstered by the neo-con philosophy of the Bush administration. Not only was Israel's special relationship with the United States intact but it had also been strengthened.

That was so until the 9/11 attacks on the United States. The Palestinian uprising was an embarrassment to the United States and resulted in a sharp warning to the Palestinian leadership "that they have no hope of renewing negotiations for an independent state until they take decisive action to stop terrorism and violence." Sharon was similarly warned to "swiftly end the suffering and humiliation of the Palestinians" (Brown, September 20, 2001, 11).

The dual warnings clearly indicate that the Bush administration was aware of the causes of terror and violence but had clearly placed the onus for the uprising on the Palestinians. The threat to the Palestinians was clear, but there was no threat to Israel—merely a slap on the hand to give the impression that the United States was an unbiased third party in the conflict. The Salafi-jihadists were delighted. The more Israel slaughtered Palestinians, the more Muslim hostility toward the United States would soar.

Sharon well understood this situation and in an interview with the *Jerusalem Post* stated, "I have made it clear to the administration as well as to a list of countries in Europe, that while the stability of the Middle East is important to them, and is very important to Israel, we will not pay the price for that stability. We will simply not pay it" (Brown, October 17, 2001, 10). He had earlier upset the White House by comparing US coalition building in the Arab world for its War on Terror with British appeasement of the Nazis in the 1930s (Brown, October 17, 2001, 1). The War on Terror continues, as does the role of the Israeli-Palestinian conflict in that war. So, too, do Israeli concerns about the reliability of Christian support for Israel when the chips are down. Faith is a powerful weapon, but in the War on Terror it may benefit the Salafi-jihadists more than it does the Israelis. Force proved counterproductive in Israel's fight against terror by pushing the United States and the European Union toward a two-state solution of the Palestinian conflict. The Israeli use of finance to starve the Palestinians into compliance also had the same effect. Christian and Jewish faith in the United States remain a vital force in sustaining Israel by force and finance, but will they keep Israel whole or will land be sacrificed for peace?

SAUDI ARABIA AND THE WAR ON TERROR

Saudi Arabia's role in shaping the War on Terror was perhaps more complex than Israel's, if that were possible. Both were vital allies of the United States that enjoyed special relationships with Washington. Israel's special relationship was based on faith while the Saudi special relationship was based on finance. The United States and its major allies were dependent upon Saudi oil and its vast arms purchases. This was all the more the case as the price of oil soared with the 9/11 attacks and the invasions of Afghanistan and Iraq. Both Israel and Saudi Arabia were considered vital for the War on Terror: Israel for its expertise in combating terror and its strategic location as a land-based carrier on the Mediterranean, and Saudi Arabia as a land-based carrier on the Persian Gulf with easy access to both Iraq and Iran. The difficulty facing the Bush administration was that Israel accused Saudi Arabia of financing Hamas and other Sunni extremist groups hostile to Israel.

The Bush administration was thus faced with a fascinating question. What was more important to the US administration and its War on Terror: the faith-based support for Israel's special relationship with the United States or Saudi Arabia's finance-based special relationship with the United States? Both, moreover, had been criticized for inflaming Muslim hostility toward the United States.

The case against Saudi Arabia was far more damning. Bin-Laden was a Saudi citizen. So were fifteen members of the 9/11 attacks. The Saudi royal family and wealthy Saudis, including the royal family, gave generously to the charities that funded al-Qaeda and other Sunni extremist groups. Banks in the Gulf, if not in Saudi Arabia, were widely accused of laundering money that found its way to al-Qaeda and other terrorist groups. Simultaneously, the Saudi education system propagated an extremist Wahhabi vision of Islam that was anti-American and xenophobic in nature. The same doctrine was spread through the world by Saudi outreach programs. Not surprisingly, the Saudi population was hostile to the war on Iraq. American use of Saudi bases for the Iraqi invasion posed a threat to the Saudi regime and would later be rescinded. All things considered, Saudi wealth and faith worked against the War on Terror, while the Saudis were reluctant to support the use of force by the United States and its allies in the invasion and occupation of Iraq.

Finance was the foundation of Saudi Arabia's special relationship with the United States. It was supported by fears of what would happen if Saudi weapons and holy places fell into the hands of the terrorists. Given the intensity of religious fervor in Saudi Arabia, this was a clear possibility. In a curious twist of faith and force, it was fear of how faith might transform Saudi arms and wealth into terrorist force that helped keep the Saudi special relationship with Washington alive. This threat continues.

Both special relationships tied the hands of the Bush administration in fighting faith-based terror by inflaming the very Islamic extremism and anti-Americanism that was fueling the terror. Like it or not, the War on Terror was becoming a war between Abrahamic faiths, with each of the United States' main allies in the region using its special relationship with Washington to block US policies that it opposed.

An ever-greater irony is that Iran, the sworn enemy of both Israel and Saudi Arabia, was strengthened by the War on Terror as it gained control of Iraq and extended its Hizbullah network throughout the region. In the process, Iran drew closer to Russia, pursued nuclear weapons, and developed long-range missiles capable of carrying those weapons if and when they were developed. Both Israel and Saudi Arabia pressed the United States to invade Iran, but the war in Iraq that was to facilitate that invasion was such a disaster that it made the invasion impossible by, along with the war in Afghanistan, totally exhausting the United States and allied forces. Forces in Afghanistan even complained that the war in Iraq had deprived them of the men and materials needed to successfully execute their mission of stamping out the Taliban.

LESSONS LEARNED

1. Special relationships impair the United States' ability to curb the policies of its allies that fuel terror.
2. Occupation promotes more terror than it eliminates. We have seen this in both the US occupation of Iraq and the intifada uprising in Israel.
3. Conflicting faith-based alliances intensify violence and lay the groundwork for more intense wars of religion.
4. Although faith, force, and finance were key weapons in the US War on Terror, both were double-edged swords that worked at cross-purposes. As a result, force promoted faith rather than crushing it.
5. America's allies in the Middle East are going to put their interests before those of the United States regardless of special relationships.

6. Force is not just about bombing and invasions. It is the problem of what comes afterward.

7. If the primary goals of US allies in the Middle East differ, it may be impossible to find the effective balance between faith, force, and finance required to fight terror.

8. Force is not compatible with reducing the intense interfaith hostility between Shia and Sunni sects.

9. Faith-based terror groups gain popularity and efficacy by attacking United States and Israeli forces stationed in the Occupied Territories.

10. Reliance on mercenaries to achieve force objectives is counterproductive, as the mercenaries are self-serving and lack discipline.

11. A fixation with force as a cure-all ignores social support for programs vital for stabilizing occupied countries.

12. Illusions based on partial truths are a poor substitute for hard data and substantiated intelligence.

8

THE ERA OF ISLAMIC RULE (2010–2013)

America's War on Terror relied heavily on its allies in the Middle East to lock down the terrorist groups in their countries by force. The United States provided the arms and finance as required. Because there was no shared definition of terrorism, each of America's allies in the region was free to use arms and finance to crush opposition groups of all varieties. Some were terrorists while others merely wanted democracy, human rights, and equality. As a result, US policy often made the oppressive regimes of the Middle East even more oppressive.

There seemed to be little cause for worry. All of the allies in question had been in power for twenty years or more with few storm clouds on the horizon. What was the danger of a little more oppression in an already oppressive region? If oppression, grinding poverty, despair, hopelessness, and the humiliation of Islam were the seeds of revolution and terror, the Arab world would have exploded years earlier.

The surge of Salafi-jihadist groups discussed in the preceding chapters should have been a warning of just such an explosion, but it was not. For all intents and purposes, the old order of tyrants and tribal kings was firmly in control.

Appalled by Arab docility in the face of oppression and foreign domination, the moderator of the Al Jazeera program *Opposing Views* asked the question, "Why are Arabs more tolerant of tyrants than any other people on the face of the earth?" (Qassem, 2010). This wasn't his view alone, for the question had earlier been posed to the program's viewers,

75.3 percent of whom agreed with the proposition that the Arabs were, indeed, the most docile people on earth.

No sooner had the Al Jazeera program aired than the Arab world erupted in rage as Arab youth poured into the public squares of Tunis and Cairo screaming for jobs, dignity, and justice. What a marvelous sight it was, with banners, chants, and inciters hoisted on the shoulders of their colleagues like the poets of old.

The explosion began in Tunis on December 17, 2010, when a fruit peddler was stopped by a female inspector as he hawked his apples. She seized his apples. He grabbed them back. She slapped him. A scuffle ensued, and he was beaten by two of her colleagues (Fisher, 2011). Other reports say the peddler was selling vegetables, but the results were the same. Angry and humiliated, the vendor demanded restitution from the local authorities who brushed him aside. His fruit gone and his honor destroyed, the vendor set himself ablaze in front of a public building. Less than a month later, mass protests would force Tunisia's president of twenty-three years and close ally of the United States to flee the country.

The suicide by flames could well have been written off as insanity if the humiliation and despair of the fruit peddler had been his alone. It was not. Other protest suicides followed throughout the region despite warnings by government clerics that the Koran banned suicide, as covered by most of the Egyptian newspapers that participated in the Arabic Press Consortium, El Journal. As the president of the Arab Federation of Psychiatrists noted, "Many people with no outlet for their own frustration, despair, and helplessness, understood how he must have felt and saw him as a kind of role model" (Okasha, 2011, 1).

Approximately six weeks after the Tunisian riots, it was the flames of Egypt, the emotional center of the Arab world, that electrified the Arab masses and sent revolution and violence spiraling throughout the Arab world.

Why did the Arab world explode in rage after decades of servility? The answer to this question will be debated for decades, but the key elements in the explosion are not hard to identify.

The despair of the Arab masses had transformed the Arab world into a vast tinderbox waiting to explode. All that was required was a spark. The explosion, however, was more than a matter of grinding poverty and a dismal future without jobs or any hope of a better life. It was also a matter of profound indifference on the part of the tyrants. Tribal kings and presidents alike believed that their security services and US backing could keep them in power forever. The uglier the public mood became, the more the tyrants retreated to their palaces while the security forces ran the country.

Ghazi al-Taube, a leading Al Jazeera commentator, stressed that the indifference of Arab leaders to the plight of the masses was nothing new (al-Taube, 2011). Arab leaders, in his view, had always been isolated from the masses. Some may have been more enlightened than others, but with the exception of the early days of Islam, there had always been a disconnect between the rulers and the ruled. Force and tyranny were the norm, not the exception. As a result, there simply were no mechanisms available for the masses to express their grievances other than protests and violence. The tighter the lid was sealed, the more mass hostilities festered until they exploded in violence. This was the case in the rage of 2011, much as it had been in the violent explosions that accompanied the era of Islamic resurgence. The contexts were different, but the root causes were the same (Palmer and Palmer, 2008).

What was new in the Arab Spring explosions was the steadfastness of Arab youth in the face of armed security forces firing live bullets, clubbing the demonstrators from horseback and camelback, and dragging female protesters away for virginity checks. The events were also covered in detail by the Arabic Press Consortium, El Journal.

The Arab Spring revolutions are better referred to as explosions because they had no identity, no organizational structure, and no ideology other than desperation and hopelessness. Nor, for that matter, did they possess a national identity or a religion. Wretchedness in the Arab world was pervasive and played no favorites. It was this wretchedness that provided a critical mass of people willing to stand firm against the tyrants. It had become their only hope. The dispossessed were nothing new in the Arab world. The new element was Facebook and other avenues of social networking. Suddenly, the dispossessed had found a way to share the intensity of their agony and humiliation. This gave birth to a new and powerful group that was referred to as the Movement of the Dispossessed, a term made famous by Mousa as-Sadr, a Lebanese ayatollah.

The Arab Spring prepared the way for rule of the Middle East by a new Islamic order, but no one was quite sure what kind of Islamic order it would be. Turkey had been ruled by the moderate Justice and Development Party with great success for the better part of a decade. Democracy and economic development had flourished, as had Turkey's efforts to join the EU. Egypt and Tunisia, having elected the Muslim Brotherhood to office in fair elections, were attempting to follow the Turkish model, and Turkey was doing its best to assist them. Saudi Arabia, in contrast, sponsored a global outreach program that preached an extremist Salafi doctrine of anti-Americanism.

Iran, for its part, continued to be an Islamic democracy that sponsored a global Hizbullah program. A much-battered Iraq claimed to be a democracy, but the country's dominant Shia population voted for leaders friendly to Iran, while the Sunni Iraqis were bogged down in tribal conflicts or joined Sunni extremist groups linked to al-Qaeda or the newly founded Islamic State of Iraq and Syria (ISIS). Syria, a predominantly Sunni country with the exception of its ruling Shia-Alawi tyrant, who was fighting for his life and the lives of his Shia-Alawi sect, had splintered into so many mainly religious militias that it was hard to keep score. Of these the most dominant and brutal was ISIS, the one that had proclaimed itself an Islamic caliphate. Israeli-occupied Palestinian areas were rapidly falling under the control of Hamas and the more violent Islamic Jihad. This was clearly the case in the Gaza Strip, but the situation in the West Bank was far from being resolved. Yemen, Libya, and the Sudan remained in a state of civil war with no end in sight. Algeria wasn't quite so chaotic, but a return to civil war against a variety of Islamic groups remained a distinct possibility. A revived al-Qaeda and ISIS were active in virtually all Sunni Muslim countries and used their bases in Syria, Iraq, Yemen, Libya, and other countries suffering from the turmoil of civil war to spread their venom throughout the region.

This impressive list of Middle Eastern countries ruled or partially ruled by Islamic creeds testifies to the power of Islamic faith in the region. Force and finance may have crippled Islam as a faith weapon from time to time in the past, but they clearly didn't eliminate it. The above list also testifies to the tremendous variety of Islamic rule throughout the region, a variety that ranges from forward-looking democracy and development in Turkey to the backward-looking extremism and violence of the Salafi-jihadist fanatics. Islamic unity, for all intents and purposes, had become impossible. Islam could rule, but it could not provide a unified front capable of applying the faith, force, and finance resources of the Muslim world to the goal of driving the United States and Israel from the region. Islam had become its own worst enemy.

This vast array of Islamic rule, then, was the picture facing the United States and its allies once the dust had settled on the Arab Spring of 2010–2012. The objective of this chapter is to illustrate the vastness of the differences between the diverse varieties of Islamic rule or partial rule and their relevance to America's War on Terror.

We begin by examining Turkey's Islam Lite, the most moderate form of Islamic rule in the Middle East, and then move to the Brotherhood's attempt to establish a moderate form of Islamic rule in Egypt. From Egypt we turn to ISIS's use of faith, force, and finance to establish itself as an Islamic caliphate destined to return the Islamic world to the pristine purity of the Prophet Mohammed's rule in seventh-century Arabia. The chapter ends with Iran's use of faith, force, and finance to expand its control over a larger portion of the Middle East. It also raises the question, which is most dangerous, ISIS or Iran?

ISLAM LITE: THE TURKISH MODEL

Since assuming office in 2002, Turkey's Islamic Justice and Development Party has built Turkey into the world's seventeenth largest economy, consolidated Turkish democracy, brought Turkey to the doorstep of membership in the EU, made Turkey a key player on the international stage, and established Turkey as the dominant Sunni power in the Middle East. The sick man of Europe has awakened.

This success was achieved by a program that blended Islamic morality, Turkish nationalism, economic liberalism, and secular democracy into a single package compatible with life in the twenty-first century. Added to the mixture is Recep Tayyip Erdogan, a leader whose charisma rivals that of Nasser. His followers called him "Papa" as he swept electoral victory after electoral victory by pitting the mass need for spiritualism against Turkey's legacy of military oppression. He has fulfilled this spiritual need by defending the right of Muslims to wear Islamic dress and pray when and where they saw fit. It is no different from the religious freedoms enjoyed by Americans, but his opponents, including Israel, have accused him of creeping Islam. It will not be long, they warn, until Turkey is turned into an Islamic state.

Israel was particularly alarmed because Erdogan also played upon Muslim emotions by opposing Israeli-US efforts to crush the Hamas government in the Gaza Strip and by defying the US blockade of Iran. All of this took place at the same time that he was vowing to cooperate with Israeli and American efforts to bring peace to the Middle East. The only caveat on these goodwill gestures was Turkey's dedication to protecting Islamic interests in the region.

Faith and force, in turn, were buttressed by Turkey's strengthening financial position and the prospects of joining the EU. As certified members of Europe, Turkish workers would have free access to the EU labor market, no questions asked. As the Turkish economy already prospered from remittances from Turkish workers in Germany, the larger EU labor market could well end fears of excessive Turkish unemployment.

The United States applauded the strengthening of a Turkish military that played a vital role in NATO's Middle Eastern activities. Turkey, as a Muslim country, was able to deploy troops in Muslim countries that found US troops abhorrent. Turkey's geographic position was also vital to NATO concerns in Eastern Europe and the newly emergent countries of the former Soviet Union. It was these force-based advantages that provided the foundation for Turkey's special relationship with the United States. US weapons poured into Turkey much as they poured into Israel and Saudi Arabia. Hopefully, from the US perspective, Israel, the Saudis, and Turkey could get along. Which special relationship would dominate US policy in the long run: faith, strategic force, or finance?

The end of the Arab Spring saw Erdogan riding a powerful crest of faith, force, and finance unprecedented in Turkish history. It is within his grasp to surpass Ataturk in the pantheon of Turkish heroes. This will surely be the case if he succeeds in rescuing Islam from the backward-looking doctrine of the Salafi-jihadist terrorists by making it relevant to the realities of the twenty-first century.

The success of moderate Islamic rule in Turkey has led both Arab and Western analysts to suggest that the Turkish model may be the solution to the United States' Arab woes. Turkey is selling the model, calling on Arabs to follow Turkey's path of pursuing Islamic morality within a secular political framework. Secularism promotes democracy and development, while Islam promotes morality and equity. The state is secular, but individuals are Muslims (No Author, *Hurriyet Daily News*, 2011). Turkish pundits have duly labeled the Turkish model "Islam Lite."

The Turkish model has refuted claims that Islam is incompatible with democracy, economic development, and modernity. As a result, many Arabs take hope that the Turkish model will serve as a model for Arab development. Turkish culture, they note, is very similar to Arab culture. Both were shaped by tribalism and Islam. While the fit isn't perfect, the Turkish experience in nation building is closer to the Arab experience than a model of development and democracy born in the British Isles. The Turkish leader also portrays the image of an Islamic leader with whom the secularists can live. Devout Muslims can have their headscarves, and more secular Muslims can have democracy and economic growth.

Religious and cultural similarities do not mean that the Turkish model is transferable to the Arab world. As an Egyptian analyst warns, the Arab revival is not a matter of this model or that. "It has to do with hard work to create economic prosperity. It has to do with the rule of law, clean elections and working to respect human rights even when strong prejudices are in place" (Amrani, 2011).

There are those, however, who worry that the Turkish model is merely a temporary stage that may eventually evolve into an Islamic state based upon Islamic law. Perhaps an ever-greater danger is the fear that Erdogan may use his powerful combination of religious faith, Turkish nationalism, and charisma to transform himself into an absolute dictator. A suspicious step in this direction was his sponsorship of a new constitution that transformed Turkey from a parliamentary republic, in which the prime minister and president were selected by the legislature, into a presidential republic in which the president was selected by popular election. The new constitution was approved in 2017 and Erdogan was elected president, a far more powerful position than he had occupied before. Along the way, Fethullah Gülen, a revered Islamic cleric who had worked closely with Erdogan in building the Justice and Development Party, accused him of becoming a dictator. The battle was joined and Gülen, now residing in the United States, was accused of plotting an attempted religion-based coup. Thousands if not hundreds of thousands of suspected Gülen supporters have been arrested or stripped of their government jobs. Erdogan has also demanded that the United States extradite Gülen to Turkey. The United States refused. US-Turkish tensions have increased apace as have differences over American support for Turkish forces in Syria and Iraq. Turkey's special relationship with the United States remains, but it is not the same relationship as before; firm cooperation between Turkey and the United States has seen this bitter personality conflict push Erdogan toward Russia and Iran. Once again, charismatic leadership could not accept competition. The United States was the victim. So was Turkey's model of moderate Islam.

EGYPT: WHY RULE BY THE MUSLIM BROTHERHOOD FAILED

Having swept to power in Egypt in the aftermath of the Arab Spring, the Muslim Brotherhood was well positioned to seize power throughout the Sunni Arab world. Not only was Egypt its international headquarters but the Brotherhood also possessed vibrant branches in all countries of the Sunni Arab world. Much as Egypt had been the centerpiece of Nasser's Arab nationalist quest for Arab unity, so the Brotherhood now intended to make Egypt the centerpiece of a moderate Sunni Islam compatible with the realities of the twenty-first century. The Brotherhood also had broader visions of Islamic unity that included ending the centuries-old rift between Sunni and Shia Islam. This was not at the top of the Brotherhood's wish list, but the Brotherhood saw little benefit for Muslims in the perpetuation of a centuries-old conflict that pitted Islam against Islam.

In this regard the Muslim Brotherhood might well be viewed as a middle ground positioned between Turkey's "lite" vision of Islam, on one hand, and the backward-looking Salafi and Salafi-jihadists, on the other. While the Islam Lite vision of Islamic modernity required Islam to work within a secular constitution, the Brotherhood in Egypt wanted secular modernity to work within the framework of an Islamic constitution.

The ability of the Brotherhood to achieve its goal of making its version of moderate Islam the dominant creed in the Sunni Arab world depended on its success in Egypt, the most dominant and influential of the Sunni Arab states and the home of Al-Azhar, the oldest surviving Islamic university and the most authoritative voice on Islamic doctrine. With the Brotherhood's control of Al-Azhar, its doctrine would become the official doctrine of Islam.

Optimism reigned, but the challenges facing the Brotherhood were so massive that the pundits of the era threw up their hands in despair and declared Egypt ungovernable. Abject poverty headed the list and gave way to a bankrupt and mismanaged economy with few resources. Economic woes led to rampant unemployment and an alienated population. Rectifying the situation would require a miracle as buildings collapsed, health care was inept, utilities were haphazard, and a failed education system turned out poorly trained graduates for which there were no jobs.

The social situation was no better. The gaps between the rich and poor were staggering, as was the unbridgeable tension between the traditional and modern segments of Egyptian culture. Not to be overlooked was a society fragmented along religious lines that pitted Muslims against a Christian minority.

Something resembling order was maintained by oppressive, hostile, and corrupt security forces over which the Brotherhood had no control. The security forces were supported by an equally corrupt and incompetent bureaucracy. It was this combination of oppression, incompetence, corruption, and greed that had fueled Egypt's Arab Spring.

Any hope that the Muslim Brotherhood may have had for solving the above problems was scuttled by the fact that Egypt's Muslim Brotherhood president reigned but did not rule. This paradox came about as the result of a fascinating struggle between faith and force for control of Egypt, neither of which was able to rule without the other in the chaos following the Arab Spring. Faith in this epic battle was represented by the Muslim Brotherhood. Force was represented by the Supreme Council of the Armed Forces (SCAF), which had seized temporary power to save Egypt from the chaos of the revolution.

What followed were negotiations between the Brotherhood and the SCAF for power sharing. The SCAF would allow fair parliamentary elections that the Brotherhood was the odds-on favorite to win, while the SCAF would win the presidential elections that followed. How could the SCAF lose when they controlled the same political organization that had returned Mubarak to office with a 90 percent majority for decades?

The deal held, and the parliamentary elections took place as scheduled. The Muslim Brotherhood, buttressed by the moderate Salafi, swept the parliamentary elections with 70 percent of the popular vote.

This led to presidential elections, which the Brotherhood contested, although it had vowed not to do so. The SCAF cried foul and used its control of the legal system to declare the parliamentary elections unconstitutional. The parliament was closed, leaving everything to depend on the presidential elections.

Both sides claimed victory in the presidential elections, but since the military counted the votes it was within the military's power to seize the presidency. Fear of the masses dissuaded the military from doing so, and the Brotherhood was proclaimed the winner. Had force lost its bite, or was the capitulation of the SCAF a strategy to buy time until the mass hostility of the Arab Spring had died down? The question will be discussed in the next chapter.

The reasons for the Brotherhood reneging on its deal with the military are twofold. First, the Brotherhood's control of a weak parliament would not enable it to pursue its moderate vision of an Islamic state. Only control of the presidency would give it complete power to pursue its political and religious objectives. Second, the Brotherhood well understood that the SCAF would never allow it to create a moderate Islamic state if the military controlled an all-powerful presidency. It was now or never. The Brotherhood had to strike while the iron was hot or face another decade of military oppression.

The Arab Spring had not destroyed the old regime. The Muslim Brotherhood needed to do just that if it were to transform Egypt into a moderate Islamic state. In addition to controlling the military and the police, it also meant controlling the legal system, the bureaucracy, the Islamic religious establishment, and the economy, all of which remained in the hands of SCAF, now the heir of the old Mubarak regime.

Added to the Brotherhood's priority list was assuring the revolutionaries that Egypt would be a democratic and just society free of corruption and oppression. It also meant convincing the United States and the EU that the Muslim Brotherhood intended to create an Islamic state on the Turkish model that strived to be a moderate member of the world community. This was not an easy task, given the deep divide in Egypt between those who embraced modernity and those who clung to their traditional ways and traditional faith. The more the Brotherhood pleased the modern segments of Egyptian society, the more it was likely to push the more traditional segments of Egyptian society into the hands of the quiet Salafi, if not the Salafi-jihadists.

Brotherhood rule during its brief term in office was remarkably democratic. The parliament could not be used as a symbol of democracy because it had been banished by the military. That left a free press, the right to demonstrate, and the free existence of political parties as the most visible standards of Brotherhood democracy. Having followed Egypt's Arabic press throughout the period of Brotherhood rule, I can certify that the press was free. Demonstrations of all varieties testified to the freedom of speech, as did the multitude of political parties vying for the attention of the public. Religion was also free, with Christians participating in the Brotherhood's ruling Brotherhood Party. The problem wasn't freedom of speech, press, and religion, but too much of it. I can only describe the press during the year of Brotherhood reign as bizarre and totally irresponsible, with any relationship between fact and reality being totally incidental. So much false news was circulating that it was impossible to tell one from the other. Protests and demonstrations careened through the streets of Cairo at will. Freedom of religion was even more lethal, as Salafi-jihadist parties seized upon Egypt's unusual freedom and took root in the Sinai Peninsula and many poverty-stricken areas. The nonviolent Salafi also turned on the Brotherhood, condemning its moderate vision of Islam as the work of the devil. Freedom from oppression, in turn, unleashed a crime wave. Some criminal groups adopted a religious persona to enhance their freedom of action.

The force problem was even more trying for the Brotherhood as the military demanded complete control over its own budget and the right to do whatever it considered necessary to preserve the security of Egypt. Military demands were tantamount to eliminating the role of the Egyptian president as the commander in chief of the armed forces. The Brotherhood president refused the military's demand and found himself without a force weapon capable of returning order to the streets.

In the financial sphere, the Brotherhood restored the subsidies on food, fuel, and other vital goods that had been cut by the Mubarak regime at the urging of the United States. This helped feed the poor but made the United States reluctant to provide the financial aid required to shore up Brotherhood rule. The United States had chosen to place economic theory above political realities in its use of finance to guide the future of the Middle East. It would be up to faith to keep the Brotherhood in power and set the stage for its control of the Middle East. Military force hadn't crushed faith rule by the Brotherhood, but it had clearly crippled it. Faith had failed to control the population that had put it in office. It had also failed to mobilize them to work and sacrifice to give the Brotherhood the success in Egypt that it needed to extend its rule throughout the Sunni Arab world.

THE ISLAMIC STATE OF IRAQ AND SYRIA (ISIS)

The proclamation of ISIS, the Islamic State of Iraq and Sham (historic Syria) on June 28, 2014, was one more step in the evolution of the Salafi-jihadist organizations that began with the splintering of the Salafi terrorists from the Muslim Brotherhood in the 1950s. They, as we have seen in preceding chapters, became the violent Egyptian Salafi-jihadists of the 1970s, the core of Turabi's unified Islamic network of the 1980s, and the foundation of bin-Laden's al-Qaeda networks of the 1990s and 2000s. Each step in this evolutionary chain was built upon and extended the experience of its predecessors and was fueled by increases in the causes of terror discussed throughout this book. As the causes of terror remain, there is every reason to expect that Salafi-jihadist terror will continue to surge as it builds upon the lessons of the past. With this thought in mind, we examine how ISIS will continue to pursue its objectives and how it differs from the al-Qaeda network of which it was a part. In addition to describing how ISIS operates, we offer insights into what the next trend in Salafi-jihadist terror may look like.

The emergence of ISIS as a Salafi-jihadist cult occurred in the aftermath of the US invasion of Iraq. It was joined by many officers from Saddam Hussein's defunct army, who shared the Salafi-jihadist goal of driving the United States from the Middle East. Saddam's officers also shared ISIS hostility toward the Shia, who had gained dominance in US-controlled Iraq. This lethal mix of faith and force blended well because Salafi-jihadist doctrine called for the elimination of sin from the world by force, and Saddam's officers were well versed in brute force. The next step in the development of ISIS was its swearing of allegiance to bin-Laden's al-Qaeda network, which was embracing a variety of Islamic states that had emerged in the chaos caused by the Arab Spring. In the case of Syria, bin-Laden requested its Iraqi affiliate to initiate a Syrian al-Qaeda affiliate to be known as the Nusra Front.

A situation thus arose in which the Nusra Front was simultaneously a branch of ISIS and an affiliate of the al-Qaeda network. But who was in charge, bin-Laden's successors or the newly appointed and soon to be self-proclaimed caliph of ISIS?

The conflict began over differing visions of how to run affiliate Islamic states in Iraq and Syria. Zawahari, who at the time was leading al-Qaeda, insisted that bin-Laden's principles of running an Islamic state be followed by ISIS in both countries.

Abu Bakr al-Baghdadi, the new leader of ISIS, was young, intelligent, ambitious, inexperienced, fanatical, impatient, unrealistic, and jealous of bin-Laden's authority. At every turn he violated bin-Laden's vision of building an Islamic state capable of driving the United States from the Middle East. The list, summarized below, was gleaned from a variety of works on al-Qaeda (AQ) and ISIS (McCants, 2015; Weiss and Hassan, 2016; Lister, 2015; and Palmer and Palmer, 2008). The list is not a quote, nor are the authors cited responsible for the list. I offer the list because bin-Laden's experience and domination of the Salafi-jihadist movement highlight weaknesses that could lead to the downfall of ISIS.

- Affiliate Islamic states are to follow instructions issued by AQ Central Command. All policies and major promotions are also to be cleared by the AQ Central Command as unity and coordination are essential for success. Conflicting and contradictory policies will lead to disaster.
- Affiliate organizations are to build a popular support base within their areas of operation. You need the support of the local populations, not their hostility.
- Affiliate organizations are not to take the next step of establishing an Islamic state unless they can defend it. Defeats are demoralizing and lead to a lack of faith in the leaders of the state.
- Affiliate organizations will lose control of the populations they rule unless they can provide for their basic needs in a just way.

Barring this, the fledgling state will face hostility, rebellion, and sedition.

- Don't attempt to rule a state of the dispossessed by force. Fear and frustration will lead to hostility, rebellion, and sedition.
- A return of the caliphate is premature unless it can be justified as the will of God and defended by force. The defeat of an Islamic caliphate would devastate the Salafi-jihadist image by demonstrating that it was premature and lacked God's blessing.
- The ability to defend a caliphate is infeasible at the present time because the United States and NATO can defeat any Muslim state that currently exists. They must be destroyed before an Islamic caliphate can be viable.
- Efforts to defeat the United States and NATO require Islamic unity, including alliances with the Shia. Shia-led Iran-Hizbullah forces are fighting the United States and NATO. Let them do it. We cannot achieve our goal of Islamic purity until the United States and NATO have been defeated.
- Don't attack oppressive Muslim leaders who have sided with the West. They are pushing people into the ranks of the Salafi-jihadists.
- Don't attack Shia who are fighting for a pure Islamic state. Let them fight for us. Alliances are useful.

From the al-Qaeda perspective, ISIS was failing on all counts. The proclamation of an Islamic caliphate by ISIS was the final straw in turning the two dominant Salafi-jihadist terrorist networks against each other.

The split between al-Qaeda and ISIS wasn't merely a matter of a youthful break with their elders but also a glaring difference in philosophy that returned to the splinter of the Salafi-jihadists from a Muslim Brotherhood during the 1950s. While the Brotherhood had preached a patient heart-and-mind strategy of preparing Muslims for an Islamic state through teaching, preaching, welfare, and politics, ISIS, like the breakaway Salafi-jihadists, focused almost entirely on violence as the means of inculcating Islamic doctrine, creating an Islamic environment by eradicating sin, and destroying treasonous leaders beholden to the West. Bin-Laden's philosophy was shaped during his Turabi years as well as through his realistic experience in dealing with the United States and Iran. Faith, force, and finance were weapons, but bin-Laden was also a realist who understood the need to deploy these weapons in the face of the overwhelming power of the United States and its NATO allies.

The philosophy of ISIS, for its part, was shaped by the writings of Sayed Qutb and later reinforced by Abu Bakr Naji's book, *Management of Savagery*. Both are a rejection of the calculated patience and gradualist approach of the Muslim Brotherhood and urge violence as the surest way to achieve a return to the Prophet's rule in seventh-century Arabia.

This philosophy was ready-made for Baghdadi, the self-proclaimed caliph of ISIS. He was a man in a hurry who had a pathetic hatred of Shia. His view of reality, in contrast to that of bin-Laden, was that the chaotic US occupation of Iraq and the subsequent turmoil in Syria created by the Arab Spring were God-given signs that the time for caliphate had arrived. Delay would merely result in the consolidation of US-NATO power and the apostate Shia control of both Iraq and Syria. In a curious way, al-Qaeda was seeking a middle ground between the Muslim Brotherhood's moderation and ISIS's fanatical extremism. Both had become al-Qaeda's competitors for the soul of Islam. The Brotherhood was moderate and nonviolent. ISIS was ultraviolent.

The continued existence of ISIS testifies to its success despite its reliance on force rather than bin-Laden's strategy of caution and patience.

The reliance on force didn't mean that force dominated faith in ISIS strategy. Rather, faith provided the foundation for force. Koranic prophecy was vital because it was an indicator that the Salafi-jihadist vision of Islam was the sure path to paradise, just as many Christians look to biblical prophecy for assurance that Armageddon will lead to salvation. According to the Koran, it was in Syria that the final battle of the end of time was predicted to take place, Palestine being part of Syria at the time. The Antichrist would set the stage, and Christ would play his role in preparing the way for the Mahdi (messiah). Particularly graphic in this regard were the Salafi-jihadist portrayals of the Antichrist provided by Jean-Pierre Filiu in his book, *L'Apocalypse dans l'Islam* (Filiu, 2008).

It is these assurances of salvation that provided the foundation for recruitment and intense indoctrination once foreign recruits reached

ISIS camps. In some portrayals, the Antichrist wore a star of David. In others, he was an American cowboy. Whatever the case, the United States and Israel were depicted as conspiring with the Antichrist.

Indeed, it was difficult to find a single dimension of the ISIS enterprise that is not founded on faith. The core of ISIS, like all Salafi-jihadist organizations, is a leader believed to possess a special blessing of God (baraka) that enables him to lead his followers to an eternity in paradise. Baraka is usually blended with personal charisma that compensates for the leader's lack of formal religious credentials. Baghdadi's rise to the leadership of ISIS was recommended by the ruling council following the decline of his predecessor and was duly approved by al-Qaeda. Baghdadi was intensely devout and possessed a doctorate in the Arabic language. Studies of the Arabic language, the language of God, are so interlaced with the Koran and related Islamic scriptures that the Arabic language's holiness is beyond question. Charisma followed; Baghdadi's success in expanding ISIS territory helped create an untouchable cult of personality, accompanied by his proclamation of the caliphate in 2014.

The new caliphate, however, was far more than a base camp for a spider network established throughout the world. It was to personify God's blessing of its leader by placing ISIS at the top of the Salafi-jihadist pyramid. The leader was not merely an iman but a caliph, the successor to the Prophet Mohammed. As such, he had become the absolute leader of Islam. Bin-Laden, for all his glory, would pale in comparison. Perhaps the leader of ISIS would become the new Mahdi. But first, he had to prove his baraka by miraculous works that could only be achieved by the grace of God. It is difficult to understand ISIS strategy and its violent use of force without understanding this goal.

The faith strategies of ISIS and related groups focus on efforts to convince Muslims that the United States and its allies, including Israel, have declared war on Islam. This strategy is designed to push Muslims away from the United States and into the hands of ISIS. It also allows ISIS and related Salafi-jihadist groups to pose as the defenders of Islam while portraying the Muslim kings and dictators as American puppets and traitors to Islam. This strategy is working because the Arab kings and tyrants are falling all over themselves protesting their holiness and support for Islamic causes. Their efforts garner more snickers than cheers, which is why the tyrants and tribal kings are so afraid of elections and a free press.

The effectiveness of ISIS and related Salafi-jihadist groups in convincing Muslims that the United States and Israel have declared war on Islam has also been very successful because it is supported by Christian and Jewish extremists who delight in fanning Islamophobia. Sadly, this process has become a burgeoning feature in the psychological war between the Abrahamic faiths.

ISIS and similar Salafi-jihadist groups use social media to target desperate and hopeless audiences with its faith message of hope, redemption, and salvation, and they are adept at knowing who these target audiences are and how best to reach them. Their success in this endeavor is manifest in the volume of their youth recruits.

Mosques and religious institutions are exploited by ISIS as part of its spider networks and indoctrination centers. In this regard, it is important to note that formal mosques are sponsored by the state, while informal or public mosques spring up in vacant storefronts and other innocuous places out of the public eye. These informal mosques are so prevalent and ever-shifting that they are difficult for government officials to keep track of. Additionally, ISIS has become remarkably adept at using the international media to provide it with more coverage than it could conceivably pay for. It is negative coverage to be sure, but what is negative in the West is testimony to the ISIS claim that the United States and its allies have declared war on Islam.

The emphasis on faith is not to suggest that the leader of ISIS wasn't dedicated to the core Salafi-jihadist strategy of using force to transform the Middle East into an idealistic model of the Prophet Mohammed's rule in seventh-century Arabia. Unlike the Muslim Brotherhood that views teaching and preaching as the path to an Islamic society, the Salafi-jihadists believe that this goal can only be achieved by violence. Only force can provide Muslims with a pure environment by driving the United States and Israel from Muslim lands. Only force can make Muslims act in an Islamic manner. Only forced indoctrination can make them believe in Islam. Force is justified by the need to protect and expand the Islamic faith.

Viewed in the context of the logic of violence, only attacks on Islam by the Christian and Jewish faiths can force Muslims to defend their faith by defending themselves. In much the same manner, outrageous terrorist attacks on civilian targets in the West are the only way that the Salafi-jihadists can retaliate for outrageous Western attacks on civilian Muslim populations. Also bear in mind that Muslims, like Christians, believe in Armageddon and the Second Coming of Christ, albeit with the proviso that Christ will ultimately step aside for the new Mahdi. How curious it is that Christians paint Muslims in the role of the Antichrist while Muslims paint Christians and Jews in that role.

Given the importance of force to the Salafi-jihadist mission, it must be expected that force will be utilized in a multitude of ways. For example, ISIS thrives in chaos. Therefore, it uses violence to keep the chaos going in Iraq, Syria, Yemen, Libya, Egypt, and wherever else it can use violence for expansion or to find easy targets to defeat the United States as a display of its power. Their use of violence allows them to play the role of Samson against Goliath. Samson and Goliath appear in the Koran, including Samson's plea for God's assistance against the more powerful giant. That giant, in ISIS propaganda, is the United States and its crusade against Islam. Remember, Muslims, Jews, and Christians worship the same God—*the* God.

Yet another key element in the ISIS force strategy is a perpetual game of cat and mouse that it plays with the United States and the EU. Whenever ISIS has suffered a defeat at the hands of a major power in the Muslim world, a more dazzling attack has soon been forthcoming in the West. This strategy has enabled ISIS to extend the playing field in its cat-and-mouse game from the Arab world to Europe and North America. The longer the game lasts, the bigger the playing field becomes, and the more Western media will publicize the power of ISIS, the more Islamophobia and fear will grasp the United States and Europe. Simply put, faith as viewed by the Salafi-jihadists could not survive without the use of force. Faith is the motivator and mobilizer, but force is the means to the end.

Finance is also part of the ISIS force strategy as it attacks the economic infrastructure of host countries to weaken their ability to resist further incursions from this group. This has also enabled ISIS to meet its financial needs by operating its own businesses, including oil refining and distribution centers. Some Islamic governments, including Saudi Arabia, have been accused of financing ISIS activities. Saudi Arabia has vehemently denied this accusation, but incredibly wealthy Saudi angels have a long history of supporting extremist groups. Saudi Arabia also views ISIS as a useful force weapon against Hizbullah. This strategy does not come free. Added to the above is a long list of money laundering, robbery, blackmail, abductions, and other criminal activities justified by faith.

It would also be remiss to suggest that ISIS doesn't try to take care of the basic needs of its own people. Well-cared-for fighters are provided with sex slaves. As for occupied populations, those that go along get along, as long as their faith parallels that of ISIS. However, only the pure of heart are likely to benefit from this rule.

The same basic principles apply to the tribes. Those that support ISIS are rewarded while those that oppose it are crushed. Youth were particularly problematic, for piety doesn't always compensate for the lures of modernity, as hard as ISIS might try to erase it from their minds.

As we have seen in the above discussion, ISIS has coordinated faith, force, and finance to expand its spider network throughout the world and to promote itself as Islam's defender in America's war against Islam. This topic will be reviewed at length in the final chapter of the book when we seek solutions to the present conundrum in the Middle East.

The key point to be made is that the techniques and strategies of the Salafi-jihadists have continually adjusted to the changing environment of the Middle East and the global technologies of faith, force, and finance. What has not changed is the Salafi-jihadist organizational model based on faith and its use of force and finance as means for achieving its goal of Islamic purity. If faith is strong, in the Salafi-jihadist view, force and finance will follow. It is also faith that enables Salafi-jihadists to survive the force and finance attacks of their adversaries, including the United States and Israel. Without faith, they are nothing.

IS IRAN A GREATER THREAT THAN ISIS?

Is Iran a greater threat to peace and stability in the Middle East than ISIS is? The answer to this question depends upon whom you ask. If you ask the Saudis and Israelis, the answer is an emphatic yes. Both see Iran as a clear and present danger to their existence. Both see ISIS as a dangerous, if temporary, weapon in the war against Iran-Hizbullah. If you ask the United States and Russia, the answer is less clear. While aware of the Iranian threat, both are more concerned about ISIS than they are about Iran-Hizbullah. This is evident in the fact that the United States and Russia are inclined to use Hizbullah as a force weapon against ISIS, a topic elaborated in the next chapter.

Perhaps a better way to answer this question so vital to the future of the Middle East is to compare Iran's capacity for achieving its objectives to that of ISIS, as outlined above.

Judging by its behavior, Iran's goals as it looks toward the future of the Middle East are a blend of faith, aspirations, fear, and opportunity, all of which are influenced by its leaders' perceptions of the environment swirling around them. As perceptions vary from individual to individual, changes of leadership in Iran often lead to changes in the flexibility of policies. When moderate clerics are in ascendancy, Iran can be quite flexible. This is not the case when conservative clerics are in ascendancy.

This said, the basic principles of Iranian policy have remained consistent since the era of the Ayatollah Khomeini. These policies start with the principle that Shia Islam is the true Islam. This principle renders sustained cooperation between Shia and Sunni Muslims virtually impossible. The key word is *sustained*, for Iran does have a long history of cooperating with Sunni groups, including al-Qaeda, when it suits its strategic interest. This explains why much of the chaos in Syria, Iraq, and just about everywhere else pits Sunnis against Shia at the same time that Iran supports Sunni groups in the Israeli Occupied Territories and plays al-Qaeda against ISIS (Moghadam, 2017).

From this principle follows the belief that Sunni Islam is attempting to destroy Shia Islam. Iran, accordingly, must constantly be on the defensive against Sunni attack. The most immediate threat is the Saudi monarchy and ISIS.

The same logic dictates that Iran, as the largest and most powerful Shia country, must defend Shia Islam against Sunni aggression wherever it occurs. Saudi Arabia's blatant persecution of the predominantly Shia population in its oil rich Eastern Province is particularly irksome to Iran. By Iranian logic, the oil of the Eastern Province is Shia oil that had been stolen by the Saudi monarchy. Given this logic, Iran must reclaim the Shia Eastern Province from the Saudis. This is a matter of faith, but it is also a matter of finance. Iran feels much the same way about Iraq. Not only is 60 percent of the Iraqi population Shia but much of Iraqi oil is in the Shia areas. The Kurds also claim Iraqi oil, which makes things particularly sticky.

Protecting Shia Islam, from the Iranian perspective, requires the unity and coordination of the Shia faithful. Iran, accordingly, ardently pursues the goal of establishing a Shia crescent stretching from Iran to Lebanon. If Iran has its way, this crescent will include Iraq, Syria, and the predominantly Shia area of Saudi Arabia, the Persian Gulf, and Yemen. A dream, perhaps, but this policy is obvious in the strong ties between Iran and Shia leaders in Iraq, Syria, Lebanon, and Yemen, most of which are involved in civil wars supported by Iran. The Gulf sheikhdoms also accuse Iran of fomenting turmoil among their Shia populations.

Faith, force, and finance are all powerful assets available to Iran in its efforts to achieve its dream of Shia control of a swath of states encircling Saudi Arabia and Israel. Faith is the most important because it has enabled Iran's Shia clerics to control the government and create a faith-based security apparatus that includes the Basiji and the Republican Guards. Like much of the Gulf, Iran's economy is oil-based, which provides it with a capacity to meet the basic needs of its population and to fund a vast Hizbullah network that spans the area charted to become the Shia crescent. Oil revenues also enable Iran to purchase Soviet weapons, including nuclear reactors, and to develop rockets capable of hitting Israel. According to the Israeli press, these rockets are powerful enough to carry nuclear warheads if and when they exist. Hizbullah Lebanon is reported to have thousands of Iranian rockets strategically located on the Israeli border. Beyond question, Iran possesses the rockets to destroy the oil fields of Saudi Arabia and the Gulf kingdoms. This means that one attack on Iran by the United States or Israel would result in the Saudi oil fields going up in flames. The Saudi monarchy would not be far behind.

In addition to developing its own force capacity, Iran's ruling clerics have been skillful in forging force alliances with Russia, a strategy that has added the threat of a Russian entanglement to any US strike on Iran. While the Russians are not enamored with a nuclear Iran, they are also involved in a proxy war with NATO for control of both the Middle East and Eastern Europe. Iran is a key player in the Middle East, which could be a Russian bargaining chip for NATO concessions in Eastern

Europe. Similar implicit alliances have been made with Qatar, the Saudi nemesis in the Gulf, and Turkey, a powerful advocate of Israeli withdrawal from its Palestinian occupied territories. Particularly worrisome to the US-Saudi-Israeli block hostile to both ISIS and Iran has been the emergence of a Russian-Iranian-Turkish block that is hostile to ISIS but not to the Shia. This same force bloc has been supportive of moderate Islamic rule based on the Turkish Lite–Muslim Brotherhood model that is anathema to Saudi Arabia, Egypt, and other authoritarian countries in the region.

The link between faith, force, and finance in the Iranian case, however, is far greater than guns and rockets. Faith is also a matter of dedication, motivation, and organization.

What makes faith such a powerful weapon in the Iranian arsenal is the push-pull combination of tradition, indoctrination, and oppression. Key to Shia traditions is the ritual mourning for the treacherous assassination of Ali, the fourth caliph successor of the Prophet Mohammed. Shia traditions are a pageant of suffering and sacrifice reinforced by a religious content that directs this emotional outpouring toward the purification of the world in preparation for the return of the Hidden Imam. This tradition of suffering and clerical indoctrination has produced a dedication that makes Shia forces exceptionally motivated fighters. This was demonstrated in Khomeini's war with Iraq during the 1980s and Israel's difficulty in defeating Hizbullah forces in Lebanon. Reinforcing Shia traditions and dedication to their faith is a continuing legacy of oppression and deprivation at the hands of Sunni leaders. Faith and tradition pull Shia toward Iranian leadership, while oppression and deprivation by Sunni leaders reinforce Shia dependence on Iran for their survival and the survival of their faith.

Iran's vast military establishment is led by clerics and headed by the Elite Revolutionary Guards. At the bottom of the control pyramid, as we have seen in earlier discussions of Iran, are the Basiji, who control the countryside and support the higher-level clerical security forces. Collectively, the clerical security forces provide the force required to achieve Iran's clerical goals. They also provide a vivid example of the ability of faith to control force.

This does not mean problems don't exist. The Revolutionary Guards, in particular, have become so powerful and influential in the political and economic spheres that their authority may challenge that of the clerical elite. Popularly elected presidents, while vetted by the senior religious elite, have also demonstrated an independence that has forced the hand of the clerics on policy issues. Perhaps the best case of this was the reign of the hyperfanatic former mayor of Tehran, whose zeal in enforcing religious law and pursuing religious objectives made him a charismatic hero among the extremists while pushing the moderate clerics into revolt. The reverse of this process had occurred years earlier as a moderate president attempted to soften the enforcement of Islamic law and ease conflict with the United States and its allies. The division between extremists and moderates continues to widen as Iranian youth have become increasing restive under rigid Islamic rule while the rural areas remain wedded to hardcore Islam.

Conservatives and moderates differ on the degree to which Iran should bend to the realities of international politics. While moderates may bend, the conservatives are intent on pushing their religious goals to the limit.

Ironically, the Ayatollah Khomeini had encouraged the tensions between the moderate and extremist clergy to consolidate his power in founding the Islamic Republic. That policy has now come back to haunt Iranian policy making. Moderates want to promote Iran's core goals by negotiation. The extremists are locked into force. This gap between moderates and extremists may be cataclysmic if Iran does acquire nuclear warheads to place on its arsenal of long-range rockets.

This places the United States and NATO in a curious situation in dealing with an Iranian Islamic Republic whose regional objectives are constant and political system is stable but the direction of its relations with the West are constantly shifting as a result of shifts in the Iranian clerical elite. Adding to the confusion is the pulsating threat from the Saudi-Israeli alliance, the Russian uses of its Iran card in its revived cold war with the United States, and the ability of ISIS to establish a viable caliphate hostile to Iran and Shia Islam in Iraq and Syria, the core of Iran's idealized Shia crescent.

LESSONS LEARNED

1. Virtually all conflicts in the Middle East soon take on religious complexions.

Faith has to be constantly reinforced.

The force of a single country can be muted by the force of competing alliances.

The Arab Spring was a warning sign that ISIS is unlikely to be the last link in the evolutionary chain of the Salafi-jihadists unless the causes of the Arab Spring are addressed.

The major Salafi-jihadist organizations can be pitted against one another based upon competition over leadership.

Youth were prime recruits for the Salafi-jihadists, but occupied youth often inclined toward hostility against piety imposed by force.

9

THE OLD ORDER STRIKES BACK (2017)

The outlook for the Middle East that the United States and its allies faced with the advent of the era of Islamic rule was bleak. The old order in Egypt and Tunisia had given way to rule by the Muslim Brotherhood, a powerful moderate Islamic organization that threatened to dominate the entire Sunni Arab world. More frightening was the soaring terror spawned by ISIS, al-Qaeda, and various allied Salafi-jihadist groups. Iran was pursuing nuclear weapons en route to establishing a Shia crescent that threatened to choke Israel and Saudi Arabia. Syria, Libya, and Yemen had dissolved into civil war among a multitude of factions, many with links to the Salafi-jihadists and the Muslim Brotherhood. Wars of religion between the Abrahamic faiths beckoned, as did proxy wars between the United States and Russia. Even the Chinese were meddling in the troubled waters of the Middle East.

The US solution for coping with the era of Islamic rule was the creation of a new Middle East forged by an alliance of its regional allies. This was the central thread in America's case-by-case responses to the endless series of Middle Eastern crises spawned by the era of Islamic rule. Case by case, as former secretary of state and presidential candidate Hillary Clinton was fond of saying, was how the United States responded to crises in the Middle East. This was a strange way to operate in an intensely interconnected region, but how else could the United States function when it had so many special relationships in the region?

The four key members in the US alliance for a new Middle East were Turkey, Saudi Arabia, Israel, and, potentially, Egypt. Each had long enjoyed a special relationship with the United States, yet each was pursuing policies that the United States criticized as being averse to the creation of a new Middle East of peace and security. Each, moreover, had a different vision of what the new Middle East would look like and how the new Middle East was best achieved by diverse combinations of faith, force, and finance.

The choice of when, where, and how to use faith, force, and finance to bring peace and stability to the area was not the United States' alone. Each of the Middle Eastern members of the alliance for a new Middle East had its own ideas on the topic, as did the countries of the EU, Russia, and China. This, then, is the story of the present chapter. We begin the discussion with the United States, the lead player in efforts to build a new Middle East of peace and stability, and then move to the key members of the US alliance, including Turkey, Israel, Egypt, and Saudi Arabia.

THE UNITED STATES FORGES AN ALLIANCE OF PEACE AND STABILITY TO BUILD A NEW MIDDLE EAST

The US strategy for confronting Islamic rule centered on attacking the Salafi-jihadists and Iran-Hizbullah organizations spewing terror at the same time that it forged a new Middle East of peace and stability. It all seemed logical enough. The launching pads of the terrorists would be destroyed while a new Middle East forged by American allies in the region would prevent their return. The United States' NATO allies, major targets of the terrorists, would pitch in and do their part in assuring both the destruction of the Salafi-jihadist terrorists and the creation of a new Middle East.

The simplicity of the American plan was an illusion because the ISIS terrorist cells to be bombed were scattered throughout the region and were paralleled by a growing number of revived al-Qaeda groups and Taliban organizations. Hizbullah branches were active wherever sizable Shia populations were to be found, including the EU. It didn't mean that they were terrorists but merely potential terrorists at Iran's beck and call. Presumably this included groups allied with the US-sponsored

Shia government of Iraq. Was the Muslim Brotherhood a terrorist organization? Not really. Only those who feared its moderate brand of Islam considered the Brotherhood a terrorist organization. As every country had its own definition of terror, the list of groups guilty of terror increased each day. What all this boiled down to was the need for the United States to attack terrorist countries as well as terrorist groups. Iran was clearly a terrorist country, as were Yemen and Libya. But what was a country? Were Palestine and the Islamic caliphate established by ISIS countries? This was a tricky question, for it had much to do with international law.

The American plan to eliminate terror and create a new Middle East involved a pallet of force, faith, and finance so complex that it would take volumes to describe in detail. In line with its foreign policy, the US government responded on a case-by-case basis.

Force was the main weapon in the US arsenal as it bombed ISIS, al-Qaeda, and Taliban targets in Pakistan, Yemen, Libya, Syria, and Iraq, among others. But to what avail? Bombing alone, as US generals admitted, was not adequate to destroy ISIS and al-Qaeda operations. American and allied troops would have to fight pitched battles on the ground to dislodge ISIS from their base camps. That, however, was only half the battle, because US and allied troops would have to stay on the ground to prevent a return of ISIS militias. Once again, the United States had found itself in the costly and lengthy occupations it had hoped to avoid. American casualties increased, as did a staggering number of civilian casualties that had nothing to do with terror. Was the United States bombing the terrorists or was it bombing the victims of terror? The United States had fallen into the Salafi-jihadist trap by killing innocent Muslims. As we have seen in the preceding chapter, there would have to be retribution.

Iran, the archenemy of Israel and Saudi Arabia, by contrast, was attacked by finance as economic boycotts attempted to stop its pursuit of nuclear weapons by squeezing its economy.

Faith entered the picture as both Christian and Jewish groups continued to stimulate large aid packages to Israel. That, however, was only the tip of the faith iceberg shaping American policy in the region. As noted above, the United States had become increasingly alarmed that its attacks on terrorist targets would strengthen extremist claims that the United States had joined Israel in a war of the Abrahamic faiths.

Excessive US force threatened the Saudi use of the faith weapon as the Salafi-jihadists and the Iranians mocked the monarchy for pretending to be the defenders of Islam at the same time that they were helping the United States and Israel kill Muslims. The United States' use of faith became even stranger as it experimented with using Shia militias in Iraq to fight ISIS. What did the United States gain by training and arming Shia militias hostile to Saudi Arabia and Israel? America, it seemed, couldn't win for losing.

At the same time, Russia had stepped up its efforts to rebuild the old Soviet empire by threatening Ukraine and its Balkan neighbors. The EU and NATO became increasingly nervous and prepared their military for a war against Russian expansion. The Germans had made strident efforts in this direction that also created a twinge of concern in the EU. How was the US military, for all of its might, to cover the breadth and width of the Middle East and prepare to stop a Russian advance into Western Europe? Not to be left out, the Chinese were making expansionist moves in East Asia. The United States was faced with a choice between stopping Russian and Chinese expansion or stopping extremist terror.

The US policy also produced a number of unexpected twists, the most tragic of which was the crisis of millions of Muslim refugees created by the combination of terror and the force-based response of the United States and its allies. Next in the line of unexpected twists came the plague of Islamophobia in the United States and the EU. Islamophobia stimulated Christian and Muslim fear, and fear stimulated religious violence. It was a vicious circle. Once again, ISIS was getting its wish of a war between the Abrahamic faiths. Jews, too, were the victims of this insane war of religious hatred. So much was this the case that an Israeli cabinet minister warned the Israeli government to be prepared for a mass influx of American Jews fleeing a country long viewed as a safe haven from the anti-Semitism sweeping Europe.

How, then, did the United States' Middle Eastern allies in the old order strike back at Islamic rule, and how did they fit into the dream of a new Middle East of peace and stability? It is to these questions that we turn in the remainder of the chapter.

TURKEY AS A LINK BETWEEN THE PAST AND PRESENT

Turkey's role in the old order of the Middle East was that of an Islamic stabilizing force that kept the Soviet Union at bay during the Cold War and provided logistic support for the US invasions of Iraq and Afghanistan during the War on Terror. Turkey would have to continue to play a critical stabilizing role if there were to be a new Middle East of peace and stability.

What makes Turkey so vital to the American dream of a new Middle East free of terror and violence is Turkey's unique combination of force, faith, and finance. Force is vital to forging a new Middle East because Turkey, a member of NATO, possesses the most powerful army in the Islamic world.

As Russian expansionism and terrorist threats remain, so does the United States' special relationship with Turkey and the continued strengthening of the Turkish armed forces. There can be no effective US alliance for building and enforcing a lasting peace and stability in the Middle East without Turkish participation.

Turkish armed forces are all the more critical to forging a new Middle East of peace and stability because Turkey's Islamic faith enables it to fight Salafi-jihadist terrorist groups without precipitating images of a new crusade. Other faith advantages also abound. Turkey's blend of Islam, democracy, and modernity is a powerful faith weapon capable of countering the harsh vision of the Salafi-jihadists. Not to be ignored is the Turkish background of many of the former Islamic republics of the former Soviet Union. They, too, may have much to say about the nature of a new Middle East. No other members of the alliance possessed this combination of faith and force compatible with the American dream of creating a new Middle East.

Turkey had little to offer in the area of finance, but that deficiency could be addressed by other projected members of the alliance, Saudi Arabia in particular. Turkish hopes of joining the EU also offered hope for the increased prosperity of Turkey. Whether or not Turkey's membership in the EU materializes, its importance as a stabilizing force in the Middle East assures continued US financial and military aid. It will also provide Turkey with a strong voice in the shaping of a new Middle East.

The Turkish vision of a new Middle East featured Turkey as the industrial and political core of a Middle East ruled by the Turkish model of democratic Islam compatible with the twenty-first century. Steps in this direction included active Turkish support for rule by the Muslim Brotherhood in Egypt and Tunisia. Turkey was and is also an active supporter of Hamas rule in the Gaza Strip and of an independent and sovereign Palestinian state that includes the West Bank as well as the Gaza Strip. So vigorous was the Turkish leader Erdogan in supporting this vision that Turkish pundits accused him of wanting to revive the Ottoman Empire. Islam, in the pundits' view, was being blended with popular support to boost the charisma of the Turkish leader.

The merit of the Turkish vision of a new Middle East is that it provides a tested version of fighting the extremist faith of the Salafi-jihadists. It does so by promoting a moderate democratic version of Islam capable of meeting the spiritual and economic needs of Muslims in a modern framework that avoids the oppression and despair that had caused the Arab Spring and the subsequent surge of extremist terror.

Turkey's military has also been involved in crushing ISIS and other extremist groups in Syria and elsewhere in the Muslim world. This of itself has reduced the stigma of Christian and Jewish troops inflaming Muslim emotions in the region. Those who would downplay the importance of avoiding Christian and Jewish affronts to Islam need only recall the crisis caused by the publication of Dutch cartoons mocking the Prophet Mohammed that triggered months of riots the length and breadth of the Muslim world. Subsequent attacks on the Prophet Mohammed in French magazines resulted in terrorist attacks on the personnel of the magazine in Paris. All spoke of a new crusade against Islam to a hypersensitive Muslim audience.

While not a rich country, Turkey pursued efforts to join the EU, a union that would stimulate its economy and open avenues of cooperation between moderate Islamic governments and both the EU and the United States. The Turkish message to the United States and the EU was simple. If you want your economic and social policies to shape the future of the Middle East, incorporate the Middle East into your global structure. Turkish membership in the EU offers the first step in that process.

What Turkey offered the US alliance for peace and security in the Middle East also posed to the American dream of a new Middle East an almost insoluble set of problems. Turkey's utility in countering Islamic faith with a moderate democratic Islam was countered by two conflicting forms of faith: Turkish nationalism and Erdogan's efforts to protect and extend the power of his charisma.

Turkish force came to the fore with the use of its military to crush a Kurdish rebellion that had festered for decades in Turkey only to explode in Syria and Iraq in the aftermath of the Arab Spring. The Kurdish revolts in both Turkey and Syria were fueled by the American withdrawal from Iraq that enabled the Kurds to establish what was for all intents and purposes a Kurdish state in northern Iraq. The Kurdish rebellion in Syria and Iraq paralleled the expansion of ISIS in both countries. The Turks were more concerned with the Kurdish threat than the ISIS threat, and Turkish troops attacked the Kurds in both Iraq and Syria to prevent the creation of a Kurdish state that extended from northern Iraq to southern Turkey. There were even accusations that Turkey was using ISIS to fight the Kurds.

As if the above problems weren't complex enough to stymie US efforts to create a new Middle East, the other key players in the American alliance for peace and stability in the Middle East were vehemently opposed to Turkey's vision of what a new Middle East should look like. Turkey, aware of this reality, countered by strengthening its ties with Iran and Russia, each of which had a vision of a new Middle East that didn't include the United States.

ISRAEL STRIKES BACK AT THE NEW ISLAMIC ORDER

The replacement of the old order in the Middle East with a new Islamic order found Israel surrounded by armed Islamic militias on all sides, including the Israeli Occupied Territories within Israel itself. Terrorist attacks on Israeli targets were frequent, as were brutal Israeli responses. Many of these responses focused on the destruction of Palestinian homes. Others took the form of punitive financial boycotts that prevented food, medicine, fuel, and other vital materials from reaching the Occupied Territories. Military campaigns in Gaza, such as Cast Lead, were exceptionally brutal.

The use of faith to justify the violence of Israeli reprisals tore the Jewish world apart. A minority of Israeli soldiers refused to fight, in the name of Jewish religious and humanitarian values. Israeli organizations condemning the brutality of Israeli reprisals made a point of feeding the gory details to the global press.

The brutality of Israeli reprisals also raised questions about the utility of force and finance in maintaining control of the Occupied Territories. Force didn't stop the violence in the Gaza or in Syria's Golan Heights. There were two responses to the Israeli maximum force policy. One response was that things would have been worse without the brutality. The contrary view was that the harshness of Israeli force in crushing Palestinian resistance to Israeli occupation had been manifestly negative. The resistance appeared to increase while external support for Israel gave way to increased demands for granting independence to the Occupied Territories. It also resulted in demands that Israel be tried for crimes against humanity by the World Court. These and the United Nations' condemnation of Israel were blocked by the United States but had an adverse impact on Israel's long-cultivated image as a peace-loving country. Rather than a brave Samson, Israel had become Goliath. This of itself was an Israeli defeat in the psychological war for the Middle East. The chain of the negative consequences for Israel's excessive use of force has continued with global Jewish complaints that the Israeli policies are placing Jews at risk. This clearly is the position of the J-Street Jewish Lobby that emerged to counter AIPAC's support for Israel's iron-fisted control of the Occupied Territories.

As mentioned earlier in the book, the Palestinian issue is a matter of land—holy land. A far more dire challenge to Israel's security is that posed by Iran and its Lebanese Hizbullah subsidiary. Both have heavily armed rockets focused on Israel. Although a less immediate threat, ISIS and al-Qaeda also lurk on Israeli borders in Yemen, Lebanon, Syria, and Egypt's Sinai Peninsula.

Israel's defenses focused on helping the United States forge a new Middle East by establishing a strong cooperative relationship with both Saudi Arabia and Egypt. Turkey, as we have seen, remains problematic, as do US demands for an end to Israeli settlements and a land-for-peace solution to the Palestinian problem.

Israel has also made a point of helping groups at odds with Iran, not the least of which are Kurdish militias attempting to forge an independent Kurdish state that would stretch from northern Iraq to a large Kurdish enclave on Syria's Turkish border. The Israelis similarly offered aid to Christian groups in the southern Sudan that were rebelling against the Islamic ruler of that country. Beyond question, these policies disrupted Islamic rule in the affected countries. They also had predicted consequences such as intensified Turkish attacks on the Kurds in both Iraq and Syria. This of itself made it difficult for Israel and Turkey to cooperate in the formation of a new Middle East, as did Turkish support of Hamas rule in the Gaza Strip. Caught in the middle between two special relationships, the United States experimented with using both Kurdish and Hizbullah-type Iranian-supported groups to fight ISIS. Neither Turkey nor Israel was amused.

Israel had the most to lose, for having lost a war to Hizbullah in southern Lebanon, Israel was vitally dependent upon US support in crushing Iranian military expansion in Syria, Lebanon, and Yemen. This was all the more the case following the United States' lifting of its economic boycott of Iran that had been established in response to Iranian development of nuclear energy. Making matters worse was the developing Iranian, Turkish, and Russian alliance dedicated to the creation of a new Middle East.

EGYPT: THE UNITED STATES DECLARES COUPS THE FIRST STEP TOWARD DEMOCRACY

Egypt's Arab Spring and subsequent rule by the Muslim Brotherhood gave the United States two choices. It could follow Turkey's advice and give moderate Islamic democracy a chance to destroy Islamic extremism, or it could follow Saudi advice and keep the Muslim Brotherhood from taking over the Arab world.

While the United States dithered, the Mubarak generals seized power. The military's counterrevolutionary strategy was simplicity itself. First, the military sabotaged Brotherhood efforts to meet the demands of the masses for food, jobs, security, and everything else that had fueled the overthrow of the old regime. This task was relatively easy, for as mentioned in the preceding chapter, the generals remained in control of the military, police, bureaucracy, judiciary, economy, and religious establishment. Food, fuel, electricity, and law and order suddenly vanished. It was less of a conspiracy than each branch of the old regime doing its best to scuttle a common enemy.

This task accomplished, the generals blamed the Brotherhood government for the reign of chaos and launched a hate-fear campaign by accusing the Brotherhood of attempting to transform Egypt into an Islamic caliphate. Secular liberal groups led the charge with a smear campaign accusing the Brotherhood of stealing the Arab Spring. Rioters careened through the streets, demanding the Brotherhood's resignation. Counter-demonstrations kept pace as warnings of civil war soared.

With fear and hate at a fever pitch, Abdel Fattah el-Sisi, former head of military intelligence and then minister of the interior, poured fuel on the flames by calling for true democracy and vowing not to spill a drop of sacred Egyptian blood. This was a strange position for one of Mubarak's generals who had spilled considerable amounts of blood in attempting to crush the Arab Spring revolution.

In the meantime, anti-Brotherhood protesters had been given the green light to storm the streets at will. Brotherhood supporters countered, albeit without police protection. Violence flared and culminated in the march on June 30, 2012, where thirty million Egyptians were pleading for Sisi to save them from civil war and Islamic tyranny. Egypt's new man on horseback had arrived.

The figure of thirty million protesters was described by the BBC as a carefully staged fantasy, and even the Saudi press suggested that the figure might be as low as five or six million. Whatever the number, five million people shouting and screaming against the government was a formidable number.

Bowing to what he claimed was the popular will, Sisi overthrew a popularly elected government that had reigned for only a year. Its leaders were arrested, and an Egyptian media that had been as free as it was irresponsible during the two previous years became simply irresponsible. Headlines screamed that the Brotherhood was a terrorist organization that had declared war on Egypt. Egypt's intellectuals rushed in to proclaim that the coup was not a coup, because the military had simply bowed to the popular will as the first step in establishing a true democracy.

The next step in the counterrevolution was trickier. The Brotherhood had adopted a democratic strategy in order to prove to the world that it had nothing to fear from moderate Islamic rule in Egypt and beyond. As a result, Sisi would be forced to create the illusion of democracy if the counterrevolution were to succeed. Following a path well trod by Arab dictators before him, Sisi proclaimed a road map to democracy and appointed a handpicked transitional government to guide the way to free elections and a revised constitution. Throngs mobilized by the old propaganda ministry cheered. They had been rescued from Islamic rule, and democracy was at hand.

The difference between the democratic strategy pursued by the Brotherhood and the illusion of democracy conjured up by the military was staggering. Brotherhood rule featured a free press, freedom of speech, a multitude of political parties, and unfettered demonstrations and protests. Rule by military fiat featured none of the above. Sisi's message was simple: *Trust me while I save you from the Brotherhood.*

The Brotherhood then threw the country into political and economic chaos by launching massive protests the length and breadth of Egypt. They had to be stopped, or the military's counterrevolution was doomed.

Time was of the essence. When Brotherhood protesters approached the officers' club where they believed the deposed president was being held, the police and military opened fire, killing forty-four protesters. Sisi remained unrepentant and blamed the Brotherhood for the carnage. Pictures published by the *Guardian* proved otherwise. International condemnation rained on the head of Sisi. His blatant slaughter of innocent protesters was not leading to democracy, they claimed, but to a revived military dictatorship.

Stung by criticism from abroad and the doubts of his liberal supporters, Sisi called upon the mob to give him the power to crush violence and terrorism. It was not legal democracy that mattered but the will of the people. Thousands of youths screamed their support for Sisi, while an equal number of Brotherhood supporters called for a return of the elected government.

Violence exploded as the military and Sisi's recently revived secret police opened fire on the demonstrators. Estimates of the death toll ranged from 72 to 130. The figures of the wounded ranged in the thousands.

Sisi, far from expressing remorse, gave the Brotherhood forty-eight hours to join army-sponsored reconciliation talks. The Brotherhood responded to Sisi's call for surrender with new demonstrations. The army could either kill them or return Egypt's elected president to office. Violence was minimal, but with the passing of the deadline, Sisi's puppet government announced that all future Brotherhood demonstrations would be crushed with maximum force.

It was at this point that the United States, self-proclaimed world leader in democracy, had to choose between hopes for a Turkish-style Islamic democracy or a tinhorn dictator whom the United States could use to crush moderate Islam and democracy by force as part of America's effort to win the War on Terror by returning the old order to power in Egypt.

There seemed to be confusion on the topic. Secretary of State John Kerry, a well-known liberal, proclaimed that Sisi's coup was the first step toward democracy. Sisi responded with a tirade condemning the United States for not giving his rule adequate support. This of itself was an indicator of a nervous dictator, but it paled in comparison to the outrage that followed Senator John McCain's fact-finding mission to Egypt. Sisi, Senator McCain proclaimed, was an illegitimate leader who had seized power by a military coup.

The Egyptian press interpreted McCain's comments as punishment for Sisi's tirade against Kerry. Far worse was speculation that the counterpoint between Kerry and McCain was a cruel US conspiracy to keep Egypt in a state of chaos or, perhaps, to return the Brotherhood to power. Why else, the conspiracy mill pondered, would the US support an illegitimate military dictator against the relatively moderate Muslim Brotherhood in Egypt, arm ultra-extremist Sunni groups fighting a Shi'ite dictator in Syria, and put a Shi'ite government beholden to Iran in power in Iraq? Clever people, these Americans, at least in the mind of Egyptian conspiracy theorists and an increasingly paranoid dictator.

Sisi's rule was a blend of force, faith, and finance more bizarre and inept than that of any other Middle Eastern leader in history, including Saddam Hussein and Muammar Qaddafi. Megalomania appears to be a disease among the tinhorn tyrants of the region.

Force came first because Sisi used all the money that he could scrape up, including billions of dollars from Saudi Arabia and its allies and generous US military aid, to build what an Egyptian press claimed was the thirteenth largest army in the world. The Egyptian press, as free as the wind under the Brotherhood, now existed for the sole purpose of praising Sisi and creating the illusion that all was well in a starving country with swelling prisons, crumbling buildings, crashing trains, fuel shortages, irregular water and electricity, a deteriorating education system, sickening hospitals, unemployment, housing shortages, rampant corruption, and rapacious police who used corruption and violent shakedowns to compensate for their low salaries. Protests were illegal, sermons were dictated by a Sisi-appointed minister of religious affairs (*wafq*), and steps were taken to create a new moderate Islam devoted to justifying Sisi's oppressive rule. It became official doctrine, but it met neither the material nor spiritual needs of the masses.

Courts and a rubber-stamp parliament exist only to give the impression of democracy. When Sisi is forced to backtrack, he allows the courts to do it in the name of justice. Sisi, for his part, attempts to build charismatic faith by giving a sad portrayal of Nasser in a pathetic attempt to make himself the new Nasser. Nasser worked miracles. All Sisi does is kill Egyptians. Things were better under the Brotherhood. At least you could breathe.

How well, then, did the US strategy of keeping Egypt's military tyrant in power to fight extremist faith-based terror succeed? It didn't. All of the causes of terror we have discussed throughout the book have increased under Sisi. His much-vaunted security establishment has focused on unsuccessful efforts to crush the Muslim Brotherhood that refused to accept Sisi's coup. In the meantime, Salafi-jihadist terrorists in the Sinai remained at large. As a result of Sisi's policies, US weapons ended up killing innocent Egyptians and fueling terror. Force in this case was fueling extremist faith rather than crushing it. As for Sisi's charismatic faith, that is just another empty illusion. The Saudis used finance to keep Sisi alive, but to what avail? Can he be trusted, or is he scheming to take over the Kingdom? This thought occurred to the Saudis, and tensions between two of the United States' key allies have increased accordingly. So have America's dreams of an alliance for peace and stability in the New Middle East.

SAUDI ARABIA: CAN THE PROTECTOR OF ISLAM PROTECT ITSELF FROM ISLAM?

This question brings us to Saudi Arabia, the final member of the alliance for peace and stability in the new Middle East. How ironic it is that Saudi Arabia, the self-proclaimed protector of Islam, is largely dependent upon a very secular Christian power for its security in an era of Islamic rule. The ironies continue when it is observed that all of the multiple threats to the Kingdom are faith-based Islamic threats, while Saudi Arabia, the protector of Islam, is moving closer to a Jewish state that has slaughtered thousands of Muslims while cleansing them from their Islamic lands. Perhaps the greatest irony of all is that the most powerful weapon available for protection of the Saudis and other oil monarchies is not faith or force but finance.

What, then, are the faith-based threats to Saudi Arabia? The list is complex because each offers a different challenge to the archaic Saudi monarchy. The first and most obvious of the faith threats to the Kingdom is the Iran-Hizbullah threat. Not only is Iran more powerful than Saudi Arabia but it is also on the verge of becoming a nuclear power. While that may take time, the immediate threat is the creation of a Shia crescent that would allow Iran to surround the Kingdom with Shia populations from all sides, including Iran, Iraq, the Shia populations in the Gulf kingdoms, the Saudi Eastern Province, and the rebellion of a Shia tribal confederation in Yemen. A Shia crescent could well spell the end of the Saudi monarchy and its partners in the Gulf Cooperation Council. The Saudis have attempted to defend themselves from the crescent by launching a war in Yemen together with an Islamic alliance that it has hastily cobbled together at great expense. The Yemeni war demonstrated the futility of Saudi Arabia's attempt to build a Sunni NATO, and Saudi salvation remained dependent on its special relationship with the United States based on its massive purchases of US weapons. When the Saudi special relationship with the United States grew tense under the Obama administration, the Saudis shifted their finance to Britain. It then shifted back to the United States under the Trump administration.

The next faith-based threat to consider is the Muslim Brotherhood and the threat of a moderate and democratic Islam that has long found popularity in Saudi Arabia and the Gulf. The Saudis are spending billions to crush the Brotherhood in Egypt but have become increasingly nervous about the megalomaniac aspirations of Sisi and his huge army. They had hoped to control Sisi and use him to defend the Kingdom. That dream frayed, but both sides are doing their best to pretend that all is well.

This is not so in the case of Saudi animosity toward the Gulf kingdom of Qatar, the main financial backer of the Muslim Brotherhood in the region, and the sponsor of the freewheeling Al Jazeera media network that advocates modernity and free speech in the region. Adding insult to injury, the Qataris remained neutral on the Iran threat, as did Kuwait. Neither, it seems, wanted to be swallowed up in a Saudi-Iranian war. The Saudis struck back in 2017 by using their financial dominance in the Gulf to impose an economic and political boycott on the smaller Qatari kingdom. The United States couldn't rush to Saudi Arabia's aid, because Qatar was the sight of major US military bases in the Gulf. Turkey rushed to Qatar's aid, as did Iran, supported by Russia. Faith kept the Saudi monarchy from offering the United States bases in the Kingdom, because Saudi Arabia's Wahhabi clergy opposed a US presence on Saudi holy land.

This brings us to the next faith thorn in the monarchy's side, that being the Wahhabi clergy that the monarchy needs to justify its rule. The Wahhabis are hostile to moderate Islam, preach a Salafi doctrine that is vehemently anti-American, and fuel Salafi-jihadist doctrine within Saudi Arabia and on a global basis.

Less urgent and biding their time are the branches of ISIS and al-Qaeda that are active in the Kingdom. While figures are difficult to come by, the Saudi press continues to praise Saudi security forces for arresting homegrown terrorists. The Saudis also have experimented with supporting Sunni extremist militias, including ISIS, to fight Hizbullah-Shia militias. This policy runs the risk of arming the very militias that have vowed to overthrow the monarchy because of its deep support for the United States and Israel.

Out of public view but of concern to the Saudis is the tension between a monarchy tied to the United States and Israel, on the one hand, and its Wahhabi clerics, who preach hostility toward both, on the other. Most recently, the monarchy has called for a new Islam. Though the details for it seem vague, it is nonetheless likely to conflict with the monarchy's alliance with the Wahhabi clergy. How can the monarchy advocate a new Islam without denigrating Wahhabi Islam that is founded on the Islam of the ancestors?

LESSONS LEARNED

1. Once again, we have seen how it is impossible to treat crises in the Middle East on a case-by-case basis, because things are so interconnected that success in one area produces chaos in another.
2. Cooperation among the United States' allies in the region is tenuous at best.
3. Faith can generate force, but force finds it difficult to create faith.
4. Military coups don't lead to democracy.
5. The United States' special relationship with diverse Middle Eastern countries counters its efforts to create alliance among the same countries.
6. Arming megalomaniac dictators breeds violence, terror, and anti-Americanism.

10

SOLUTIONS TO AN ERA OF STALEMATE (POST-2017)

The unfolding drama of the Middle East entered an era of stalemate with the failed efforts of the Western powers and their Middle Eastern allies to stem the surge of Islamic rule triggered by the Arab Spring revolutions. The era of stalemate became more ominous with Western recognition that the battle against jihadist extremism was to be a long one. Battles are won but only to be crowned by a new surge of terror at a time and place of the Salafi-jihadists' choosing.

The era of stalemate is the most dangerous era that the West has encountered since the unfolding drama of the modern Middle East began with the restructuring of the Middle East in the aftermath of World War I. Europe and North America have become part and parcel of the battleground for control of the Middle East. The era of stalemate is also dangerous because we have no idea of when or how it will end or of the unexpected twists that will be afflicted on us along the way. Of these the most frightening is a war among the Abrahamic faiths fired with emotions of faith and fought with weapons so devastating that the casualties of wars past will pale by comparison.

In this chapter we examine the era of stalemate and why it continues on the relentless path toward an unknown future. We suggest that fundamental alterations in the way the West employs faith, force, and finance in dealing with the Middle East may prevent a probable tragedy from happening. We begin with the stairway to terror that transforms normally nonviolent individuals into holy warriors. From the stairway to terror, we turn to the reasons that prevailing counter-terrorist measures have failed to break the stalemate between the most powerful countries on earth and the religious fanatics. This, in turn, leads to the harsh realities that will have to be addressed by any sustainable solution to the terrorist crisis. Next come five vital steps that must be taken if the crisis of the terror is to be avoided. We conclude by examining how faith, force, and finance fit into these solutions of the crisis of terror.

THE STAIRWAY TO TERROR

The stairway to terror outlines the path that typically nonviolent individuals follow in becoming terrorists associated with organizations such as al-Qaeda and ISIS.

Step 1. Festering Frustration

Most individuals approaching the stairway to terror tend to be averse to violence. This is due in large part to their membership in kinship, religious, or ethnic groups that shape their identity and help them meet their basic needs for food, shelter, security, belonging, and spiritualism. If these core groups preach nonviolence, most of their members will be nonviolent. Few individuals in the Middle East can survive without the support of their core groups. They certainly cannot rely on their governments, because most governments in the region are as oppressive as they are inept at providing public services. They cannot go it alone, because nothing gets done in the region without the support of core groups.

The rulers understand this and go out of their way to use finance to incorporate clergy and tribal leaders into the ruling elite. This strategy leaves the masses helpless by giving them no place to turn for a solution to their despair. Thus, the stairway to terror involves both individuals and groups. Neither can be effective without the other.

Step 2: Despair Breeds Violent Groups

If a need exists, a group will emerge to fill it. This was the case of labor unions during the industrial revolution in the West, just as it was with the rise of the Muslim Brotherhood in Egypt following World War I. The greater the despair, the more extremist groups will form. They may be ad hoc groups, such as the surge of Salafi-jihadist groups of the 1970s, or they may be established groups alienated by the regime. This, as we have seen, was the story of the fall of the shah of Iran as a result of his alienation of the clergy. When the shah's financial support of the clergy ended, a formerly docile clergy turned against him.

Step 3: Seeking and Risk Taking

Despair forces people to seek a solution to their misery. For many people, God is the solution. It may also be an ideology such as Marxism or a charismatic nationalist leader such as Nasser. Whatever the case, this step is crucial, because the individual has taken a substantial risk by breaking with core groups and incurring the hostility of the regime. This step does not make the individual a terrorist, but it opens his or her mind to indoctrination by group leaders.

Several factors may impel individuals to take this critical step toward resistance and potential violence. These include the intensity of the despair, the pervasiveness of the stimuli, the appeal of the Salafi-jihadist groups, and the absence of less risky alternatives for need fulfillment.

Step 4: Weeding Out the Chaff

The path to the Salafi-jihadist religious solution often takes the form of core groups of students and workers who are promised a paradise in a heaven paved with glory, respect, and prosperity. However, leaders of small groups find it difficult to meet the members' needs and are torn by group-dynamic tensions that involve status and faith in the spiritual baraka of the leader. Recall that in the earlier discussion of Egypt, some ninety Salafi-jihadist groups simply faded away. Individuals may simply drop out of the group and attempt to return to a normal life, if that is possible. It may not be easy, because they have already been branded by the authorities and caused problems to their community.

Step 5: Becoming a Warrior for God

Dissatisfaction with the capacity of small groups to meet their spiritual and material needs usually leads the more dedicated group members to shift to larger prestigious groups headed by a charismatic spiritual leader whose baraka indicates the gift of God's grace. It is this grace that makes him their guide and that guarantees their salvation in heaven. Indoctrination and discipline increase. There is also a change in identity as they accept the supreme guide of the organization as their spiritual leader. In the process they develop a new persona as a soldier of God. As success and status increase, so does the hope of an eternity in paradise and membership in a spiritual vanguard that will rule the world in the name of God.

It is these core groups that came together to form bin-Laden's al-Qaeda network. It is similar groups, having laid a foundation throughout the Islamic world, that have allied themselves with ISIS and al-Qaeda for strategic reasons including financial support and enhanced prestige.

Step 6: Consolidation and Globalization

Throughout the course of this book we have seen the expansion of the Salafi-jihadists terror organizations from small groups to international organizations whose faith, force, and financial wings now span the globe. The faith weapon of these organizations offers salvation to the dispossessed in extremist mosques, schools, social networks, and secret cells throughout the world. The force weapon of these organizations is terror by indoctrinated, trained, and disciplined true believers who view themselves as soldiers of God charged with saving humanity by restoring the purity of Islam. Finance ranges from donations from the poor to money laundering in international banks and to oil exports.

THE FAILURE OF PREVAILING COUNTER-TERROR

The answer to the riddle of failed counter-terror efforts begins with the failure of counter-terror measures to address the general principle that most people possess a basic need for faith in God to provide for a better life and salvation from their despair. This principle, while far from being absolute, does have numbers on its side—lots of numbers, as evidenced in the appeal of organizations such as the Muslim Brotherhood, Hizbullah, ISIS, and al-Qaeda. This is all the more the case because the despair, hopelessness, humiliation, deprivation, and oppression that characterize daily life in much of the Middle East intensify the spiritual need for salvation.

To make matters worse, the dispossessed have no other place to turn to for help and hope. They cannot turn to the authoritarian leaders of the region to resolve their despair, for there are no peaceful means of redress in the authoritarian countries of the region. As a result, frustration and anger build until they simply explode, as they did in the Palestinian intifadas and the Arab Spring revolutions.

Government-sponsored mosques abound in the Middle East, but Islam as preached in government mosques does not offer a spiritual solution for the dispossessed because it tends to be too formal, legalistic, esoteric, and supportive of authoritarian tyrants to meet the dispossessed's spiritual need for salvation. It may preach a glorious view of heaven, but it does not get down to the gut-level needs of the dispossessed. How could it, when the leading clergy are controlled by the ruling elite? The minister of religious endowments in Egypt writes the Friday sermons to be preached in the government mosques, all of which stress the Islamic need for national unity as a religious obligation. He has even suggested that the masses should work free for the good of God and country. Other clerics have called for love of the army as a religious duty. All of the authoritarian leaders of the region call for national unity, but there is no national unity. If there were, they would not have to keep on calling. What choice do they have when there is little faith in either the authoritarian governments that rule the region or the official versions of Islam that they sponsor?

This situation means that the dispossessed are pushed toward religious groups that will resist the oppression of the region's authoritarian regimes. Some are nonviolent groups such as the Muslim Brotherhood, while others, such as the Salafi-jihadists, advocate violence. Whatever the case, establishment Islam will not be a major force in countering ISIS, al-Qaeda, and related terrorist groups, because it fails to offer a solution to the despair of the masses. As a result, religious movements resisting the authoritarian regimes in the region are not only flourishing but have soared in the era of satellites, social media, and cyber warfare. Given the despair and intensity of Islamic faith in the region, nonviolent religious groups such as the Muslim Brotherhood are the only faith option available to the United States in fighting the violent extremist radicals.

Faith may also explain why the relentless battles in the era of stalemate have become increasingly bloody, with heavy casualties on all sides. Perhaps this is because the shifting religious paradigms of all three Abrahamic faiths are moving in the direction of growing extremism that is supportive of violence.

An alternate explanation for the excessive violence of the era of stalemate is that extremists are more passionate about their faith than moderates are. I doubt if this is the case, but there can be little doubt that the extremists are more emotional and less earthbound than the moderates. They also tend to view the scriptures as literal commands rather than allegorical suggestions. This in turn makes them more absolutist and less flexible in finding solutions to Middle Eastern problems. This does not mean that the extremist view of what God wants is the correct version but merely that the extremists are the driving force in the conflicts of the Middle East. That does not make it right, but it does make it a reality in understanding why the drama of the Middle East is unfolding the way that it is and what can be done about it.

This, then, brings us to the overwhelming use of force as the dominant weapon used to break the era of stalemate in the Middle East. In large part, force has failed because the critical questions of when, where, what kind of force, and how much force is required to curb extremism and violence without being counterproductive have yet to be answered. American, Israeli, and EU military and intelligence leaders have been candid on the topic.

What we do know is that bombing alone, as US generals have admitted, was not able to defeat faith-motivated extremists. This led to admissions that there would have to be boots on the ground. Just a few boots would not do, because once the boots left, the jihadist radicals would come back. This, of itself, was a cause for stalemate, because few countries were anxious to put boots on the ground for a long period of time. No boots, no victory. This meant that the boots would have to stay on the ground if they were to stop the jihadist threat. Like it or not, the United States and its EU allies would have to occupy much of the

Middle East. None of the lessons learned throughout the book were as painful as those of occupation, not the least of which was US occupation of Afghanistan and Israeli occupation of Palestinian-ruled areas of Israel.

The stalemate also persists because the task of breaking it is so massive that the United States cannot do it alone, as hard as it may try. Alliances are formed with America's Middle Eastern allies but fail as a result of tensions and conflicts among their members, each of which has a different vision of what a future Middle East should look like and how best to get there.

As the United States has special relationships with all of the allies in its alliance designed to create a new Middle East, key US policies invariably offend a key ally, and coordination and compromise break down. Not only do America's special relationships make alliances difficult and solutions impossible but they also draw the United States into battles that heap more Muslim hostility on the United States as they deplete US resources. The Saudi war in Yemen is a case in point.

Adding to the prolonged stalemate in the Middle East is the reality that the struggle in the Middle East is but one of several global conflicts confronting the United States and its NATO allies. Choices for limited resources have to be made. This is all the more the case as global conflicts that hinted at a new cold war between the United States and Russia quickly spawned proxy conflicts in the Middle East.

Alternative force strategies such as arming puppet regimes like Sisi, the world's new Saddam Hussein, merely pushes more people into the ranks of the dispossessed. The extremists win again.

The picture is much the same in efforts to arm Muslims to fight Muslims. The United States arms and trains Muslim militias much as it armed and trained bin-Laden's al-Qaeda forces in Afghanistan. Perhaps the United States should ask itself, why should Muslim groups and governments fight for the United States? Odds are, they will exploit the United States for their own purposes and then turn against it. Arming the enemy of our enemy is a short-run strategy at best.

Counterforce is also increasing as the Salafi-jihadists and their Hizbullah counterparts increase in sophistication and military capacity. Foremost among these adjustments was the adoption of the Shia strategy developed by the Ayatollah Khomeini for transforming faith into force, including the establishment of a powerful Hizbullah network centered in Lebanon.

Further sophistications were provided by bin-Laden's strike-and-hide strategies, developed after his flight from Afghanistan. This strategy has become far easier in the era of stalemate as the Middle East continues to splinter into a multitude of countries and nonstate actors. This process will become even more prevalent as civil wars continue to afflict almost half of the countries in the region, including Iraq, Syria, Israel, Yemen, and the Sudan, to mention but a few. Count on the number to grow with despair and extremism increasing throughout the region.

Finally, force has failed because the use of force by the United States and its allies has been so blatant that they have alienated our natural Islamic allies, about 95 percent of whom do not want to return to a time warp of seventh-century Arabia.

The more the United States alienates their natural Muslim allies, the more the allies fear the country and the more the United States is seized by an Islamophobic fear factor reminiscent of fear of Nazis in World War II and the Red fear during the Cold War. Rather than seeing a "commie" under the bed, they now see a Muslim. Not only have the terrorists turned the force war into a stalemate but they are winning the psychological war by forcing both Americans and the world's Muslims into a war of religions that could well destroy all concerned.

The use of finance to defeat Islamic extremism and terror has also been a flop. The aid programs of the United States go largely to prop up authoritarian leaders such as Egypt's Sisi, who uses our aid and the billions pumped in by Saudi Arabia and its Gulf allies in a failed effort to build what he claims to be the thirteenth largest army in the world. Sadly, this army is being used to crush moderate Islamic currents overthrown by a military coup while it fails to conquer the terrorists in the Sinai. No wonder the Egyptian press has listed more new Egyptian Salafi-jihadist groups than anyone can count. And what will the United States do if Sisi falls or invades Saudi Arabia?

Finance has not been used to address what the United States has defined as the causes of extremism and terror. The United States complained bitterly that Israeli settlement building was a major obstacle to peace in the region yet in 2016 provided Israel with a $36 billion aid package despite a blatant increase in Israel's settlement building. As a result, Israel's faith-based special relationship with the United States prevented the Obama administration's use of finance to end what the United States had designated as a major cause of extremism and terror. This of itself was not going to solve the extremist-terrorist issues, but US presidents repeatedly stated that it was a critical issue. Bernie Sanders, in his campaign for the presidency, headlined this problem by calling for an end to the settlements.

The diverse explanations for the persistence of the era of stalemate outlined above constitute an interconnected chain in which each link impairs efforts to deal effectively with the others. The best example of this situation has been the US policy of treating each link in the chain of enduring violence in the Middle East on a case-by-case basis. This policy helped the United States to turn a blind eye to the terror-supporting policies of the allies with which it had a special relationship but it has also blinded the United States to steps critical to breaking the era of stalemate. Also prolonging the era of stalemate have been the psychological traits of key leaders responsible for guiding the struggle against stalemate on both sides of the battle line. Their perceptions were influenced by various concerns of faith and finance as well as perceptions of the need for force.

HARSH REALITIES AND LESSONS LEARNED

Terror and violence will continue as long as the lethal combination of mass despair and religious extremism continues. Any effort to bring peace and stability to the Middle East will have to address one or the other, if not both.

Terror is what each country in the world says it is. There is no meeting of minds on the topic. As a result, coordination and cooperation are haphazard at best.

Technological changes are occurring so rapidly in all areas that the application of faith, force, and finance may outpace solutions to the terrorist problem as soon as they are conceived.

Faith is vital because it is impossible to take faith out of the Middle East equation. Faith is not only a key motivator and organizer of much of the tension in the Middle East but is also a key element in the equation that transcends both regional and international boundaries.

Force alone is not going to solve the problem because it is a temporary solution that can only be sustained by occupation. It also stimulates more violence and conflict than it eliminates. It is essential to balance hard force and soft force. The use of hard force may be critical in traditional warfare but disastrous in countering psychological warfare. The two are linked because excessive collateral damage from hard force may provide a psychological advantage to the Salafi-jihadists by turning Muslims against the United States and EU. Hard force threatens and destroys while psychological warfare uses soft power to convince, motivate, discredit, and demoralize. Both may be critical to fighting terror, depending upon the circumstances.

Finance is vital to ease the despair that plagues the region, but finance does not buy love, loyalty, or gratitude. This is because the use of finance in the Middle East is not charity but a political weapon.

The lessons learned throughout the book also make it clear that the United States cannot end terror or bring peace and stability to the Middle East by itself.

American alliances with its regional allies are also unlikely to bring peace and stability to the region because all of the United States' allies in the region are pursuing policies that the United States has condemned as being causes of terror. US allies in the region also find cooperation difficult because of their competing interests. The United States complains bitterly but does nothing because of its special relationships with its Middle Eastern allies. They respond to American pressure by claiming that the United States is forcing them to commit suicide, and they resist accordingly.

This means that the goal of accomplishing peace and stability in the Middle East is pursued within a global context that includes both a revival of the Cold War and the prospect of a global war of religions among the Abrahamic faiths.

Establishing peace and security in the Middle East would seem to be a universal objective that takes priority over national and regional concerns. However, that is far from being the case, as each key country or group with a stake in the Middle East continues to pursue its own interests and those of its leaders regardless of the global consequences of its policies. This, as we have seen, has been the history of the modern

Middle East, including the present era of stalemate. Globalization is taking root everywhere except in ending terror by bringing peace and stability to the Middle East.

FIVE VITAL PROBLEMS TO BE ADDRESSED

Such, then, are the challenges facing the search for solutions to the surge of terror afflicting the world. Compelling logic dictates that only an international alliance can bring peace and stability to the Middle East.

Recall that a tragedy is a predictable disaster that the actors in the drama lack the will to stop. And so it is with the drama of peace in the Middle East and the world beyond. How could it be otherwise? The United States wants to be great (again). Russia wants to be great (again). China wants to be great (again). Britain wants to be great (again). So do France and Germany and the EU. Israel and Turkey want to be pure again. The Islamic extremists want Islam to be pure again. The Christian extremists long for Armageddon, for only they and Jews who convert to Christianity will experience the second coming of Christ. And so the story goes and goes and goes. Muslims, too, long for the second coming of Christ, for his return is vital for the appearance of a Mahdi, the final Messiah for which the Jews still long. Faith, be it religious faith, nationalism, or dreams of charismatic power, is not to be denied. Neither is the human lust for power, wealth, security, and spiritual ties to God. How well they blend together.

While prospects for the creation of the global alliance required to solve a global terrorist problem are dim, the search for partial solutions to a global crisis follows its relentless course. Whatever the case, any solution to easing the threat of global terror must address five key problems.

Stopping the Terrorists

The terrorists responsible for much of the blatant violence throughout the world have to be stopped. The finger points directly at ISIS, al-Qaeda, and other Salafi-jihadist groups. Whether it also points to Iran's Revolutionary Guards and Hizbullah affiliates remains a matter of debate in global circles. The Trump administration supports this view, but Russia heatedly rejects it.

Preventing the Despair Base of Terror

The brutal authoritarian regimes that are responsible for the wellspring of despair that fuels Salafi-jihadist extremism must be replaced with governments that can meet the material and spiritual needs of their subjects. This includes providing their subjects peaceful means of conflict resolution such as fair elections and free speech.

Preventing Religious Extremists from Exploiting the Despair of the Masses

Countries and organizations supporting virulent visions of Islamic and other forms of religious extremism must curb their activities.

Working with Islam

The world's 1.6 billion-plus Muslims must be convinced that the United States and NATO have not declared war on Islam. Except for an extremist minority, the world's Muslims are America's natural allies in the war against the Salafi-jihadist extremists. The War on Terror cannot be won without their support. Allowing panic over Islamophobia to push them into the hands of the extremists is to fall into the trap of the Salafi-jihadists, who can only win if the United States and its allies radicalize the Muslim world.

Resolving Conflicts that Trigger Violence in the Middle East

These terror-triggering conflicts include the Palestinian-Israeli conflict, the Turkish-Kurdish conflict, and the Sunni-Shia conflict that has endured since the earliest days of Islam.

In the remainder of the chapter we examine various uses of faith, force, and finance that are likely to take center stage in the struggle to end the global terrorist threat posed by the five key causes of terrorist violence outlined above. While the focus is on the future, be warned that it is likely to be an uncertain future in which dreams, fears, and illusions play a dominant role. Such is the nature of tragedies.

SOLUTIONS

The five critical problems prolonging the War on Terror can be resolved without causing more terror or exacerbating the Cold War with Russia and the looming war of the Abrahamic faiths. The suggested solutions to the struggle against terror aren't easy, but they are empirically grounded in the faith, force, and finance lessons learned from a century of conflict in the modern Middle East.

Stop the Terror without Accentuating the Causes and Facilitators of Terror

Stopping terror starts with defeating the terrorist militias on the ground. This is as essential to winning the heavily psychological faith war against terror as it is to winning the military and financial wars against terror. From the force perspective, defeating the Salafi-jihadist militias on the ground destroys the military base camps they require to train, arm, supply, deploy, and communicate with their terrorist networks throughout the world. The more terrorist organizations are deprived of their base camps, the more difficult this process becomes. In the same manner, defeats of ISIS on the ground can severely cripple the financial resources upon which its operations depend.

Defeats on the ground also take their toll psychologically and theologically as they shatter the impression that the leaders of Salafi-jihadist groups possess a special baraka (blessing of God) that is leading them toward victory in the violent cosmic battle to return Islam to a time warp of seventh-century Arabia. Defeats shatter baraka and have to be explained and revived by frantic compensatory victories that strain the resources of the terrorists. The loss of baraka soon leads to a loss of personal charisma and, ipso facto, faith in the mystical and superhuman powers of the leaders.

Declining religious and charismatic faith in Salafi-jihadist leaders, in turn, creates severe psychological problems for the Salafi-jihadists by sowing doubt, discontent, suspicion, and blame games within their ranks. As a result, discipline weakens and defections increase. So does maneuvering to replace the leader and his appointed lieutenants up and down the organizational hierarchy. This process is accelerated by the death of a leader as the struggle for succession requires the new leader to establish his religious and charismatic authority. Replacements can be found, but loyalty to their authority takes time to establish and is difficult to maintain. This problem is prevalent in affiliated groups, many of which have ambitious leaders of their own. This process was evident in the splintering of ISIS from al-Qaeda. It was also evident in the power struggles in Iran following the passing of the Ayatollah Khomeini.

The need to defeat the terrorist on the ground is not an issue of debate. What has been debated is the wisdom of prolonged occupation of liberated ISIS territories to prevent their return. The pain of occupation was drenched in blood in Iraq, Afghanistan, and Israeli-occupied Palestine and may be counterproductive. This is all the more the case because US occupation of Muslim land supports the psychological-theological warfare of the Salafi-jihadists by implying that the United States has declared war on Islam. This creates a vicious circle by providing the Salafi-jihadists with the recruits they need either to reoccupy liberated land once the United States leaves or to shift their resources to 101 swamps in the Middle East that are ripe for occupation by one Salafi-jihadist group or another. If this trend continues, the United States could find itself mired in the Middle East longer than it has been mired in Afghanistan, and with the same results. Perpetual occupation is far more likely to increase terror than defuse it.

Prevent the Despair Base of Terror

Salafi-jihadists or equally violent extremist groups will exist as long as oppression and economic exploitation leave the peoples of the Middle East no escape from their despair except religious or ideological extremism. This has been the story of the modern Middle East. It was also the story of the surge of communism in Russia and China and the rise of fascism in Germany and Italy.

There are numerous ways in which the United States could fight Salafi-jihadist terror by ending the despair of the peoples of the Middle

East. The first of these is for the United States to stop supporting oppressive regimes in the region in hope that tyranny will bring peace and stability to the region. Oppressive and exploitive governments don't bring peace and stability. They bring religious extremism, violence, and terror.

Easing the despair base of terror could also be achieved by the effective use of foreign aid and other financial weapons to build hope among the masses for a brighter future. This would take the wind out of Salafi-jihadist propaganda sails and fight the impression that the United States and NATO have declared war on Islam. Sadly, a lion's share of US foreign aid goes to support the very tyrants who are increasing terror by fueling the despair that drives the dispossessed into the hands of the terrorists. It is true that the United States cannot always dictate where its aid goes. The tyrants are sovereign leaders, and it is they who decide who gets what in their countries. As a result, the supporters of the tyrants get most of what there is to get, while the plight of the dispossessed deepens. It is these same tyrants who block NGOs from aiding the dispossessed of their countries because they fear that people who help the poor will incite revolt. The United States could force the issue but claims to avoid meddling in the internal affairs of allied countries.

Use Moderate Islam as a Solution to Extremism

How, then, is the United States to prevent religious extremists from exploiting the despair of the masses when it has failed to stem the despair base of terror? The answer to this conundrum is that the United States must support a moderate vision of Islam that resists tyranny, fights Salafi-jihadist terror, and advocates a forward-looking Islam compatible with life in the twenty-first century.

Impossible? Not at all. The Prophet Mohammed was a forward-looking reformer whose goal was to bring peace and stability to Arabia by eliminating the main causes of conflict that had turned the region into a tribal war zone. Greed was condemned, charity for the poor made one of the key pillars of the faith, killing Muslims was forbidden, and Christians and Jews were allowed to live in peace among Muslims in return for a minor tax that absolved them from military service. Justice was to be honest and fair, and polygamy was reduced to four wives, a sharp decline from the unlimited polygamy practiced in the era. The Prophet Mohammed was a merchant and as such believed in capitalism. It was, however, capitalism with responsibility for the good of the people.

The point to be made is that Islam is not of itself the source of despair-fueling terror. The core of the problem is the Islamic clergy who are serving the rapacious elite rather than Islam's humane objectives.

This leads to a dilemma. The Salafi-jihadist terrorists agree that the crisis in the Middle East has been caused by tyrannical leaders and the sycophant clergy who support them. Indeed, they require the tyrants and sycophant clergy to push the dispossessed into their ranks.

It is true that government-controlled clerics issue religious decrees (fatwas) denouncing the Salafi-jihadists as apostates. The implication of these decrees is the warning that the followers and supporters of the Salafi-jihadists will go to hell rather than paradise. This warning also applies to the use of mosques for recruiting terrorists, training them, and giving them shelter. In some cases, senior clerics have urged the masses to help the police identify suspected terrorists with little proof required. This, in turn, unleashes witch-hunts and has become an excuse for excessive police brutality.

The difficulty with this approach is that the senior clerics issuing decrees against the terrorists also issue decrees justifying oppressive rule and gross economic inequalities. Who, then, is the enemy? Is it the Salafi-jihadists, the tyrannical governments, or the clergy that serve the tyrannical governments? To quote a common Arabic phrase, "All have blood on their hands."

A final solution to the terrorist crisis, accordingly, requires that the United States and its allies stop supporting the tyrannical leaders and the sycophant clergy who support them, without enabling the Salafi-jihadists to seize power.

This means that faith must prevent the dispossessed from ascending the stairway to terror by encouraging the masses to resist oppressive regimes in a nonviolent way that includes peaceful demonstrations and silent sabotage.

While this may seem impossible, it is precisely the pattern that the Justice and Development Party used to overthrow tyrannical military rule in Turkey. It is also the pattern that the Muslim Brotherhood has pursued throughout its long history in Egypt. Demonstrations continue under the reign of Sisi, a brutal and inept tyrant, despite the slaughter of innocent marchers by the police and military. Sisi branded the Brotherhood a terrorist organization, as did the Saudis, when its only sin was calling for democracy, justice, equality, and an end to oppression by the security forces. The oppression has intensified, but so has the resistance of the Muslim Brothers. Such is the power of moderate Islam. Moderate Islam is the United States' best bet if it wants to stem the dramatic flow of young Muslims into the ranks of the terrorists.

The monarchy in Jordan attempted to ban the Brotherhood but gave up on the task as being too risky despite intense pressure from Saudi Arabia and Egypt to crush the Brotherhood. The Jordanian electorate wanted the seductive blend of moderate spiritual faith that offered the pathway to paradise blended with democracy, justice, schools, health care, and equality that the Brotherhood has to offer, as do the masses of most of the Sunni Arab world.

This combination of moderate spiritual faith that offers the pathway to paradise blended with democracy, justice, and equality has made the Brotherhood the archenemy of the Salafi-jihadist terrorists who can't compete with the Brotherhood's mass appeal. Why should people live in a brutal time warp of seventh-century Arabia when they can achieve paradise in a twenty-first century environment that blends spiritualism, democracy, and modernity in a convenient package? Ironic, is it not, that both the puppet tyrants bolstered by the United States and the Salafi-jihadist extremists want to destroy moderate Islam?

Like it or not, moderate Islamic organizations such as the Turkish Justice and Development Party and Muslim Brotherhood offer the United States and NATO the best way of weaning youth from the stairway to terror.

A further advantage of supporting moderate Islam is that it alleviates Muslim fears that the United States and NATO have declared war on Islam at the same time that it promotes democracy and resists the oppression and exploitation that fuels much of the terror in the region. This is not to suggest that faith solutions to the terrorist crisis in the Middle East will be easy. Faith solutions are, however, a critical element in a broader package that involves force and finance strategically targeted to defeat the Salafi-jihadists.

Yet another step in preventing Islamic extremists from exploiting the dispossessed of the Islamic world is to pressure Saudi Arabia to curb its propagation of a Wahhabi doctrine that is manifestly anti-Western. As a former British ambassador to Saudi Arabia states in the sharpest of terms, Saudi support for Wahhabi-Salafi doctrine does promote terror (Wintour, 2017, 1).

A major step in this direction would be making special relationships between the Western powers and Saudi Arabia dependent on the toning down of their Wahhabi doctrine and curbing its perpetuation throughout the world. Western support of Gulf countries such as Qatar that are forward-looking in supporting moderate Islam and freedom of the press could also facilitate this process.

There is no need for the United States to force moderate Islam on anybody. It is already what most Muslims want. All that is required for the United States and its NATO allies to make moderate Islam a dominant force in defeating extremist Islam is to bring democracy to the authoritarian leaders of the region whose policies are promoting the most virulent forms of extremist violence. Once moderate Islam achieves a position of power, the role of the United States and its NATO allies is to make it effective in meeting the material needs of the people that it rules. Spiritualism will take care of itself.

The standard response to this suggestion is that the governments of the Muslim world are too fragile for either democracy or moderate Islam. It is precisely this fragility that is breeding terror and fueling Salafi extremism.

Another objection to this suggestion is that the United States needs Saudi financial arms purchases to keep its arms industries afloat. The United States and NATO thus face a cruel choice between faith and finance. Is that perhaps why they rely on force?

Integrate Muslims into the World Community

Working with Muslims means incorporating them as partners in a world community in which all three Abrahamic faiths can look forward to a future of peace and harmony.

The logic for incorporating Muslims as partners in the global community begins with the observation that the world's 1.6 billion Muslims are already part of that community. They aren't going away, and excluding them from partnership in the global community is a recipe for perpetuating the present era of stalemate. It is also a recipe for fueling a looming war of the Abrahamic faiths. The future offers little hope for Islamophobes, as Islam is the fastest growing religion in the world; it is already the dominant religion in much of Africa and is projected to become the majority religion in Europe within the next two decades.

There are also compelling reasons for welcoming Muslims into the world community. Muslims have suffered more from Salafi-jihadist violence than any other people on earth. Few want to live in a time warp of seventh-century Arabia and most want to be rid of Salafi-jihadist violence. Rather than declaring war on 1.6 billion Muslims, it would make much more sense to let Muslims join in the battle against the Salafi-jihadist terrorists. This would also enable the United States and its NATO allies to concentrate their military force on carefully targeted Salafi-jihadists rather than giving the impression that the United States has declared war on Islam by imposing collective punishments on innocent Muslims.

Yet another compelling reason for welcoming Muslims into the world community is that they make good citizens. Recent studies published by Pew and Gallup, for example, presented statistics indicating that Muslims were among the most productive people in the United States (Nowrasteh, 2016).

The Salafi-jihadists, for their part, would love to see the United States and NATO declare war on the world's Muslims.

The first step in integrating Islam into the global community is to promote moderate Islam. This is because moderate Islam is a forward-looking faith compatible with the global community in the twenty-first century. It is also because Islam is fully compatible with moderate Christianity and moderate Judaism and shares a common interest with moderate members of its sister faiths in destroying extremist violence in all of its varieties.

A second step in integrating Muslims into the world community is to help Muslim countries establish governments in which democracy, opportunity, and moderate religion are allowed. Moderate Islam has a far greater appeal than extremist Islam and can defeat extremist Islam. This is because it is effective in meeting both the spiritual and material needs of the population.

The third step in defeating Islamic extremism is to stop declaring war on Islam. This, as noted above, merely fuels terror by turning Muslims against the United States and forcing Muslims to defend their faith.

The fourth step in this process is to avoid the Islamic trap. The Islamist trap was a clever ploy that I first discovered in Egypt's Arabic press that was designed to make moderate Muslims who opposed corrupt, oppressive, and exploitive leaders appear to be terrorists. As a result, a Muslim, rather than being the equivalent of a Christian or a Jew, was made an evil symbol in the Western psyche.

The most vital and difficult step in integrating Muslims into the global community is to prevent Christian and Jewish extremist groups from provoking Muslim hostility and fueling Islamophobia in the West. Much to the delight of the Salafi-jihadists, Muslims respond in kind to hostility, and the groundwork for a war of the Abrahamic faiths picks up steam. How sad it is that the extremists of all three faiths believe that they will be led to victory by the same God.

Resolve Conflicts Triggering Violence in the Middle East

Conflicts triggering terror and violence in the Middle East are as old as Islam itself. This is clearly the case of the conflict between Sunni and Shia Muslims that continues to fuel terror and violence during the present era. The Arab-Israeli conflict began in the World War I era as did the Kurdish drive for independence from Turkey, Iraq, Syria, and Iran. These perennial cancers have been joined by a relentless series of recent conflicts, including the disastrous Saudi-led invasion of Yemen and the Saudi-led attempt to punish Qatar for advocating free speech and supporting moderate Islam, democracy, and peaceful negotiations with Iran. The United States is knee-deep in all of these conflicts, with no end in sight.

Ending these conflicts is vital to the United States and NATO because the conflicts fuel terror, create tensions that make alliances for peace and stability in the region close to impossible, and deepen US involvement in a new cold war with Russia and a looming war of the Abrahamic faiths. As a result, US forces and resources are torn in so many directions that coherent policy becomes virtually impossible.

The common denominator in all of the above crises is America's one-way special relationship with its key Middle Eastern allies, one that prevents the United States from addressing what has repeatedly been criticized as a major cause of terror and instability in the Middle East. This doesn't mean that the special relationships have to stop but that they must be reciprocal relationships that bring an end to the causes of terror and avoid drawing the United States into regional conflicts counter to its interests in the region.

This being the case, the only way for the United States to extricate itself from these perpetual and deadly crises is to make the continuation of its special relationships with its Middle Eastern allies contingent upon their willingness to end the practices that are fueling terror.

The United States must also drop the illusion that it can treat crises in the Middle East on a case-by-case basis. One reason is that Islam views both its land and its faithful as an indivisible nation. Travesties perpetrated against Muslims anywhere in the Islamic world go viral throughout the Muslim world almost instantly. This is a certainty in the cyber age and cannot be stopped.

This also means that the United States must avoid being drawn into reverse proxy wars—that is, it must avoid allowing its Middle Eastern allies to draw it into regional battles that are destabilizing the region, promoting terror, and stimulating endless religious conflicts that will tie up US troops for decades to come. Saudi Arabia's involvement of the United States in its futile invasion of Yemen is a case in point. Saudi Arabia's monarchy has its own tribal and Wahhabi-Salafi interests, but as we have seen throughout earlier chapters, they are often a far cry from US interests in bringing peace and stability to the region. The same principle applies to all of the Middle Eastern countries with which the United States maintains a special relationship. The United States must define its own interests rather than be swayed by countries who refuse to reciprocate America's special relationship with them.

Ultimate Solutions

The solutions surveyed above are partial solutions, no one of which is likely to solve the devastating problems of the Middle East. To be fully effective, they would have to be applied simultaneously over time.

The closest example of such an undertaking was the EU's incorporation of twenty-five profoundly unstable Eastern European countries into the European Union. All benefited from EU prosperity, law and order, democracy, and freedom of the press and religion. Things are not perfect, but the region is far more stable today than it was in the post–World War II era.

Similar suggestions have called upon the United Nations to internationalize the key trouble spots in the region until peace and stability can be established in a democratic framework. A key element in these suggestions is the division of high-conflict countries into one or more independent countries.

Other suggestions have called for closer but less binding relations between various parts of the Middle East and the EU, United States, and Russia. The options are endless.

How curious it is that all of the ultimate suggestions reviewed above are attempts to undo the consequences of a war that occurred one hundred years ago.

As it is impossible to turn back the clock, these partial suggestions for bringing peace and stability to the Middle East may offer the best hope for ending the era of stalemate.

WORKS CITED

Al-Taube, Gazi. April 21, 2011. Why are the revolutions succeeding now? *Al Jazeera*. In Arabic.

Al-Zaiyat, Mansour. August 11, 2002. Sharia and life series: Islamic groups and violence. Interviewed by Mahir Abdullah. *Al Jazeera*. http://www.aljazeera.net/programs/shareea/articles/2002/8/8-11-1.html (accessed August 11, 2002; site discontinued). In Arabic.

Amrani, Issandr. September 19, 2011. Which Turkish model? *Al Masry Al Youm*. In Arabic.

Bill, James A. 1988. *The Eagle and the Lion*. New Haven, CT: Yale University Press.

Brog, D. 2006. *Standing with Israel*. Lake Mary, Florida: FrontLine.

Brown, Derek. September 20, 2001. Middle East timeline: 2000. *Guardian Unlimited*. https://www.theguardian.com/world/2001/oct/17/israel (accessed May 5, 2004).

Brown, Derek. October 17, 2001. Middle East timeline: 2001. *Guardian Unlimited*. https://www.theguardian.com/world/2001/oct/17/israel (accessed May 5, 2004).

Close, R. October 14, 2004. Intelligence and policy formulation, implementation and linkage: A personal perspective. Remarks at 13th Arab-US Policymakers Conference, Washington, DC, September 12–13, 2004. Published in *Saudi-US Relations*.

Crosby, D. 2011. *Faith and Reason*. Albany: State University of New York Press.

Crosby, D. 2018. *Partial Truths and Our Common Future: A Perspective Theory of Truth*. Albany: State University of New York Press.

Eban, Abba. January 23, 1994. Israel's Eban: Momentum for peace. *Orlando Sentinel*. http://articles.orlandosentinel.com/1994-01-23/news/9401250757_1_soviet-union-israel-syria.html (accessed January 23, 1994).

Eizenkot, G. September 13, 2015. The Gideon doctrine, the changing Middle East and IDF strategy. *Jerusalem Post*. https://www.jpost.com/Jerusalem-Report/The-Gideon-Doctrine-412594 (accessed September 13, 2015).

Evans, M. D. 2004. *The American Prophecies*. New York: Warner Faith. 2004.

Filiu, J. P. 2008. *L'Apocalypse dans l'Islam*. Paris: Fayard.

Fisher, Marc. March 26, 2011. In Tunisia, act of one fruit vendor sparks wave of revolution throughout the Arab world. *Washington Post*. https://www.washingtonpost.com/world/in-tunisia-act-of-one-fruit-vendor-sparks-wave-of-revolution-through-arab-world/2011/03/16/AFjfsueB_story.html?utm_term=.ace43607d2d3 (accessed March 26, 2011).

Fraser, T. G. 1980. *The Middle East, 1914–1979*. London: Edward Arnold.

Ghannouchi, Rached. January 25, 2016. Tunisia holds the key to defeating ISIS. *Time*. http://time.com/4189180/tunisia-holds-the-key-to-defeating-isis/ (accessed February 5, 2016).

Holden, D. and R. Johns. 1981. *The House of Saud*. London: Pan Books.

Husaini, I. M. 1956. *The Moslem Brethren*. Beirut, Lebanon: Kyayat's College Bookstore.

Kahane, R. M. 1974. *Our Challenge*. Radnor, PA: Chilton Book Co.

Kessler, Glenn. March 30, 2009. Clinton calls years of Afghan aid 'heartbreaking' in their futility. *Washington Post*. http://www.washingtonpost.com/wp-dyn/content/article/2009/03/30/AR2009033002479.html (accessed March 30, 2009).

Lacy, R. 1981. *The Kingdom: Arabia and the House of Sa'ud*. New York: Harcourt Brace and Jovanovich.

Lister, C. R. 2015. *The Syrian Jihad*. London: Oxford University Press.

Lustick, I. S. 1988. *For the Land and the Lord*. New York: Council on Foreign Relations Press.

Mackey, S. 1996. *The Iranians*. New York: E. P. Dutton & Co. Inc.

McCants, W. 2015. *The ISIS Apocalypse*. New York: St. Martin's Press.

Mearsheimer, J. J. and S. M. Walt. 2007. *The Israel Lobby and US Foreign Policy*. New York: Farrar, Straus and Giroux.

Meyer, R. 2015. *Spiritual Defiance*. New Haven, CT: Yale University Press.

Moghadam, Assaf. April 14, 2017. Marriage of convenience: The evolution of Iran and Al Qa'ida's tactical cooperation. *CTC-Sentinel*. https://ctc.usma.edu/marriage-of-convenience-the-evolution-of-iran-and-al-qaidas-tactical-cooperation/ (accessed April 14, 2017).

Mustafa, H. 1995. *The Political System and the Islamic Opposition in Egypt*. Cairo: Markaz al-Mahrusa. In Arabic.

Nasr, S. H. A. 1988. *Who Rules Egypt?* Cairo: Arab Future Publishing House.

Nasser, G. A. 1955. *Egypt's Liberation*. Washington, DC: Public Affairs Press.

No Author. September 15, 2011. Erdogan offers 'Arab spring' neo-laicism. *Hurriyet Daily News*. http://www.hurriyetdailynews.com (accessed September 15, 2011).

Nowrasteh, Alex. August 24, 2016. Muslim assimilation: Demographics, education, income, and opinions of violence. https://www.cato.org/blog/muslim-assimilation-demographic-education-income-opinions-violence (accessed August 24, 2016).

Nye, J. S. Jr. 2011. *The Future of Power*. New York: Public Affairs Press.

Okasha, Ahmad. February 7, 2011. Escape from Suffering and Oppression. *Qantara.de*. https://en.qantara.de/content/interview-with-ahmad-okasha-escape-from-suffering-and-oppression-0 (accessed February 7, 2011).

Palmer, M. 1973. *The Dilemmas of Political Development*. Itasca, IL: F. E. Peacock Publishers, Inc.

Palmer, M. and P. Palmer. 2008. *Islamic Extremism*. New York: Rowman and Littlefield.

Pappe, I. 2006. *The Ethnic Cleansing of Palestine*. Oxford: Oneworld.

Pasha, Hasan Youssef. 1983. Interviews by author. Cairo.

Qassem, Fysal. November 23, 2010. Why don't the Arabs revolt? An episode of *Opposing Views*. *Al Jazeera*. In Arabic.

Rodinson, M. 1969. *Israel*. New York: Monad Press.

Sheffer, G. 1996. *Sharett: Biography of a Political Moderate*. Oxford: Clarendon Press.

Tyler, P. 2012. *Fortress Israel*. New York: Farrar, Straus and Giroux.

US Government. November 30, 2006. Measuring stability and security in Iraq. Report to Congress.

US Government. 2007. Prospects for Iraq's stability: Some security progress but political reconciliation elusive. National Intelligence Estimate for 2007. National Intelligence Council.

Weber, M. 1947. *The Theory of Social and Economic Organization*. New York: Macmillan Co.

Weiss, M. and H. Hassan. 2016. *ISIS*. New York: Regan Arts.

Wintour, P. July 13, 2017. Saudi Arabia boosting extremism in Europe, says former ambassador. *Guardian*. https://www.theguardian.com/world/2017/jul/13/saudi-arabia-boosting-extremism-in-europe-says-former-ambassador (accessed July 13, 2017).

Zonis, M. and C. A. Mokri. 1991. The Islamic republic of Iran. In *Politics and Government in the Middle East and North Africa*, ed. T. Y. Ismael and J. S. Ismael, 114–50. Miami: Florida International University Press.

Zurcher, E. J. 2004. *Turkey: A Modern History*. London: I. B. Tauris.

INDEX

Abrahamic faiths, 8; Arab-Israeli conflict and, 37; War on Terror and, 129

Afghanistan: al-Qaeda in, 117–120; global terror, counter-terror and, 117–120; Soviet Union and, 71, 79–80; US and, 79–80; US reconstruction efforts, 119–120

Al Jazeera (network), 169

al-Qaeda, 4, 82; in Afghanistan, 117–120; bin-Laden restructuring of, 117–120; ISIS split from, 144; Saudi support of, 128; September 11, 2001 attacks, 115

anti-American sentiment: ISIS strategy and, 146–147; Saudi, 128

Antichrist, 145–146, 148

anti-Semitism, 158

Arab docility, 131–132

Arab-Israeli War, 17, 40, 49–50; Abrahamic faiths and, 37; Syria and, 73. *See also* Six-Day War

Arab leaders, indifference to masses of, 133

Arab nationalism, 63; Nasser and, 47–48

Arab Spring revolution(s), 2–3, 132–134, 154; dispossessed and, 133; in Egypt, 3, 163–167; in Israel, 3; vacuum created by, 3

Arab unity, Egypt and, 40–49

Arafat, Yasser, 108

Armenia, Turkey and, 24–25

arms purchases: as power, 12–13; Saudi, 12–13, 72, 93

al-Assad, Hafez, 74–75, 103; faith and, 74–75; force and, 75

as-Sadr, Mohammed Sadiq, 105

Ataturk. *See* Kemal, Mustafa

ayatollah. *See* Khomeini, Ruhollah

Baathism: in Iraq, 75–76; Muslim Brotherhood and, 74; in Syria, 73–74

al-Baghdadi, Abu Bakr, 143, 146

Balfour Declaration, 30

al-Banna, Hasan: assassination of, 29; charisma of, 28–29; Muslim Brotherhood and, 27–29

baraka (divine inspiration), charisma and, 84

al-Bashir, Omar, 111, 112–113

Basiji, 106

Begin, Menachem, 79

Ben-Gurion, David, 50, 53

bin-Laden, Osama, 72, 80, 109, 143; al-Qaeda network restructuring, 117–120; Hussein and, 121; in Pakistan, 117; philosophy, 144–145; September 11, 2001 attacks, 113; strike-and-hide strategies, 178; Turabi and, 112, 112–113; War on Terror and, 115

Britain: arms sales, 12–13; Balfour Declaration, 30; Egypt occupation, 27;

in, 15; US strategy for building new,
156–158; World War II and, 39–62.
See also modern Middle East; tyrants,
Middle East; *specific countries*
moderate Islam: extremism and, 185–188;
promoting, 189; supporting, 187
modernity: in Egypt, 44–45, 141; Islam
and, 25–26; reformism and, 25
modern Middle East, 1–2; conflicts in, 20;
World War I and, 19–38
Mohammed, 10, 54, 185–186; cartoons
scorning, 9
monarchies: Egyptian, 26–27; Iraqi
parliamentary, 34; Saudi, 57–58,
70–71, 90–93; Saudi, Wahhabi
establishment and, 91–92
morality attacks, 84
Mubarak, Hosni, 80–81, 163; Muslim
Brotherhood and, 87; Salafi-jihadists
and, 86
Muslim Brotherhood: Baathism and, 74;
al-Banna and, 27–29; economics and,
38; in Egypt, 64–65, 67, 138–142, 163,
164–165; founding of, 27–28;
moderation, 145, 187; Mubarak and,
87; Nasser and, 43–44; Sadat and,
64–65; Salafi-jihadists and, 81, 88;
Salafi-jihadists versus, 88–89; Saudi
Arabia and, 168–169; SCAF and,
139–140; Sisi and, 164–166
Muslims: integrating, into world
community, 188–190; Palestine and
cleansing of, 125; refugees, 158;
violence against, 189

Nasser, Abdel, 40–49; Arab nationalism
and, 47–48; charisma of, 42, 46; on
Islam, 43–44; Muslim Brotherhood
and, 43–44; Six-Day War and, 63; Suez
Canal control and, 41–42
nationalism: Arab, 47–48, 63; in Egypt,
27; Kemalism, 24–25; post-World War
II, 39; in Turkey, 24–25
NATO. *See* North American Trade
Organization
neo-con philosophy, 116, 121
North American Trade Organization
(NATO), 136
nuclear weapons: Iran, 3; Israel, 51, 53

Nusra Front, 143

Occupied Territories, 68–69, 69–70,
125–126; maintaining control in, 162
oil kings/ruling elite, 4–5, 14
Ottoman Empire, 21–22;
dismemberment of, 19; Iraq and, 33;
World War I and, 22

Pakistan, bin-Laden in, 117
Palestine: Arab state in, 33; Britain and,
31, 49; Green Line, 69, 70; Israel and,
107–108; Israel and uprising by, 126;
Jewish homeland, 20, 21, 30–33;
Muslim cleansing from, 125; Six-Day
War, 49
Palestinian Liberation Organization, 108
Palestinians, 32, 33
political Islam, 9–10
populism, 25
power: arms purchases as, 12–13; of faith,
5–6, 7–10; of finance, 5–6, 12–15; of
force, 5–6, 11–12; hard, 11; of religious
faith, 99; Sadat, 67; soft, 11, 15
preemptive strike, 12
Prophet Mohammed, 10, 54, 185–186;
cartoons scorning, 9
protest suicides, 132
puppet regimes, 77; in Iran, 59–62

Qaddafi, Muammar, 101, 103
Qatar, Saudi Arabia and, 168–169

Reagan, Ronald, 107–108
reformism, 25
refugees, 3; Muslim, 158
regional control, 13–14
religious decrees (fatwas), 186
religious extremism, 63–77, 99, 181;
despair exploited by, 182; in Egypt,
64–68; in Iraq, 75–76; in Israel, 68–70;
Jewish extremism, in Israel, 69;
Muslim hostility provoked by, 190; in
Saudi Arabia, 70–72; Six-Day War and,
79; in Syria, 73–75; in Turkey, 160. *See
also* Islamic extremism; Jewish
extremism; Salafi-jihadist extremists
religious faith, 62; Erdogan and, 137;
force and, 37; power of, 99

ABOUT THE AUTHOR

Monte Palmer, professor emeritus at Florida State University, has served as a senior fellow at the Al-Ahram Center for Political & Strategic Studies, in Cairo, and director of the Middle East Centers at AUB (American University of Beirut) and FSU. He worked as a consultant for various governmental and international organizations, including USAID and the World Bank. In the process, he participated in numerous survey research projects with Arab scholars and created a unique database on the politics, culture, and religion of the Middle East.

His books include *The Arab Psyche and American Frustrations*; *Islamic Extremism* (with Princess Palmer); *Egypt and the Game of Terror* (a novel); *Politics in the Middle East*; *Political Development: Dilemmas and Challenges*; *The Egyptian Bureaucracy* (with Ali Leila and El Sayed Yassin, in Arabic and English); *The Evaluation and Application of Survey Research in the Arab World* (with Mark Tessler, Tawfic Farah, and Barbara Ibrahim); and *Political Development and Social Change in Libya* (with Omar El-Fathaly).